Diplomacy
and
Revolution

Diplomacy an

U.S.-Mexican Relations und

THE UNIVERSITY OF ARIZONA PRESS
TUCSON, ARIZONA

Revolution

ilson and Carranza

MARK T. GILDERHUS

About the Author . . .

MARK T. GILDERHUS has a special interest in the diplomatic history of the United States in the twentieth century. His articles on relations between the U. S. A. and Mexico have been published in a number of professional journals. Dr. Gilderhus, an associate professor in the Department of History at Colorado State University, joined the faculty there after earning his master's degree and his Ph.D. from the University of Nebraska. He holds a bachelor's degree from Gustavus Adolphus College.

The photographs on the preceding pages are from the Library of Congress collection.

THE UNIVERSITY OF ARIZONA

Copyright © 1977
The Arizona Board of Regents
All Rights Reserved
Manufactured in the U.S.A.

Library of Congress Cataloging in Publication Data

Gilderhus, Mark T.
    Diplomacy and revolution.

    Bibliography: p.
    Includes index.
    1. United States — Foreign relations — Mexico.
2. Mexico — Foreign relations — United States.
3. United States — Foreign relations — 1913-1921.
4. Mexico — Politics and government — 1910-1946.
5. Wilson, Woodrow, Pres. U.S., 1856-1924. 6. Carranza, Venustiano, Pres. Mexico, 1859-1920. I. Title.
E183.8.M6G5   327.73'072   76-26388
ISBN 0-8165-0630-2
ISBN 0-8165-0561-6 pbk.

To Nancy, Kirsten, and Lesley

Contents

Preface

Shortly before his inauguration as President of the United States, Woodrow Wilson remarked to a friend, "It would be the irony of fate if my administration had to deal chiefly with foreign affairs."[1] As a former professor, university president, and one-term governor of New Jersey, Wilson regarded knowledge of domestic affairs as his expertise. He lacked diplomatic experience and won election on a platform calling for domestic reform. His belief in the utility of reform profoundly conditioned his approach to foreign relations.

When the structure of international politics collapsed in the second decade of the twentieth century, Woodrow Wilson's response to war and revolution was a vision of world order in which the United States served as a model for the rehabilitation of humankind. As a goal, he envisioned a stable, peaceful community of free, independent states, each with representative, constitutional governments, competing fairly in the marketplace, respecting the rights of property, and adhering to the principle of equal commercial opportunity. As a means, he advocated reform. Through the eradication of militarism and imperialism, he proposed to eliminate conditions that caused war. Simultaneously, a process of social improvement and moral uplift would eliminate the need for revolution.

For successive generations, scholars have explored the dimensions and implications of Wilson's messianic vision. Most have agreed that Wilson and his contemporary, Vladimir I. Lenin, articulated different and opposed terms in the categories of political discourse. Sharp controversy has been provoked, however, by remaining questions. Two modes of explanation have developed, the first bearing especially on motives, the second on consequences.

Proponents of the idealist model have argued that the president's policies resulted largely from his ideological commitments. As Arthur S.

Link has maintained, ". . . idealism was the main drive of Wilson's thinking about international affairs." The president disliked foreign policies
defined exclusively in material terms; he insisted that "human rights" take
precedence over "property rights," and he often pursued abstractions.
Wilson's "missionary diplomacy" expressed a Christian sense of obligation to other human beings, as well as his conviction that political liberalism possessed greater ethical legitimacy than other ideologies. Wilson
had faith in the uniqueness of the American historical experience and
asserted a conception of mission by which the United States' role in world
affairs was "not to attain wealth and power but to fulfill the divine plan
by service to mankind, by leadership in moral purposes, and above all by
advancing peace and world brotherhood."[2]

Other scholars have employed a materialist model of explanation.
They have held that Wilson's conception of world order in effect served
the material needs of the American capitalist system. As William Appleman Williams has argued, Wilson externalized the well-being of the United
States by seeking conditions in the outside world to insure the security
and prosperity of the nation. Moralistic righteousness became a function
of economic imperatives, as Wilson fused Calvinism with capitalism and
embraced an "imperialism of idealism" which made the preservation of
the American system at home dependent upon overseas extension.[3]

Each perspective has yielded significant and enduring insights. Nevertheless, together they confront historians with a conceptual dilemma. The
idealist model asserts the primacy of ideology in shaping Wilson's behavior but has difficulty accounting for more tangible influences. Conversely,
the materialist model treats ideology as justification and rationalization
for self-interested behavior. In extreme form, each position makes unwarranted claims; together they form a false and artificial duality. To
account for multiple causes, historians must devise categories and terms
that are sufficiently precise to illuminate interpretive questions and are
sufficiently flexible to accommodate a multifaceted reality. Such is the
difficulty in coping with the many dimensions of Woodrow Wilson.

Wilson's response to the Mexican Revolution during the ascendancy
of Venustiano Carranza[4] illustrates many of the characteristics of Wilson's
conduct of foreign relations and affords opportunity to investigate the un-
folding of his vision of international order in a determinate setting. Much
of the existing scholarship on the Mexican question employs either the
idealist or the materialist model of explanation.[5] To moderate the conceptual dilemma which has resulted, this study uses a variation of the
interpretive method suggested by N. Gordon Levin.[6] Levin's characteri-
zation of Wilson as "liberal capitalist" has particular utility as an analytical
device. It denotes the values to which the president adhered. It also con-

notes a process of interaction between ideal and material components in his thinking and suggests the manner in which he extended his formulation to other people of the world.

Wilson filtered and refracted reality through sets of assumptions and predispositions as most diplomatists and statesmen have done. Unlike some, however, he claimed that his possessed a universal validity. As Levin explained, Wilson characteristically defined his goals at home and abroad within the context of "liberal capitalism" — that is, "a system of socio-political values and institutions characterized by political liberty, social mobility, constitutional government, and the capitalist mode of production and distribution."[7] Such a formulation brought ideal and material components into a reciprocal and dialectical relationship.

Wilson infused his thinking with a dogmatic ideology. His sense of history disposed him to regard political liberalism as the most advanced and enlightened form of political organization and instilled a conception of the United States as the champion in the struggle for human liberty. Such convictions shaped in part his perception of material interest. Wilson accepted economic capitalism as a legitimate foundation to sustain political liberalism but attempted to insure freedom within the marketplace, asserting that enterprisers and entrepreneurs must eschew the pursuit of special advantage and behave with appropriate regard for the principles of fair play and equal opportunity. On such grounds he developed an anti-imperial position that affirmed the right of self-determination for all people, a commitment that repeatedly clashed with the wishes of economic interest groups in the United States and with his own crusading, Protestant sense of obligation and responsibility to others. Paradoxically, the ambiguities of Wilson's position on occasion had the effect of justifying the extension of American ideals and institutions into foreign areas on grounds that foreign peoples actually willed it. Throughout, a tension existed between Wilson's emphasis on the right of self-determination and his claim to universality for the principles of liberal capitalism.

Wilson first acted on his assumptions in response to the Mexican Revolution. Consistently, he defined his goals and purposes within the context of liberal capitalism as he strove for the creation of a stable, constitutional government that could implement necessary reforms and would fulfill Mexico's international obligations as he understood them. But his position never remained static. Situational analysis is the tool used here to move within Wilson's range of perception, where relationships between ideology, material interest, and other concerns are scrutinized in specific sets of circumstances.[8] Components within the categories of Wilson's thought often conflicted. Further, his effort to reform the conduct of international relations collided with the wishes of other powers and the aims of special interest groups in the United States. Indeed, the competition between Wilson's vision and other pressures provided a dynamic for change in this thinking.

Although Wilson's policies toward Mexico manifested a degree of continuity between 1913 and 1921, his perceptions and points of emphasis underwent constant alteration as circumstances shifted. At the outset, the Mexican Revolution concerned principally the question of the presidential succession. Wilson accordingly defined his goals in political terms and justified them on ideological grounds. During the early phases, he assumed an identity of mutual aspiration with Mexicans. For him, the pursuit of American goals in effect supported Mexico's right to self-determination. Later, as the revolution focused more on social and economic issues and became entangled with the perplexities of World War I, the demands of burgeoning Mexican nationalism defied the precepts of liberal capitalism, and Wilson's faith in a commonality of purpose broke down. His attempt to circumscribe the Mexican upheaval within the bounds of liberal capitalism conflicted with Venustiano Carranza's desire to act independently of the United States, perhaps the most radical dimension of the Constitutionalist ascendancy. For Wilson, the defense of concrete interests became ever more important, a process that produced an acute tension between ideological commitments and material concerns. For eight years Wilson tried to reconcile the affirmations of the Mexican Revolution with his vision of international order. In the end he never found a way.

Acknowledgments

In the course of completing this view of Woodrow Wilson, I have acquired a multitude of debts — intellectual, financial, and personal. I have used the works of many scholars and have profited from most. Research grants from the University of Nebraska, the School of International Relations at Denver University, the National Endowment for the Humanities, and Colorado State University aided me immensely. David F. Trask of the State Department Historical Office, Philip A. Crowl of the Naval War College, and Michael C. Meyer of the University of Arizona guided and encouraged me at the outset. William H. T. Beezley of North Carolina State University shared his knowledge and endured long conversations. At Colorado State University, Harry Rosenberg arranged for a partial reprieve from teaching duties. My colleagues, George M. Dennison and Liston E. Leyendecker, read much of the manuscript. I benefited from their criticism and friendship. In times of lethargy, my wife Nancy helped me in countless ways and urged me "to get the damn thing done." Our young daughters, Kirsten and Lesley, took little interest in Wilson and Carranza but filled the hours away from the typewriter with engaging enterprises. This book is dedicated to them and to their mother.

M. T. G.

ARIZONA

Tucson

Nogales

Nogales

Naco

NEW MEXICO

Columbus
Newman

Naco Bisbee
Douglas
Palomas
El Paso
Ciudad Juárez

Agua Prieta Carrizal

Namiquipa

BAJA CALIFORNIA

BAJA CALIFORNIA SUR

SONORA

CHIHUAHUA

Ojinaga
Chihuahua C

Guaymas
Empalme
Esperanza

Santa Isabel
Parral

SINALOA

DURANGO

Mazatlán

ZAC

NAYARIT

Guadalajara

JALISCO

COL
M

Mexico
1910·1920

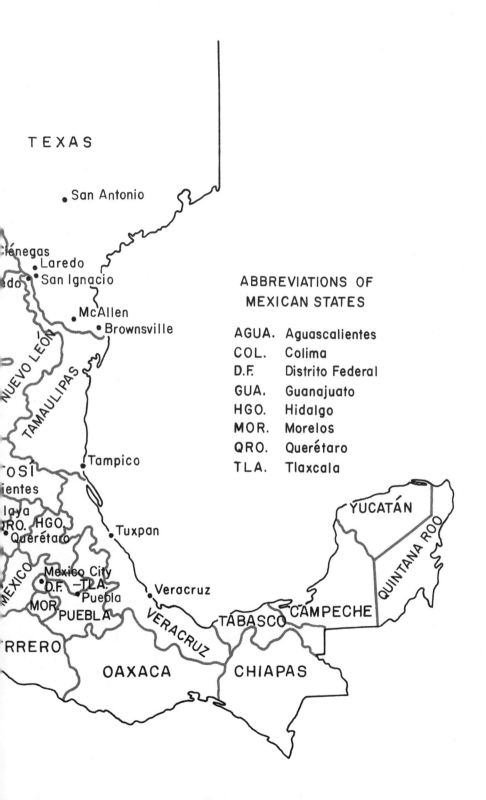

TEXAS

• San Antonio

Ciénegas
• Laredo
do   • San Ignacio

• McAllen
   • Brownsville

NUEVO LEÓN

TAMAULIPAS

• Tampico

OSÍ
ientes
laya
RO. HGO.
• Querétaro

• Tuxpan

MÉXICO
Mexico City
D.F. –TLA.
Puebla
MOR
PUEBLA

• Veracruz

VERACRUZ

RRERO

OAXACA

CHIAPAS

TABASCO

CAMPECHE

YUCATÁN

QUINTANA ROO

ABBREVIATIONS OF
MEXICAN STATES

AGUA.   Aguascalientes
COL.   Colima
D.F.   Distrito Federal
GUA.   Guanajuato
HGO.   Hidalgo
MOR.   Morelos
QRO.   Querétaro
TLA.   Tlaxcala

Chapter 1

The Mexican Question:
Wilson's Intervention

*Woodrow Wilson became President of the United States
at a portentous time in the Mexican Revolution. Two weeks
before his inauguration on 4 March 1913, General Victoriano Huerta deposed Francisco I. Madero's government
from power and established himself as provisional president.
The consequences had far-reaching effects.*

Huerta's Coup d'Etat

Mexico traditionally occupied a place of special importance in United
States foreign relations. During the nineteenth century, Mexico served as
a target for American expansionists and investors. In 1848 the United States
stripped Mexico of half of its territorial domain. Later, when President Porfirio Díaz established a stable regime and invited foreign investment to
promote economic development, Americans acquired a large material stake.
By 1911 they had laid out more than one billion dollars, an amount that
accounted for more than one-fourth the total of direct American investments in foreign countries and exceeded that of any single European group.
The annual volume of trade also expanded from $7,000,000 in 1867 to
$117,000,000 in 1911, when Americans conducted more commerce with
Mexicans than all the Europeans in combination. As David M. Pletcher
remarked, "Mexico was truly an economic satellite of the United States."[1]
The onset of revolution in November 1910 challenged American interests and influence. Francisco I. Madero's effort to wrest the presidency
from Porfirio Díaz plunged the Republic into violence and spurred incipient nationalism. Mexicans demanded the prerogative to determine their
own destiny. Struggling ambivalently with the consequences, President
William Howard Taft contemplated military intervention but doubted his
capacity to control the course of events. When Díaz fled into exile in May
1911, Taft acquiesced in the outcome. Although Madero's subsequent inability to insure the peace distressed him, the American president, unlike

American Ambassador Henry Lane Wilson, never accepted the proposition that responsibility to insure order had devolved upon the United States. Nevertheless, the overthrow of Madero relieved him.[2]

Disaffected regiments in the Mexican army rebelled against the government early on the morning of 9 February 1913. Following ten days of warfare in the streets of Mexico City, the fighting ended when General Victoriano Huerta, the army chief of staff, betrayed his superior. After arresting Madero and his cabinet by arrangement with the insurgents, Huerta claimed the provisional presidency. On 19 February Madero and Vice-President José María Pino Suárez resigned under duress, and Foreign Minister Pedro Lascuráin, the legal successor, designated Huerta the next in line by naming him secretary of *gobernación*. When Lascuráin then retired and a frightened Congress ratified the transaction, the general became the provisional president in a technically legal fashion. He would govern until new elections.[3]

The Taft administration accepted Huerta's regime as "legally established" but hesitated to bestow diplomatic recognition. Contrary to Ambassador Henry Lane Wilson's advice, Secretary of State Philander C. Knox required as prerequisites an "earnest disposition to comply with the rules of international law and comity" and readiness to settle "outstanding questions," such as American claims and the Chamizal controversy.[4] New concerns then intruded. On the night of 22 February Madero and Pino Suárez were killed under mysterious circumstances while en route to the federal penitentiary. Although spokesmen for the provisional government explained that they died accidentally when a raiding party tried to set them free, rumors suggested the possibility of assassination.[5] With less than two weeks to serve, Taft left the question of recognition to his successor.

The coup d'état shocked Woodrow Wilson. From the outset, his commitment to the principles of liberal capitalism shaped his response to the Mexican question. "One of the chief objectives of my Administration," he proclaimed on 11 March 1913, "will be to cultivate the friendship and deserve the confidence of our sister republics of Central and South America and to promote in every proper and honorable way the interests which are common to the people of the two continents." The United States, he maintained, had nothing to seek

> except the lasting interests of the people of the two continents, the security of governments, intended for the people, and for no special group or interest, and the development of personal trade relationships between the two continents which shall redound to the profit and advantage of both and interfere with the rights of neither.

But, he added,

> . . . we can have no sympathy with those who seek to seize the
> powers of government to advance their own personal interests
> or ambitions. . . . As friends . . . we shall prefer those who
> protect private rights and respect the restraints of constitutional
> provision. Mutual respect seems to us the indispensable foun-
> dation of friendship between states as between individuals.[6]

Wilson envisioned a liberal-capitalist community in the western hemisphere. The constituent nations, united by congruent interests and mutual
ideals, should share reciprocally in the benefits and responsibilities. Wilson presumed a common purpose with Latin Americans and asked that
political leaders subordinate selfish goals to the collective good. If they
should refuse, he reserved the prerogative to judge. Wilson, no less than
his immediate predecessors, regarded the western hemisphere, particularly the area bordering on the Caribbean, as a region of special importance
in which the United States had special obligations. Wilson also insisted
upon peace, order, and stability as necessary conditions to insure prosperity
and security.[7] Although he intimated some readiness to dispense with coercion if Latin Americans would comply with his prescriptions, he conveyed no inclination to abandon the practice of overseeing the hemisphere.
Paternalism and ethnocentrism colored his perceptions. His expectation
of deference necessarily disposed him against Victoriano Huerta.

Huerta promised order but could not provide it. In the state of Coahuila,
Governor Venustiano Carranza objected on legal grounds. When Huerta
served blunt notice of Madero's ouster on 18 February — "Authorized by
the Senate, I have assumed the executive power, the president and his
cabinet being prisoners" — Carranza appealed to the Coahuila state leg-
islature, holding that "the Senate, in conformance with the Constitution
does not have the authority to designate the first magistrate" and "cannot
legally authorize General Huerta to assume the executive power."[8] Accordingly, the legislators withheld recognition, urging other Mexicans to do
similarly; then Huerta secured his title in ostensible compliance with constitutional forms and threw Carranza into a quandary. Before committing
himself irretrievably to revolt, Carranza considered accommodation with
Huerta. Simultaneously, he marshaled support in Coahuila.

Neither a radical nor a proponent of lost causes, Carranza had ante-
cedents in the Porfiriato. A professional politician, he served successively
as municipal president of Cuatro Ciénegas (his hometown in Coahuila), as a
state legislator, and as a senator in the national Congress. The experience
shaped him politically. Carranza characteristically balanced commitment

against expediency in uneasy equilibrium. He derived his values from the liberal traditions of the nineteenth century, favoring federalism and constitutionalism as alternatives to centralism and authoritarianism. Nevertheless, he cultivated cordial ties with President Díaz until the onset of presidential elections in 1910 posed difficult choices of large consequence.[9]

As the scion of well-to-do Coahuila landowners, Carranza accepted the tradition of apportioning political power among the better classes but insisted that they use it wisely and fairly. By such criteria, the Díaz regime fell short. By 1910 it practiced favoritism shamelessly and distributed rewards arbitrarily. Since Carranza attributed such abuses to the influence of the so-called *científico* clique around the president, he sided with other landowners and political leaders of *anti-científico* persuasion who sought change within the Porfirian system. The effort failed, and Carranza gravitated toward Francisco I. Madero, a fellow Coahuilan, who had challenged Díaz more directly by declaring his candidacy for the presidency.[10] Carranza's association with Madero developed as much from convenience as from conviction; it always suffered a degree of strain.

Although Carranza was unobtrusive in the revolution in November 1910, Madero cultivated his support, choosing him as secretary of war in a provisional cabinet and then as interim governor of Coahuila. Carranza later won election to the office in his own right. Once Madero became president in November 1911, he squabbled with Carranza over the control of state militia in Coahuila. Nevertheless, no known evidence substantiates the allegation that Carranza intended to rebel.[11] Indeed, early in 1913 he alerted Madero's brother, Gustavo, to a possible military revolt.[12] The uprising in Mexico City on 9 February probably held little surprise for Carranza, but the consequences dismayed him.

Carranza objected to Huerta's exercise of arbitrary power and felt threatened by the implications for himself and his state. As a civilian, he prized respect for the constitution, in part because the position of men such as himself depended upon it. If generals could force presidents into retirement, they could menace governors as well. Carranza had no desire to relinquish his office or to have it taken from him. His choices were difficult, however. Either resistance or submission could entail unwanted consequences. Opposition could result in civil war. Carranza had no guarantee that he could stand against Huerta and the federal army. Conversely, accommodation might fail if Huerta refused to concede Carranza's prerogatives as governor or to accept the political status quo in Coahuila.[13]

Maneuvering cautiously, Carranza assembled military forces and felt out prospective allies. He also tried to negotiate, hoping among other things to gain time. Carranza's emissaries to Mexico City, Eliseo Arredondo and Rafael Arizpe y Ramos, initially hoped for an agreement. Huerta reportedly would let Carranza retain his office and control the state militia.[14] Then the understanding broke down. Huerta may have backed away from it, or it may have had less solidity than the negotiators believed. When leaders in the government urged Carranza to "collaborate with us in the work of peace which we intend to undertake and carry out at any price," he refused to yield. By the first week in March 1913 he knew that dissidents in Sonora, Chihuahua, and elsewhere would serve as allies. He therefore repudiated the provisional government in secret terms dispatched through the American Embassy in Mexico City, insisting that Pedro Lascuráin, the rightful successor, take office until new elections. Later he publicly charged Huerta with "treachery and murder," asking that Mexicans resist "the shameful satisfaction of ignoble ambitions."[15] The breach had become irreparable.

Carranza proclaimed his goals on 26 March 1913. The Plan of Guadalupe defined them in political terms. Carranza intended to heighten his appeal by shunning divisive social and economic issues. The presidential succession preoccupied him. The plan maintained that Huerta had committed an act of "betrayal" by his "illegal" and "unpatriotic" seizure of power. It further disavowed the provisional government and designated Carranza as "the first chief" of the Constitutionalist forces, who promised to install a legal government in power through free elections.[16] The drive against Huerta bloodied the Republic of Mexico for sixteen months.

Election of Huerta

Woodrow Wilson agreed with Carranza's contention that Victoriano Huerta had taken power by treachery and murder. Such disregard for the rudimentary principles of constitutional government not only violated his moral and ethical sense but also jeopardized his vision of a hemispheric community. Leaders in the Wilson administration had reason to think that insurgents in Central America might emulate Huerta's example if it went unopposed. Rather than sanction such consequences, the president devised the test of "constitutional legitimacy," in which he asserted the right of the United States to inquire whether new governments took office in compliance with their national constitutions. If selfish violations of legality took place, he reserved the right to deny his sanction. He stated his objection to Huerta succinctly: "I will not recognize a government of butchers."[17]

Although precedents in American diplomatic usage supported the president's position, Wilson disregarded more conventional criteria. Most European powers extended recognition on the grounds that Huerta would best insure order. Ambassador Henry Lane Wilson and officers in the State Department argued similarly. According to John Bassett Moore, the counselor, nonrecognition defied "the *de facto* principle." Still the president persevered, reasoning that the restoration of a legitimate government capable of recognition would resolve the difficulty. Early in May 1913 he and Secretary of State William Jennings Bryan considered the possibility of mediation, but before they acted, they wanted information. Both believed that

Ambassador Henry Lane Wilson sympathized with Huerta. Indeed, they suspected that an attachment to Republicanism and special interests had contaminated the integrity of the entire diplomatic corps.[18]

To obtain reliable judgments, again they broke with convention. In May, Wilson sent William Bayard Hale, a journalist, friend, and former Episcopalian clergyman, on a mission to Mexico City as a special executive agent, instructing him to investigate the legality of the provisional government and the rumors that Henry Lane Wilson had aided the overthrow of Madero. Hale re-enforced the president's preconceptions by depicting Huerta as a debauched tyrant and Henry Lane Wilson as a scheming conniver. Leaders in Washington also dispatched Reginaldo F. del Valle, a Californian of Mexican descent and an acquaintance of Bryan's, as a special agent to the Constitutionalists. Although the rebels' sincerity of purpose impressed him, he described Carranza as narrow, stubborn, and unfriendly to the United States. Later, when de Valle traveled to Mexico City, his tactlessness sparked a feud with William Bayard Hale, and Henry Lane Wilson denounced the presence of both. To dissipate the confusion, the administration withdrew del Valle and Wilson in the middle of July. Later the president asked for the ambassador's resignation.[19] Although the first experiment with special executive agents ended inauspiciously, Wilson used them again and again.

Mexicans meanwhile vied for advantage. Huerta cultivated Henry Lane Wilson but obtained a liability; he also courted support in the United States. One agent, Oscar J. Braniff, thought Secretary Bryan's ignorance of Mexico a special obstacle.[20] Carranza also dispatched confidential agents to Washington. Roberto V. Pesqueira, a Constitutionalist from Sonora, exploited American antipathies toward Huerta while using the pseudonym F. González Gante. He worked closely with Sherburn G. Hopkins, a Washington attorney. Together they confidently predicted success.[21]

Since Wilson's aversion to Huerta initially implied no special commitment to the Constitutionalists, Carranza appealed to the American people early in April for patience and understanding. Later he sought favor by promising a claims commission and instructing subordinates to respect foreign property rights. He hoped especially for a relaxation of American export restrictions. In May 1912 the Taft administration imposed an embargo on the sale of arms to antigovernmental forces in Mexico. After the coup of February 1913 the embargo ironically permitted Huerta to purchase war materials in the United States but denied similar privileges to the Constitutionalists. Carranza wanted the Americans to enforce the measure against his enemy or to lift it. The embargo worked no insuperable hardship, however. Traffic in contraband along the border supplied his forces with munitions.[22]

President Wilson mounted a more active campaign against Huerta in the summer of 1913. Choosing to mediate the Mexican question, he urged that the rivals arrange a cease-fire and schedule elections; Huerta should stand aside as a candidate and the United States would recognize the new government. The president designated another executive agent to convey the terms.[23] John Lind, a Swedish immigrant and a former Democratic governor of Minnesota, had neither diplomatic experience nor knowledge of Mexico, but he possessed the president's trust. His chance of success was slim. The mediation scheme presumed a low estimate of Huerta's resourcefulness and determination to retain power.

Lind proposed the plan to Foreign Minister Federico Gamboa at Veracruz in the middle of August 1913, cautioning that Wilson might lift the arms embargo, recognize the belligerency of the Constitutionalists, and consider military intervention unless Huerta consented. Later he suggested the possibility of a loan, but neither threats nor blandishments could prevail. Gamboa characterized the proposition as "strange and unwarranted," since Mexican law already provided guarantees to hold elections. Indeed, the provisional government had scheduled them for 26 October. Later Gamboa remarked that provisional presidents under Mexican law could not succeed themselves in office, and Lind misconstrued the observation to mean that Huerta would not run. His optimism misled President Wilson, who prohibited all arms shipments to Mexico late in August and told the United States Congress that he would "wait" and "vigilantly watch" the course of events. Since he could "not thrust our good offices" upon Mexico, he would give "the situation . . . a little more time to work itself out in the new circumstances."[24]

A multitude of difficulties closed in on Victoriano Huerta in the autumn. To suppress mounting criticism, he dissolved the Chamber of Deputies on 10 October, asking that the electorate choose new representatives, in addition to a president, in the election two weeks later. Huerta prepared cunningly, unwilling to relinquish power. While disclaiming his candidacy in public, he encouraged it in private, confiding that he would remain in office should he receive a mandate. To disqualify other contenders, he counted on the electoral laws, which required a president to receive a clear majority among ballots cast by one-third of the eligible voters. As Michael C. Meyer observed, Huerta's "calculated plot to divide the opposition, to confuse the voters, and at the same time to maintain the sham of trying to meet all legal technicalities worked perfectly."[25] Huerta remained in office.

An Affair of Honor: Fall of Huerta

The outcome confirmed Woodrow Wilson in his opposition. A misperception of British policy further encouraged him. The British decision to recognize Huerta had distressed leaders in the administration since the spring. Now a coincidence heightened their concern. On 11 October, the day after Huerta dismissed the Chamber of Deputies, Sir Lionel Carden presented his credentials as the new British minister to Mexico. Carden reportedly held Americans in low esteem and also had connections with S. Weetman Pearson (Lord Cowdray), a large English investor in Mexican railroads and petroleum. Wilson and Bryan interpreted Carden's arrival as a studied affront. Indeed, they perceived it as evidence of nefarious design. Encouraged by John Lind, they transformed Huerta into an agent of British imperialism.[26]

Wilson, Bryan, and Lind believed that Lord Cowdray and British oil interests had determined British policy in an effort to secure special economic favors from Huerta. For Americans to acquiesce in their view would strengthen an illegitimate regime, violate the principle of self-determination, and place American oil producers at a disadvantage. Such an understanding distorted actuality. Peter Calvert has demonstrated that British oil companies possessed no such overweening influence.[27] The Foreign Office wanted access to Mexico oil but not at the cost of alienating the United States. Foreign Secretary Sir Edward Grey had intended no offense when he recognized Huerta, but the Americans acted on their misimpression nevertheless.

President Wilson attacked British policy in his celebrated address at Mobile, Alabama, on 27 October. He also asserted with Latin Americans a common opposition to European imperialism. As he explained, the issue pitted "material interests" against "human rights, national integrity, and opportunity." The American struggle at home against vested privilege had counterparts in Latin America where the inhabitants had fallen subject to "foreign capitalists" seeking "concessions." But Wilson prophesied "emancipation" and urged that the United States assist in bringing it about. Americans should champion the Latin American cause "upon terms of equality and honor" and seek "the development of constitutional government throughout the world."

Again Wilson articulated an integrated vision of liberal-capitalist community in the western hemisphere and arrogated the principal responsibility to himself. His anti-imperialist inclinations served simultaneously to uphold American ideals and American interests. To frustrate British designs would safeguard the right of self-government and open new opportunities for American enterprise. Wilson justified his assertions on ideological grounds. Although "the United States will never again seek one additional foot of territory by conquest," he could "not turn from the principle that morality and not expediency is the thing that must guide us." He would "never condone iniquity because it is most convenient to do so."[28] Despite the implication of readiness to go to great lengths, tactical questions disturbed him. Wilson disliked the reckless use of military force and hesitated to employ it unless he could rationalize it on principled grounds. Nevertheless, late in October he contemplated a naval blockade and perhaps a declaration of war. He acknowledged ambivalently that "many fateful possibilities are involved. . . . I lie awake at night praying that the most terrible of them may be averted. No man can tell what will happen while we deal with a desperate brute like that traitor, Huerta."[29]

Secretary of State Bryan made the American position even more explicit. Late in November he informed foreign embassies in Washington of the relationship between American aims in Mexico and Central America, where the United States intended "to secure peace and order" by defending "the processes of self-government." He maintained that "usurpations like that of General Huerta menace the peace and development of America as nothing else could" by making "the development of ordered self-government impossible" and placing "the lives and fortunes of citizens and foreigners alike in constant jeopardy." The United States aimed "to isolate General Huerta entirely; to cut him off from foreign sympathy . . . and to force him out." Bryan hoped to accomplish the goal "without irritation or impatience" but cautioned, "If General Huerta does not retire by force of circumstances it will become the duty of the United States to use less peaceful means to put him out." At the same time, he disavowed any interest in "special or exclusive advantages." In Mexico as elsewhere, the United States would "show itself the consistent champion of the open door."[30] Bryan's formulation was classic.

British authorities responded incredulously. Some reasoned that Wilson's position implied a "de facto American protectorate." Others anticipated intervention. But Foreign Secretary Sir Edward Grey shunned confrontation. In the middle of November he stated that "we cannot support [Huerta] in any way against the United States." Later, he persuaded Washington that he meant no ill will. The Wilson administration, in Calvert's phrase, "deluded itself into believing that the British government was pursuing a policy actively hostile to its own in Mexico and, having done so, deluded itself out again."[31]

President Wilson also tried to enlist the Constitutionalists as more active allies. In November 1913 Special Agent William Bayard Hale suggested an arrangement. If Carranza would accept mediation, the United States would support him. Further, if he would guarantee foreign lives and property, the Americans would relax the arms embargo. But Carranza wanted no such dependency, which could limit his freedom to act and could have adverse repercussions in Mexico. He demanded total victory, not mediation, and regarded additional commitments to foreigners as unnecessary. He had already promised fair treatment. Later he instructed Special Agent Roberto Pesqueira to discuss only the relaxation of export restrictions and got his way. On 3 February 1914 Wilson lifted the arms embargo on shipments to Carranza but left it in force against Huerta.[32] The president hoped for decisive consequences.

Constitutionalist armies under Generals Alvaro Obregón, Francisco Villa, and Pablo González advanced steadily during the early months of 1914. Villa took the city of Torreón early in April, opening the way to Mexico City. Other forces moved against Tampico, a port city of special importance to foreigners. Since the turn of the century, American and British nationals had invested huge sums of capital to develop facilities there and in the outlying oil fields.[33] In 1914 Mexico produced 21,000,000 barrels of petroleum, the third highest in the world. As Robert E. Quirk remarked, "the area around Tampico was the richest in the Republic and a valuable prize for any faction. . . ."[34]

The prospect of large-scale fighting unsettled American residents, who counted on the United States naval squadron in the harbor to protect them. As rebel forces drew near, Rear Admiral Henry T. Mayo, the American commander, proclaimed his neutrality but reserved the right "to take all necessary steps" to safeguard American interests. Later Secretary of State Bryan suggested a plan to defend the city through neutralization but failed to win Mexican consent. Meanwhile, hundreds of foreigners took refuge in Tampico. An incident then occurred. It provided Woodrow Wilson with a pretext for military intervention.

On 9 April 1914 Mexican soldiers in the federal army arrested a small party of sailors from the U.S.S. *Dolphin* when they violated a restricted zone. When General Ignacio Morelos Zaragoza, the federal commander, learned of the episode, he released the Americans and apologized, but his verbal apology failed to satisfy the American commander. Admiral Mayo regarded the removal of men at gunpoint from a United States vessel, even a whaleboat, as a "hostile act, not to be excused." When he demanded as satisfaction a formal apology and a twenty-one-gun salute, Woodrow Wilson sustained him in it.

The president and his family had left Washington for a long weekend at White Sulphur Springs, West Virginia. When Wilson learned of the incident, he construed it as an affront to American honor and then transformed it into a crisis. Without full knowledge, he claimed, "Mayo could not have done otherwise." Later he instructed Nelson O'Shaughnessy, the chargé d'affaires in Mexico City, to warn of consequences of the "gravest sort" unless "the guilty persons are promptly punished." O'Shaughnessy, hoping to advance a flagging career, pressed Huerta, who at first dismissed the matter as unimportant. Morelos Zaragoza's apology should suffice. Further, a salute would violate Mexico's "national dignity and decorum." Equally intransigent, Huerta exploited the incident to build political support through appeals to Mexican patriotism.[35] Nevertheless, Wilson told reporters on 13 April, "The salute will be fired." On the next day the cabinet endorsed Wilson's claim that Mexico had treated the United States with "studied contempt" and had flouted "the rights of American citizens and the dignity of the government." Only Bryan had misgivings. On 15 April O'Shaughnessy suggested a compromise to which Huerta grudgingly acceded. Mexico would fire a salute if the United States would do so simultaneously. But Wilson rejected accommodation, choosing instead to intervene.

The president interpreted the crisis as "an affair of honor." For Wilson, it symbolized Huerta's malfeasance and confirmed the illegitimacy of his regime. Such conditions allowed no compromise. Until the incident at Tampico, Wilson had shunned the use of force. Now he persuaded himself that he shared with the larger body of Mexicans a commitment to higher purposes and, further, that he could cooperate with them in establishing a legitimate government. Such convictions proved crucial in the decision to intervene. Paradoxically, Wilson intended intervention to defend Mexico's right to self-determination.

The administration first planned to deprive Huerta of revenue and supplies by seizing the customs houses at Tampico and Veracruz and by establishing a naval blockade. The scheme changed abruptly on 19 April when Washington learned that the German steamer *Ypiranga* soon would dock at Veracruz with a shipment of arms for Huerta.[36] To head it off and perhaps also to avoid damaging oil installations at Tampico, where government and rebel forces had massed, the president chose only Veracruz as his target. On 20 April he asked the Congress for authority to use the armed forces "to obtain from General Huerta and his adherents the fullest recognition of the rights and dignity of the United States." A combined force of navy and marines disembarked on the following day.

Wilson anticipated little difficulty. Indeed, he premised the undertaking on the assumption that the customs house would fall quickly and easily. As he expected, contingents of the federal army withdrew, but other Mexicans resisted stubbornly. When Wilson learned that two hundred had died, he became "pale, parchmenty," and "positively shaken." He also miscalculated in another respect. He had hoped that Constitutionalists would welcome the intervention, but only Francisco Villa approved. Carranza warned that "the invasion of our territory . . . violating the rights that constitute our existence as a free and independent entity, may indeed drag us into an unequal war."[37] Mexicans had not identified with Wilson so much as he with them. Unwanted complications unnerved him. To avert them, he accepted the mediation offer of Argentina, Brazil, and Chile.

A conference of mediation convened late in May at Niagara Falls, Canada, but settled nothing. The United States insisted upon the removal of Huerta and the creation of a new government to hold elections. The spokesmen of Huerta and Carranza replied that the purview of mediation could not extend to Mexico's internal affairs. When at last an innocuous protocol required the contending factions to constitute a provisional government through direct negotiations, the advance of Constitutionalist armies had rendered the agreement irrelevant. On 15 July 1914 Victoriano Huerta fled into exile, leaving a caretaker government behind him. It fell on 15 August when General Alvaro Obregón took the Mexican capital.[38] The Constitutionalists then attempted to consolidate their triumph amidst an upsurge of political particularism.

Carranza: First Chief of a Divided Party

Huerta's departure eliminated the principal political adhesive among Constitutionalists. Without a focus of mutual opposition, they had little in common. Indeed, political fissures appeared even before the final triumph. During the march on Mexico City, Venustiano Carranza and Francisco Villa had quarreled. Villa, a former bandit, had fought with Madero in 1910. As commander of the powerful Division of the North, he shared a hatred for Huerta, but, chafing in his role as subordinate, he offended Carranza by acting independently. Carranza suspected that Villa harbored political ambitions, and he maneuvered to keep him in check. Once established in Mexico City, Carranza refused either to call elections or to take office as provisional president, ruling instead by fiat in his capacity as first chief. Such methods further antagonized Villa, who denounced Carranza as a dictator. Although Obregón tried to mediate, Villa called for Carranza's removal from power on 30 September, alleging that the first chief had violated the Plan of Guadalupe and had inflicted "many insults and slights" upon the Division of the North.[39]

Carranza moved simultaneously toward a break with Emiliano Zapata. Zapatistas had fought independently in the struggle against Huerta. Agrarian questions in the southern state of Morelos preoccupied them, and they demanded radical changes. In the Plan of Ayala, they advised expropriation to break up *latifundia* (large landed estates), to reconstitute traditional *ejidos* (communal pastures), and to place land in the hands of the Indian farmers (*campesinos*) who worked it. Although Carranza made overtures to them in the middle of August, Zapata required that Constitutionalists embrace the Plan of Ayala and amalgamate with him. Since Constitutionalist leaders often came from the landed and commercial classes and usually took a moderate stance on the land question, Zapata perceived them as natural enemies.[40]

Less obvious distinctions divided Carranza and his followers from Villa and his. John Womack observed that each possessed military organizations and "seemed incoherent conglomerations of rival elements, with former Maderistas on both sides, as well as many parvenu revolutionaries and even some old *científicos* and Reyistas." Nevertheless, fundamental differences in style, temperament, and aspiration set them apart. The Villa movement, a kind of primeval anarchism, affirmed profound discontent but few well-defined goals. Womack described it as "restless and hard to please, utterly free, unconscious, overwhelming." More "a force of nature than of politics," the Villistas, "cowboys, muleskinners, bandits, railroad laborers, peddlers, refugee peons," had "no definite class interests or attachments" and "could give their populism no real point." They were "commotion rampant." Unlike the *campesinos* of Morelos, they lacked a sense of communality and land hunger. Many had commercial ambitions. How they intended to use power never became clear.[41]

In contrast, Carranza and his adherents stood for regularity and legitimacy. Although many favored social and economic reform to bring about moderate change, the leaders had the greatest interest in political questions. They intended neither to realign the established order drastically nor to destroy hierarchical relationships. Rather, they aspired to replace old elites. Carranza himself defined his purposes in legal terms. Unlike Zapata and Villa, he lacked a broad mass following and an independent base of support. Indeed, since he derived much of his power from military leaders such as Alvaro Obregón and Pablo González, he could maintain his position only by insisting upon adherence to constitutional forms and the pre-eminence of civilian authority. Concerns that encouraged his revolt against Huerta also disposed him against Zapata and Villa. By refusing to subordinate themselves, they threatened the political edifice of the Carranza movement as it had evolved by 1914. Carranza could not tolerate the challenge but lacked the means to put it down.

Although generals such as Alvaro Obregón and Lucio Blanco regarded Villa and Carranza as expendable, they preferred reconciliation to fratricide and called upon military leaders to settle political questions at a convention. When the delegates assembled in the city of Aguascalientes in October 1914, they claimed to possess political sovereignty. Villa and Carranza first professed readiness to submit, but each qualified his position with conditions. When the Convention then selected Eulalio Gutiérrez as provisional president, Carranza refused to step aside, insisting that the assemblage had no authority to order him about. Gambling, the first chief forced the generals to choose.[42] When Villa and Zapata cast their lot with the Convention and Obregón sided with Carranza, Mexico again drifted into civil war.

Intervention Explained

The first crusade in Mexico revealed several dimensions in Wilson's liberal-capitalist conception of hemispheric order. Wilson first bridled at Huerta's methods. They impressed him as prototypical of atavistic militarism, a condition that he perceived as uncongenial to representative democracy. Wilson objected on principled grounds and with due regard for possible ramifications elsewhere in the hemisphere. In this instance liberal ideals complemented and reinforced material concerns. The defense of each depended upon the preservation of order within a constitutional framework.

Wilson first deprived Huerta of support, then moved more actively against him. Perhaps the most crucial element in the decision to intervene was Wilson's capacity to link Huerta with British imperialism and to identify his own aims with those of the Mexican people. He intended intervention to safeguard Mexico's right to self-determination and to serve his own anti-militarist and anti-imperialist proclivities. He could justify the decision on grounds that he shared with Mexicans a commitment to higher purposes. For Mexicans, in contrast, the intervention implied an American hegemony. The question of dependency posed the most difficult issue for Wilson and Carranza during the Mexican Revolution.

Chapter 2

The Question of
De Facto Recognition

*Woodrow Wilson hoped that the demise of Victoriano
Huerta would facilitate the consolidation of a liberal-
capitalist party in Mexico. When the collapse of the Constitutionalist coalition dashed his expectation, the Mexican
question took on new dimensions. At the same time, the onset of World War I made the establishment of a legal, constitutional order in Mexico even more pressing.*

Mexican Factions

The impending split among the Constitutionalists startled American
leaders. Secretary of State Bryan deemed it "suicidal" for Villa and Carranza "to fall out at this time." Seeking to bring them into "hearty cooperation," he intimated the possibility of diplomatic recognition late in July
1914, conditioning it on "the spirit" with which they carried out "a transfer
of power." Unless they eschewed "punitive or vindictive action toward priests
and ministers of any church," provided "a most generous amnesty" for op-
ponents, and displayed "the utmost care, fairness and liberality" in their
treatment of foreign interests, particularly in "the delicate matter" of Huerta's
"legitimate financial obligations," the "most dangerous complications may
arise."[1]

Nevertheless, American leaders lacked effective leverage and hesitated to back either faction against the other, although Carranza and Villa
both maintained lobbyists in Washington seeking support.[2] At this juncture,
the Wilson administration had scant basis for a choice on ideological grounds.
Further, each leader had the capacity to injure Americans. Villa's power
in the borderlands impressed Americans; presumably, he could take reprisals. Carranza had similar capabilities in the oil fields.[3] Rather than risk

the consequences of making a choice, Wilson preferred compromise and reconciliation.

As World War I began in Europe in August 1914, President Wilson sent another executive agent to Mexico. Paul Fuller, a New York attorney and a Democrat, impressed upon the Mexicans the need to cooperate but accomplished little. Meanwhile, Villa gained prestige in Washington. During the late summer and early fall of 1914, he appeared as the most likely to prevail. Further, his readiness to please contrasted favorably with Carranza's obstinacy.[4] Still, the administration shunned overt partisanship. The Convention of Aguascalientes confirmed the collapse of the Constitutionalist coalition, though Carranza as first chief retained the name. Meanwhile, President Wilson temporized, biding his time.

Officially, the United States took a neutral stance. The difficulty lay in sustaining it. Issues at stake in the Mexican civil war repeatedly impinged upon American concerns. Carranza introduced the question of Veracruz during a visit with Special Agent Paul Fuller early in September, complaining that Americans still held the port. Wilson then ordered them to evacuate the city as a sign of his desire "to bring about speedy establishment of a truly just and representative government in Mexico," but he had to move gingerly. Both Carranza and Villa desired Veracruz. Wilson also wanted to insure the safety of Mexicans who had collaborated with the occupying forces. Once he had obtained such guarantees from each faction, American troops withdrew late in November 1914. As Wilson explained, the city had been left to Carranza, whose army possessed the adjacent territory, but the Americans had not surrendered it.[5] Difficulties along the border also affected the United States. When rival forces besieged the Constitutionalist garrison at the border town of Naco, Sonora, and the fighting threatened Naco, Arizona, General Hugh L. Scott, the commander of the Southern Department, attempted an impartial adjustment. Early in January 1915 he devised an agreement with Mexican leaders to neutralize Naco, Sonora, and to maintain the status quo at Nogales and Agua Prieta.[6] Related troubles along the border presented difficulties throughout the year.

At the end of 1914, Villa and his allies in the Convention had the advantage. They dominated northern Mexico and also possessed the capital. Carranza meanwhile withdrew to Veracruz. Although Constitutionalist forces held scattered outposts in the North at Agua Prieta and Nuevo Laredo, their influence concentrated on the periphery. Their control of port cities enabled them to import war materials and to obtain revenues. Otherwise, they occupied the weaker position politically and militarily.[7] To compensate, Carranza tried to extend his base of support and to mobilize a mass following by broadening his appeal beyond political questions. Political duress, together with changing perceptions and realities, accounted for his change in tactics. Beginning late in 1914 he issued a series of decrees in which he promised comprehensive "reforms" to satisfy "the economic, social and political needs of the nation." Carranza envisioned gradual, moderate reform carried out by paternalistic means. His decree of 12 December 1914 outlined the essentials for insuring "the equality of Mexicans among themselves." He wanted

> agragrian laws that will favor the formation of small property, dissolving *latifundio* and restoring to the villages the lands of which they were unjustly deprived; fiscal laws intended to establish an equitable system of taxation on landed property; legislation to improve the condition of the rural peón, the worker, the miner and in general the proletarian classes; establishment of municipal liberty as a constitutional institution; bases for a new system of organization for the Army; reforms in the electoral system to insure effective suffrage; organization of an independent judicial power as much in the federal government as in the states; revision of the laws relative to matrimony and the civil state of persons; dispositions that will guarantee strict fulfillment of the Laws of the Reform; revision of the civil, penal and commercial codes; reforms in judicial procedures to make the administration of justice more expeditious and effective; revision of the laws relative to the exploitation of mines, petroleum, water, forests and other natural resources of the country in order to destroy the monopolies created by the old regime and to avoid the formation of others in the future; political reforms that will guarantee the true application of the constitution of the republic and in general all the other laws that are considered necessary to insure to all inhabitants of the country effective and full enjoyment of their rights and equality before the law.[8]

Such aspirations conformed in some respects with Woodrow Wilson's reformist assumptions but deviated in others. The question of property rights and subsoil mineral resources especially entailed potential difficulties. On 7 January 1915 Carranza proposed "a complete and radical change in the nation's petroleum legislation," envisioning more stringent regulation so that private companies could neither monopolize the industry nor deprive Mexico of a just share in the profits. Until such laws took effect, he required that work in the oil fields cease unless his government consented to it. When the State Department promptly protested that "serious complications and consequences will result if the right assumed of destroying property . . . is carried into effect," Carranza retreated but established a Technical Commission on Petroleum to investigate the question.[9] Mexico and the United States disputed over it for more than two decades.

During the early months of 1915, the physical safety of Americans in Mexico held more concern than Carranza's future plans for reconstruction. Conditions in Mexico City especially worried Americans. Factionalism beset the Convention as Villistas and Zapatistas bickered over the goals and methods of the revolution. Further, since neither Villa nor Zapata accepted Eulalio Gutiérrez as their superior, the provisional president broke with them in January 1915, hoping abortively to establish an independent government. Constitutionalist leaders seized the opportunity to advance. When General Alvaro Obregón moved into Mexico City late in January without resistance, he encountered appalling conditions.[10]

Inflation and fiat currency had rendered the peso almost worthless. Food scarcities threatened famine. Zapatistas forayed into the city and shut off the water supply for a time. Nevertheless, Carranza remained in Veracruz. J. M. Cardoso de Oliveira, the Brazilian minister who had taken charge of American affairs, believed that the first chief intended to punish Mexico City for supporting his enemies. Also Carranza wanted to force the diplomatic corps to Veracruz. Claiming the conduct of diplomacy as his "exclusive province," he invited the diplomats to move on repeated occasions but earned only a reprimand. The State Department upbraided him for lacking appreciation of "the established conventionalities of international intercourse." Meanwhile, foreigners in Mexico City complained of indignities and impositions, charging among other things that Constitutionalists had starved the city to force workers into the army and that Obregón had incited mobs to loot foreign businesses.[11]

The difficulties of possessing Mexico City persuaded Constitutionalist leaders early in March that they had acquired "a white elephant." When they intimated the possibility of withdrawal, they alarmed Secretary Bryan, who anticipated violence against foreigners. Obregón's alleged efforts "to arouse opposition" against them especially worried him. Since the United States was "not in a position to protect Americans and other foreigners from a riot," Bryan wondered whether "it may be necessary to speak out more emphatically than we have done." Deeply anxious and perplexed, President Wilson wanted to alert Carranza that "he is running a very serious risk," that Obregón's "extraordinary and unpardonable course had renewed talk of joint action by several of the chief governments of the world."[12]

To dramatize the point, the Navy Department dispatched two vessels to join the squadron at Veracruz, and the State Department lodged a protest, charging on 6 March that Constitutionalist leaders had "willfully brought about" a "deplorable situation." Indeed Bryan held Carranza and Obregón "personally responsible" for injury to foreigners. The first chief in reply thought the note so impertinent that it deserved no response, but still he denied allegations of wrongdoing, attributing them to "reactionaries" who wanted to provoke trouble with the United States. A short while later, Constitutionalist forces marched out of Mexico City, leaving the capital to their adversaries.[13]

The plight of Americans still worried their leaders. In Washington, Robert Lansing, the counselor of the State Department, contemplated "the possibility" of employing force if Carranza and Obregón persisted in "their present policy." Since unilateral action would incite Latin Americans and burden the United States with responsibilities, he urged the utility of joint intervention with Argentina, Brazil, and Chile (the A.B.C. powers). Wilson responded favorably, observing that the multilateral approach was "in thorough accord with what we are hoping in the Americas." He still considered intervention no more than "a remote possibility," although he had warned explicitly of it a few days earlier. His note to Carranza on 11 March cautioned of "the grave dangers which threaten" Mexico "from without." To speak less frankly would conceal "a terrible risk which no lover of Mexico should wish to run."[14]

Carranza's Goals

Constitutionalist leaders mounted a campaign in the spring of 1915 to counter American mistrust. Eliseo Arredondo, Carranza's confidential agent in the United States, and Charles A. Douglas, a Washington attorney, distributed propaganda and cultivated people with influence in the Wilson administration. John Lind served as one liaison. During his mission in 1913, he had concluded that Carranza, "with all his shortcomings," could best insure stability and equal treatment for Americans. Lind had advised the Constitutionalists during the Niagara conference and responded favorably when Charles A. Douglas asked for help.[15] Richard H. Cole of Pasadena, California, also assisted. Cole had had ties with Constitutionalists since the negotiations over the evacuation of Veracruz. Mexican mining interested him; possibly he hoped for concessions. He also had a connection with William Jennings Bryan through Richard L. Metcalfe, Cole's cousin, an intimate of the secretary of state and an associate editor of *The Commoner,* Bryan's newspaper in Lincoln, Nebraska. At Arredondo's request, Cole took Metcalfe to Washington and also courted other friends of Bryan's.[16]

Douglas, Arredondo, Lind, and Bryan met in the middle of April to discuss the question of recognition, but other matters diverted them. On 12 April General Victoriano Huerta had disembarked at New York City. Although the Mexican consul general had urged the arrest of "this monster shame of humanity," the United States government had not interfered, and Arredondo expected further difficulty. Nevertheless, he told the Americans of Carranza's desire for friendly relations.[17] Lind later pressed the same point upon Secretary of the Interior Franklin K. Lane, maintaining that Villa lacked "utterly all discipline mental or moral," while Carranza was "absolutely honest, patriotic and patient." Only he could pacify Mexico "without outside assistance." As Lind appraised the alternatives, "It was Carranza or military intervention."[18]

In Mexico, meanwhile, the Battle of Celaya pitted Villa against Obregón. Retrospectively it gave credence to Lind's position. For ten terrible days in the first two weeks of April, Villa dissipated his forces, throwing infantry and cavalry against entrenched positions and machine guns. By his own estimate, the assault cost 6000 casualties. Celaya marked a turning point. Villa's power began to recede. John Lind emphasized the point in a memorandum to President Wilson on 19 April, arguing that the Constitutionalists had established their military superiority and deserved recognition.[19]

Taking a similar position, Arredondo urged the first chief to reassure Americans by defining his goals in a manifesto. Carranza consented on 23 April, outlining a seven-point program that called for political changes to insure constitutional government, an amnesty law, the separation of church state, a secular system of public education, and agrarian reform. Although Carranza upheld the use of expropriation in carrying out agrarian reform, he rejected confiscation. He agreed also to respect property "acquired legitimately," as long as it constituted neither "an odious privilege" nor an "irritating monopoly." He promised further to protect foreigners in "their liberty and their property" and to assume responsibility for the financial obligations of the Constitutionalist government.[20]

When Arredondo, Douglas, and Lind displayed the draft in Washington, Wilson and Bryan suggested some changes, particularly the deletion of a sentence that held clergymen accountable for political acts; they also desired additional assurances that Constitutionalists would accept "just foreign claims" and "legitimate" financial responsibilities, such as those of Huerta's government. Arredondo believed that such "small modifications" would suggest "a good disposition to achieve peace quickly" and "inspire full confidence." He recommended that Carranza accept them and publish the document "as quickly as possible."[21]

The first chief, initially ready, told his subordinates that the United States at last understood "the justice of our cause" and accepted the Constitutionalists as "the only party capable of carrying out the social and political reforms which the people demand." American "moral support" would aid in a "definitive triumph" over "reaction." But his generals had misgivings.[22] Obregón thought the manifesto promised too much to foreigners. Benjamin Hill warned against undue concessions to the Roman Catholic Church. There was also reason to think that Washington would respond unfavorably. Rumors suggested that the United States might try to establish a provisional government around a member of Madero's cabinet. Vowing to resist such a scheme, Carranza deferred promulgation of the manifesto until a more propitious time.[23]

American Considerations

Woodrow Wilson still preferred a coalition as the best means to establish order and legitimacy. But Carranza opposed such a course, and American leaders contemplated other alternatives. Perhaps they could bring about the retirement of the established leaders and create a government among secondary chiefs. Such a scheme partook of fantasy but stirred the imagination. Special Agent Duval West's mission to Mexico encouraged the idea. In February 1915 President Wilson asked West, a lawyer from San Antonio and a "deserving Democrat," to "assess the character and purposes of the principle [*sic*] men down there" and to evaluate "the moral situation."[24] West conferred with Villistas, Zapatistas, and Carrancistas and concluded that none of them could pacify the Republic. Carranza's steadfastness of purpose impressed him, but West doubted that the first chief could establish peace. Carranza lacked military ability. His subordinates often refused to obey his orders and "would, undoubtedly, set General Carranza aside and bring about further differences," even "if the movement were successful." West perceived little high-mindedness. The "common people" had gained nothing. The "main factor in the revolutionary game" was "purely selfish."[25] Such impressions disappointed Woodrow Wilson, but he had wanted "the truth." The first chief's draft manifesto struck him as "a very sensible document," but he could not anticipate "much prospect of real control by Carranza" in light of West's report.[26]

While the crisis resulting from the sinking of the *Lusitania* engaged American leaders in May 1915, officers in the State Department considered other options. Leon J. Canova, the chief of the Division of Mexican Affairs, developed a plan supporting Eduardo Iturbide, a former governor of the Federal District, for the provisional presidency. Canova, formerly a newspaper reporter, had gone to Mexico as a special agent in the summer of 1914 and had aided Iturbide in making an escape from Mexico City, the Constitutionalists, and possible execution. Canova believed that Iturbide had the capacity to rule Mexico, but Secretary Bryan doubted it and distrusted him because of his ties with Huerta. Another possible candidate, Manuel Vázquez Tagle, formerly the minister of justice in Madero's cabinet, had refused to resign when Huerta took power and possessed a shadowy claim to the presidency, but he held little appeal for Carranza and Villa.[27]

Other difficulties heightened the urgency, especially when the proponents of Victoriano Huerta set in motion a plot to regain power. Operating out of the United States, they planned a revolt among the exiles. Beginning late in 1914, Pascual Orozco, Jr., a leading instigator, commissioned lieutenants to carry out raids across the border into Mexico.[28] Further, early in 1915 other Mexicans in sympathy with Huerta composed the Plan of San Diego. An exotic scheme urging an uprising among Mexicans, Indians, and Negroes in the American Southwest, it called for the seizure of "Texas, New Mexico, Arizona, Colorado and Upper California, of which states the Republic of Mexico was robbed in a most perfidious manner by North American imperialism," the execution of white oppressors, and eventual annexation to Mexico. News of the plan occasioned some anxiety in Texas, but American authorities had trouble taking it seriously. When one of the leaders, Basilio Ramos, was arrested and indicted in McAllen, Texas, the judge dismissed the case, observing, "You ought to be tried for lunacy — not conspiracy against the United States." Nevertheless, supporters of the plan raided periodically into the lower Rio Grande Valley during the spring and summer of 1915 and often incited Texas Rangers and vigilantes to indiscriminate retribution against Mexican people.[29]

When Victoriano Huerta arrived in New York on 12 April, intending to launch a new movement, he had secured assurances of German support. During his exile in Barcelona, Spain, Franz Rintelen von Kleist, an agent in the German secret service, had outlined an alluring proposition. Germany would support Huerta's effort to regain the presidency with money and arms. The intelligence division of the German General Staff had formulated the scheme, hoping to precipitate war or intervention by the United States. In either case, Germany would profit by reducing the capacity of Americans to provision the Allies and to influence the course of European events. In New York Huerta obtained further commitments from Rintelen and attachés of the German Embassy, Karl Boy-Ed and Franz von Papen. Meanwhile, Huerta concluded plans with Pascual Orozco, Jr., to unleash the revolt on 28 June.[30]

Huerta aroused immediate suspicion. Bryan anticipated "some kind of a scheme," and agents of the Justice Department kept watch. When they learned of the plot and German complicity in it, they promptly crushed it. When Huerta met Orozco near the border on 27 June at Newman, New Mexico, federal agents arrested them for violating American neutrality laws. Orozco later escaped and was gunned down by Texas Rangers in September. Huerta died at Fort Bliss in the following January.[31] Although the plot aborted, the evidence of German collusion gave further incentive to settle the Mexican question.

President Wilson had already addressed the issue. On 2 June 1915 he appealed to Mexican leaders, asking that they cooperate. Americans wanted "nothing for themselves" but insisted upon serving "their neighbor." Wilson promised "active moral support to some man or group of men . . . who can rally the suffering people of Mexico . . . return to the constitution of the Republic . . . and set up a government at Mexico City which the great powers of the world can recognize." He asked that Mexican leaders "act together, and . . . act promptly for the relief and redemption of their prostrate country." Otherwise, the United States would decide upon means "to help Mexico save herself and her people."[32]

Wilson still preferred reconciliation and compromise among the factions but understood more fully the impediments. He considered other choices. When Bryan suggested the possibility that Carranza "might exert an influence that would justify his recognition," Wilson acknowledged that he would capitalize on "anything that events may open to us, even the recognition of Carranza if he should develop the necessary influence and begin to bring real order out of chaos." The president hoped his appeal would "precipitate things" and "open either this or some other channel of action."[33] Opportunistically, he awaited the response.

Initially he had reason for hope. Roque González Garza, the executive officer of the Convention, asked that Carranza and Villa support "a unification of revolutionary elements." Later González Garza proposed an armistice and a coalition but succeeded only in intensifying factionalism within the Convention. Zapatistas especially scorned the American initiative. Cardoso de Oliveira, the Brazilian minister, reported that one of them, Antonio López Soto y Gama, delivered "inflammatory speeches in the course of which the United States, President Wilson, Secretary of State Bryan, Mr. West, and myself are insulted in the most unwarranted, cruel and unbearable manner." Before Roque González Garza could accomplish his goal, he fell from power. Francisco Lagos Cházaro, a Villista from Chihuahua more acceptable to Zapatistas, became the provisional president.[34]

Villa by this time occupied a tenuous political position. As the civil war turned against him, he could ill afford to alienate the United States. At the same time, if he submitted too readily to American wishes, he could antagonize his allies and further divide the Convention. Villa responded to Wilson's appeal on 10 June in a conciliatory but noncommittal fashion. While cautioning that "outside intervention" menaced Mexico, he invited "to concord all the Mexican people so that we may united work for the establishment of the revolutionary principles." He also blamed the civil war on Carranza and disputed Wilson's claim that no "central authority" existed in Mexico. Later he asked for Carranza's cooperation but could not have expected much, except perhaps that his request might influence American attitudes toward him.[35] Carranza already had rebuffed the United States.

Constitutionalist agents in Washington had urged that Carranza reply sympathetically. John R. Silliman, a special agent of the State Department attached to the first chief at Veracruz, believed that Constitutionalist leaders had "well received" Wilson's appeal and that Carranza would respond in an "appreciative, friendly and serene" manner. But again the imperatives of politics intruded. Carranza's generals took offense. Cándido Aguilar regarded the American proposal as "an attack on the independence and sovereignty of the Republic." Francisco Murguía thought it an "absurd pretension of the White House," an "intervention" which probably had the support of Wall Street bankers. An officer in Mazatlán remarked lightly, "What a witty man Mr. Wilson is."[36] Carranza replied indirectly nine days later on 11 June through a manifesto to the Mexican people. He conceded nothing. Insisting that Constitutionalists possessed effective sovereignty over most of Mexico, he decided that his government had satisfied the "essential condition" for recognition. Also, attaching the seven-point program prepared but unpublished in April, he promised fair treatment to foreigners and legitimate foreign rights.[37] Carranza gambled that Americans had no choice except him.

Intransigence of Carranza

Wilson's appeal also stirred Mexican lobbyists in the United States to action. Charles Douglas told John Lind of a "very satisfactory" talk with "our friend," probably Secretary of State Bryan, who "practically said that if Carranza strengthens himself, as he seems to be doing, that there ought to be nothing in the way of quick recognition." Still convinced that Carranza was "the only man in sight" who could restore order, Lind aided in "a publicity campaign" which promised "big results in getting Carranza and his cause . . . before the American people." Constitutionalist agents worked energetically, understanding that the United States still might prefer their rivals.[38]

A variety of schemes took shape in the summer of 1915, some of them a bit odd. Leslie M. Shaw, a secretary of the treasury under Theodore Roosevelt, advised Robert Lansing to support Félix Díaz, an anti-Carranza leader in exile and the nephew of the former dictator. Díaz allegedly had the support of wealthy Mexicans and a commitment from Andrew Carnegie to provide funds "to buy off the generals in the opposing factions." Leon J. Canova claimed that Villa, Zapata, Eulalio Gutiérrez, Félix Díaz, and others would unite in opposition to Carranza if President Wilson would approve.[39] More credible proposals originated with Nelson Rhoades, Jr., a consulting engineer from Los Angeles, California; his associate, James R. Garfield, a prominent attorney from Cleveland, Ohio, the son of a president, and the secretary of the interior under Theodore Roosevelt; and General Hugh L. Scott, the army chief of staff. They had Villista ties, most notably with Enrique C. Llorente, Villa's confidential agent in the United States, and General Felipe Angeles, another emissary, formerly Villa's chief of artillery. Villa's military capability in the borderlands impressed Garfield and Rhoades. They worried about the possibility of reprisals. The security of the frontier also concerned Scott, who described himself as "a Villa man." After peace returned to Mexico, Scott intended to put Villa "in school at Fort Leavenworth where he might learn the rudiments of morals."[40]

Rhoades, Garfield, and Scott urged the creation of a coalition government and insisted that the Wilson administration designate someone around whom the Mexicans could coalesce. Villa reportedly would step aside if necessary. James Garfield ruled out Carranza, because he "failed to keep order" and used his power "in an arbitrary fashion." Garfield preferred someone "who derives his right through the legal succession of Madero's cabinet," such as Manuel Bonilla, the former secretary of communications, or perhaps General Angeles.[41] General Scott also thought highly of Angeles, "a very attractive man, quite steady . . . high-minded and loyal." Angeles assured Scott that he wanted unity within the revolutionary ranks, but Carranza, whom Villa called "an old *chivo*," had made it impossible. Enrique Llorente similarly apprised others in the Wilson administration, suggesting that if the first chief remained obstinate, the United States could bring him around with an arms embargo.[42]

A shake-up in the State Department buoyed anti-Carranza hopes. On 8 June Secretary of State Bryan resigned his position as "an act of conscience" to protest the president's policy on the *Lusitania* question.[43] When Robert Lansing, formerly the counselor in the State Department, succeeded him, James Garfield applauded, remarking "what a relief Bryan's resignation has brought to everyone." Lansing, a specialist in international law, possessed a technical expertise which his predecessor never had. Also a harder man, he put less faith in the readiness of nations to do good and was less likely to let sentiment intrude upon policy making. He believed that the geopolitics of World War I especially required the establishment of a stable government in Mexico.[44]

Carranza's inflexibility meanwhile had further disenchanted Wilson with the coalition alternative. Nevertheless, he insisted that Carranza go "the full length of conciliation and conference with all factions." The president wanted a gesture of unity, but the first chief refused. Special Agent John Silliman reported that Carranza would not accept recognition "conditioned on conciliation."[45] Lansing's position at the outset resembled that of Rhoades, Garfield, and Scott. On 5 July Lansing rejected recognition of "the old aristocratic party," as Wilson had done all along, asserting that "the restoration of responsible government must come through the revolutionary element now composed of hostile factions." The problem was "harmonizing" them. Since Carranza probably would resist, Lansing wanted to retire the principal leaders and cooperate with the "lesser chiefs" in organizing "a coalition provisional government." If it represented "unquestionably . . . the bulk of the revolutionary element," the United States could justify recognition.[46]

Although Lansing's ideas impressed the president as "an excellent foundation . . . for planning something definite and final," Wilson had misgivings. He wondered whether Angeles and Bonilla had much support and if Iturbide had connections "with that scoundrel, Huerta." He also suspected that "without the present factional leaders, who seem to represent the strongest . . . we would be in a wallow of weaknesses and jealousies down there, unless some man . . . would be commended by our confidence" to the others. Since Villa had "again and again offered to eliminate himself," Wilson wanted to challenge the others "to follow his example" but thought it necessary to "play these men as they are." Since Carranza had spurned the others, perhaps "the A.B.C. group" and "their associates" could propose a conference of unity.[47]

The possibilities of multilateralism impressed Wilson and Lansing. Among other things, such an approach could foster cooperation, diffuse responsibility, and divert criticism away from the United States. Colonel Edward M. House, Wilson's confidant and adviser, took credit for the idea, claiming that he had suggested it as early as January 1915. When at last the president acted late in June, he instructed the secretary of state to ascertain whether "the A.B.C. men" would "cooperate with us in advice and political action (recognition and the like) in bringing order out of chaos there."[48]

Mounting troubles along the border further encouraged him. They became a source of deep tension in the summer of 1915. In July Constitutionalist forces violated the status quo agreement of January 1915 by seizing Naco and moving against Nogales. Robert Lansing protested, holding General Plutarco Elías Calles "personally responsible for any act which might jeopardize the lives and rights of American citizens."[49] Bandits and freebooters crossing the border back and forth also contributed. To avert unwanted incidents, the War Department had prohibited "hot pursuit" by American forces into Mexico. Although Henry C. Breckinridge, the acting secretary of war, thought such restrictions undesirable "from a military standpoint," he understood that Washington alone should decide "a matter of such importance as an invasion of Mexican territory." Nevertheless, General Frederick Funston, the commander of the Southern Department, complained that his officers could not tell at a distance whether "armed marauding bands" originated in Mexico or the United States. When he requested authority to pursue and capture them, his superiors allowed him some discretion but required that he exercise "the greatest moderation and caution . . . lest . . . plans of peaceful solution be nullified by the inception of an armed conflict on the border."[50]

A series of raids near Brownsville, Texas, late in the summer instilled an expectation of war. American military dispatches reported that "Mexican armed bands" periodically entered the United States, "robbing and terrorizing American citizens," and that Constitutionalist authorities either could not or would not prevent such violations. Indeed, Constitutionalist soldiers allegedly participated in them. General Funston warned that "a single act of indiscretion by a subordinate commander on either side may start a conflagration that will extend along the entire border and result in an international crisis."[51]

The plight of Mexico City also distressed Americans. Each time rival factions took the capital, the inhabitants suffered. In the middle of July Cardoso de Oliveira regarded "the situation" as "hopeless." He expected "nothing good." American residents often concurred, complaining of forced loans, looting, rape, and murder. Late in July they appealed to Washington 'in behalf of the suffering millions of pacific men, women and children in this country who are victims of hunger, cruelty and violence." When Constitutionalist forces regained the city after several days of sporadic street fighting early in August, General Pablo González promised order and justice but failed to reassure the Americans.[52]

The implications of German policy also distressed leaders in the Wilson administration. Robert Lansing particularly worried about the effects of German imperialism in the western hemisphere. The Huerta-Orozco conspiracy heightened his mistrust. On 11 July Lansing recorded his "conclusion" that

> the German Government is utterly hostile to all nations with democratic institutions. . . . Everywhere German agents are plotting and intriguing to accomplish the supreme purpose of their Government.
>
> Only recently has the conviction come that democracy throughout the world is threatened. Suspicions of the vaguest sort only a few months ago have been more and more confirmed. From many sources evidence has been coming until it would be folly to close one's eyes to it.

Lansing believed that "German agents have undoubtedly been at work in Mexico arousing anti-American feeling and holding out false hopes of support" so that "this nation will have trouble in America and be unable to take part in the European war if a repetition of such outrages as the *Lusitania* sinking should require us to act." To counter, he urged "the Cultivation of a Pan American doctrine with the object of alienating the American republics from European influence, especially German influence." He also advised "the maintenance of friendly relations with Mexico." To accomplish it in his judgment required the recognition of "Carranza's faction which seems to be the stronger."[53]

Recognition of Carranza

Lansing employed a multilateral approach in his efforts to bring about the recognition of a government in Mexico. He later characterized the negotiations with diplomats from Argentina, Brazil, Chile, Bolivia, Guatemala, and Uruguay as "difficult" and "tedious." Although he claimed to have favored the recognition of Carranza all along "as a matter of expediency," the Latin Americans so disliked the first chief that he "doubted very much whether they could be brought to accept him." Such resistance required "delicate handling."[54]

Lansing explored the possibility of joint action during the first week of August. While explaining that the United States accepted "the right of revolution against injustice and tyranny" and respected "the sovereignty of Mexico," he held that "personal ambition and personal greed were the causes of the factions; that no one faction represented the revolution, but that all of them combined represent it." Therefore, "we must seek for a new government among the factions and see if their differences could not be adjusted." The six Latin-Americans regarded Carranza as "impossible." Since they believed that disorder would continue even if he triumphed, they preferred a candidate "who would draw the secondary chiefs to him."[55]

The deterioration of Francisco Villa's position obstructed such plans. As his power ebbed in the summer of 1915, Villa became less solicitous of foreign interests, resorting to pillage and forced loans on occasion. At the end of July, observers such as Zachary L. Cobb, the collector of customs at El Paso, dismissed him as a "permanent factor" but still regarded his force as a "temporary menace to their own people, to foreign rights and as possible tools for Huertistas." George C. Carothers, a vice-consul at Torreón and a State Department agent with close ties to the general, similarly warned that Villa's only "present object is to accumulate American gold" and further that "only the strongest measures will stop the despoiling of American and other foreign property."[56]

Secretary Lansing attributed Villa's "arbitrary demands" to his "desperation . . . to maintain himself financially." To ease Villa's plight and to preserve the option of bringing him into a coalition, Lansing wanted to relax restrictions on the shipment of cattle from Mexico to the United States to relieve "his strained financial condition." The idea puzzled Woodrow Wilson who wondered why the United States should strengthen Villa at a time when "the force of events" might eliminate him. Lansing replied that "it would very much embarrass" the Pan American initiative "if Villa should prove himself unworthy of consideration by his continued acts of agressions [sic] against foreigners." Lansing did not wish to deal only with the Constitutionalist faction, reasoning that "Carranza seems so impossible that an appearance, at least, of opposition to him will give us an opportunity to invite a compromise of factions."[57]

Lansing and the Latin Americans appealed to Mexican leaders on 11 August, asking that they attend a conference of unification "far from the sound of cannon, and with no other inspiration save the thought of their afflicted land." Among "the first steps necessary to the constitutional reconstruction of the country," the Pan-American powers urged "the immediate call to general elections" as "the first and most essential." Woodrow Wilson approved the document but questioned the wisdom of calling an immediate election. By this time his order of priorities had shifted. No longer defining his goals primarily in political terms, Wilson understood that social and economic issues had become enmeshed with the presidential succession. He intended to accommodate demands for change, insisting that "a provisional government essentially revolutionary in character should take action to institute reforms by decree before the full forms of the constitution are resumed." He now regarded such a course as "the original program of the revolution" and "probably an essential part." He also advised against any attempt to eliminate Carranza. "It would be to ignore some very big facts." Since the first chief had achieved some measure of military superiority, he would "somehow have to be digested into the scheme and, above all, the object of the revolution will have to be in any event conserved."[58]

Carranza had quite different expectations. Indeed, early in August he anticipated the possibility of a war with the United States. He believed that enemies had deliberately provoked a crisis by spreading "false information" about conditions along the border and in Mexico City. If intervention occurred, he expected that it would take multilateral form; hence, he regarded the Pan-American initiative as a threat. To the presidents of Argentina, Brazil, and Chile, he protested against interference in the internal affairs of Mexico and instructed Arredondo to do similarly in Washington. Constitutionalists perceived little chance of recognition. Arredondo suspected that the State Department had deceived him. Charles Douglas lamented that "the administration does not want to recognize Carranza at all."[59]

Francisco Villa in contrast saw in the Pan-American appeal an opportunity to court support. In a conciliatory reply on 16 August he claimed still to possess "the power and resources with which to continue the present struggle" but nevertheless accepted "the good offices of their excellencies, for the purpose of bringing about a conference of delegates representing the recognized contending factions of Mexico." Zapata took a similar stance. But the Constitutionalists stalled. They inquired whether the Pan-American note had the approval of each participating government. Carranza then characterized the proposition as "a political error," citing the United States' position in the American Civil War as a precedent to support his claim that no nation could meddle in the internal affairs of another.[60]

Carranza withheld a reply for almost a month. In the interim, he arrived at a more accurate appraisal of American aims. After despairing initially, Arredondo speculated whether Wilson and Lansing really expected Carranza to accept the invitation. Perhaps they only wanted a sign of accommodation to justify recognition.[61] Carranza acted on this assumption in his response of 10 September. Again he rejected compromise with his adversaries but propitiated the Americans. Although he ruled out all discussion of Mexico's domestic affairs "by mediation or on the initiative of

any foreign government," he acknowledged the "sincerity and noble desires of the Governments of your excellencies" and invited the Pan-American
powers to meet with him "for the purpose of discussing Mexican affairs
from the international point of view."[62] His clever *démarche* had an immediate effect in Washington.

Although Lansing cautioned that "the revolutionary crisis" had en-
gendered "particularly dangerous conditions" and urged that Americans
leave territory under Villa's control "without any delay whatsoever," he
characterized Carranza's position as "not unreasonable." He rejected the invitation to confer but thought Carranza had shown "a better disposition . . .
than [in] any previous action." Further, "the situation has changed materially. . . . Villa's power has waned, his forces have disintegrated, and many
of his ablest lieutenants have abandoned him. . . ." In contrast, the Constitutionalists "undoubtedly" had more strength and cohesion than ever
before. Indeed, Lansing "almost" had concluded that "they are so dominant that they are entitled to recognition." Reasoning similarly, President
Wilson authorized Lansing to consider with the Pan-American powers the
possibility of recognizing Carranza as "the *de facto* head of the Republic."
Emphasizing the point, Wilson wanted it "clearly understood" that "we
think the acceptance of the Revolution absolutely necessary." He wanted
also to "keep faith" with Villa and Zapata, suggesting some kind of a conference to intimate that "the best and most helpful thing for them to do
is let us know confidentially the terms upon which they will submit to Carranza."[63]

When the Pan-American diplomats assembled at the Hotel Biltmore
in New York City on 18 September, the Latin Americans still hesitated to
embrace Carranza, although they agreed to investigate the question independently and to recognize a government "as soon as possible." Lansing
meanwhile decided against a formal conference with Mexican leaders,
choosing instead to consult with factional agents already in the United
States. During the next three weeks, Arredondo and Douglas worked to
win over the Latin Americans and confidently predicted success. On 7
October Arredondo detailed his case in a long memorandum. Since Carranza effectively controlled Mexico and had demonstrated his readiness
to deal fairly with foreigners, his government had earned the right of recognition.[64] On the following day Enrique C. Llorente, Villa's confidential
agent, denied that the Constitutionalists wielded real authority throughout
Mexico, but such objections had little effect. On 9 October the Pan-American
powers consented to recognize Carranza. Once each participating government had ratified the decision, Robert Lansing sent formal notification
ten days later. The telegram reached Carranza at the Hotel Salvador in
Torreón. On learning the news, he remarked only, "It is good. I had hoped
for it."[65]

Recognition Explained

Critics later questioned the wisdom of recognition. General Hugh Scott regarded it as "a mistake," "a mystery." He claimed that he "never knew why."[66] For leaders in the Wilson administration, recognition was a calculated gamble. Once Carranza established some measure of military supremacy, they hoped that he would insure order, adhere to the principles of liberal capitalism, and frustrate the aims of German imperialism.

The German question especially preoccupied Robert Lansing. Although he doubted Carranza's capacity to insure the peace and mistrusted him for his "harsh and improper treatment" of Americans, Lansing believed that the United States had no viable alternative.

> Germany desires to keep up the turmoil in Mexico until the US is forced to intervene; *therefore, we must not intervene.*
> Germany does not wish to have any one faction dominant in Mexico; *therefore, we must recognize one faction as dominant in Mexico.* When we recognize a faction as the government, Germany will undoubtedly seek to cause a quarrel between that government and ours; *therefore, we must avoid a quarrel regardless of criticism and complaint in Congress and the press.*
> It comes down to this: Our possible relations with Germany must be our first consideration; and all our intercourse with Mexico must be regulated accordingly. It is the only rational and safe policy under present conditions. . . .[67]

President Wilson conceived of recognition more as a device to advance the cause of the Mexican Revolution and simultaneously to circumscribe it within the bounds of liberal capitalism. He told Colonel House explicitly that a government worthy of recognition must "guarantee religious freedom, give amnesty for all political offenses, institute . . . land reform . . . give protection to foreigners, and recognize their just claims." Wilson too had misgivings about Carranza's capabilities and intentions but still expressed satisfaction, declaring in his annual message to Congress early in December that "we have stood the test. Mexico's fortunes are in her own hands . . . we have at least proved that we will not take advantage of her in her distress and undertake to impose upon her an order and government of our own choosing."[68] For Wilson, recognition reconciled the demands of self-determination with the principles of liberal capitalism. But he premised the decision on the expectation that Villa and Zapata would acquiesce in it. That delusion proved his undoing.

Chapter 3

The Punitive Expedition

*De facto recognition bestowed respectability upon the
Carranza regime. Twenty-eight nations, including the principal European powers, extended recognition after the Pan-
American decision.[1] In the meanwhile, the United States
and Mexico moved toward more regular relations. This effort was ruined, however, by the unanticipated consequences
of recognition.*

Border Raids

Woodrow Wilson tried to stabilize relations with Carranza in the
autumn of 1915. On 19 October 1915 he prohibited the shipment of arms
to Villa but permitted them to Carranza.[2] He also planned to send an ambassador. On the advice of Colonel House, he chose Henry P. Fletcher, a
professional diplomat characterized in the press as "one of the able men
of the corps." A lawyer by training, Fletcher had participated in the Cuban
campaign of 1898 as a Rough Rider; then, after entering the diplomatic
service four years later, he occupied posts in Cuba, China, Portugal, and
Chile, where he held the rank of ambassador. Fletcher had a reputation
for astuteness; he knew Spanish, and, as a Republican, he had ties with
important party leaders such as Theodore Roosevelt and Leonard Wood.[3]
Wilson and his advisors undoubtedly chose him to undercut partisan opposition in the Congress. Republican critics, such as Senator Albert B. Fall
of New Mexico, disliked recognition and questioned the wisdom of sending
an ambassador. Fall opposed the nomination on the grounds that Carranza's

government lacked authority and legitimacy.[4] As the presidential election of 1916 drew near, such criticism became even more astringent.

Francisco Villa also took offense at recognition. Defiantly he declared that the war in Mexico was just beginning. Reportedly he felt that Americans had violated "his confidence." Nelson Rhoades, Jr., regarded him as an "extreme danger" to Americans in Mexico. General Hugh Scott believed that recognition had "the effect of solidifying the power of the man who had rewarded us with kicks on every occasion, and of making an outlaw of the man who had helped us." Villa owed nothing to the United States. He had no expectation of recognition "and his bridle is off."[5]

The vulnerability of Americans along the border held special concern. Early in October Secretary of the Treasury William Gibbs McAdoo proposed an eccentric scheme to safeguard them through the creation of a neutral zone and the purchase of Baja California. Later Zachary L. Cobb, the collector of customs at El Paso, warned of possible reprisals, and Robert Lansing advised Americans in Mexico to seek places of safety.[6] Meanwhile, Villa retired from Chihuahua into Sonora, stating late in October that he had concluded all dealings with Americans. When he attacked the Mexican border town of Agua Prieta early in November, Americans further outraged him by permitting the transport of Constitutionalist troops through United States territory. Some observers then speculated that he might capitulate, perhaps even seek asylum in the United States. Carranza's government had promised amnesty to his subordinates if they would surrender unconditionally but had declared Villa an outlaw.[7] No one could foretell his intentions.

In the Senate the debate over Fletcher's nomination persisted. On 6 January 1916 Albert B. Fall inquired how the Wilson administration could have extended recognition when in fact no government existed. The controversy grew more acute on 10 January when a band of Villa partisans seized seventeen American mining engineers from a train near Santa Isabel, Chihuahua, and murdered sixteen of them. Although Villa disclaimed responsibility, the atrocity outraged Americans. Secretary of State Lansing immediately asked that Carranza apprehend and punish "the perpetrators of the dastardly crime." Later he warned that "a grave crisis with far-reaching consequences" could develop, since the massacre had "caused intense excitement" and "severe criticism."[8]

Republicans and Democrats in the Congress appealed for strong measures. Theodore Roosevelt considered the episode "an inevitable outcome" of maladroit policies. Senator Fall regarded it as confirmation of Carranza's incompetence and Wilson's timidity. The *New York Times* reported that nothing had "so stirred" official Washington since the sinking of the *Lusitania*. Nevertheless, the president stood his ground, putting faith in Carranza's readiness to uphold his obligations.[9] The Santa Isabel massacre delayed confirmation of an ambassador. Henry Fletcher waited in Chile, "all packed up . . . one foot in the stirrup," thinking "it would be extremely embarrassing to return here." When he finaly won acceptance, ironically he took the oath of office on 9 March 1916, the very day that Francisco Villa attacked Columbus, New Mexico.[10] Eleven crisis-filled months followed before Fletcher occupied the Embassy in Mexico City.

American observers such as Zachary Cobb and George Carothers knew of Villa's movement toward the border but could not anticipate his purpose. Shortly after 4:00 A.M. on 9 March 1916, about 485 Villistas invaded Columbus. For nearly three hours, they terrorized the residents, pillaged the town, and engaged members of the Thirteenth Cavalry Regiment in sporadic street fighting. When at last they withdrew, leaving part of the central plaza in flames, cavalry under Major Frank Tompkins pursued them into Mexico, taking a heavy toll. Villistas killed eighteen Americans, wounded eight, and gained some booty. For their effort, they lost horses, arms, and nearly a hundred dead.[11]

Why Villa undertook such a costly venture puzzled Mexicans and Americans. A packet of captured documents, presumably lost by a courier during the raid, provided some insight into his state of mind. It contained the copy of a letter to Emiliano Zapata, dated 8 January 1916, which showed that Villa had planned the raid for some time. Villa held Americans responsible for his eclipse and asked that Zapata join with him in striking against them. He could restrain his subordinates no longer. Americans had shut off the arms supply and had supported Carranza, "the enemy." Villa considered such acts as "offense" to the Mexican people and to their "national sovereignty." "All the generals and chiefs" in his command believed that the United States had become "the common enemy of Mexico." While charging that Carranza had permitted the White House to choose cabinet ministers and had given away valuable property to Americans, he asked that all "honorable" Mexicans defend their "integrity and independence" and prevent "the sale of the motherland" to the United States. Villa and his men had resolved never "to exchange another round with Mexicans, our brothers." Rather, they would attack the Americans "in their lurking places" and demonstrate to them that "Mexico is a land of free men."[12]

Desperation and irrationality accounted in part for the decision to attack Columbus. In all likelihood, Villa did not calculate his intended consequences very carefully. Probably he wanted to embroil Carranza with the United States, thereby setting his principal adversaries at odds. Probably he also hoped to secure horses, weapons, and supplies. In addition, he had personal grudges against the Columbus State Bank, which had denied him funds, and against Samuel and Louis Ravel, local merchants, who had sold him defective ammunition and reneged on other commitments once the embargo took effect. He may have desired revenge. Finally, his connections with German nationals may also have encouraged him. Two of his associates, Felix Sommerfeld and Dr. Lyman B. Rauschbaum, had ties with Franz Rintelen von Kleist and Karl Boy-Ed. They may have incited him, seeking to bring about American intervention.[13]

The effect of elusive German influence has remained largely a question of speculation. At the time, some Americans suspected the worst. Soon after the raid, Brigadier General John J. Pershing was told by Luis Cabrera, one of Carranza's advisers, that "Villa was unquestionably aided and abetted by German agents." American newspapers published similar allegations. But Count Johann von Bernstorff, the German ambassador in Washington, admitted to no complicity. Indeed, he believed that President Wilson benefited politically from his subsequent decision to send a punitive expedition into Mexico.[14]

Villa's attack upon the United States provoked an immediate crisis. Upon learning the news shortly before noon, Robert Lansing conferred with Secretary of War Newton D. Baker and alerted Carranza that "a most serious situation" had arisen. Although the United States would suspend judgment "until further facts can be learned," Lansing expected that the first chief would do "everything in his power to pursue, capture, and exterminate the lawless elements." Later in the afternoon he told Eliseo Arredondo that the attack had resulted from "a definite plan . . . to compel this Government to invade Mexico." Lansing hoped that Mexico would not object "to the pursuit by American troops," since "hot pursuit by a punitive expedition" differed fundamentally from a "deliberate invasion by an expeditionary force with the intent to occupy Mexican territory." To oppose American policy would play into Villa's hands.[15]

Lansing assumed that American forces would take chase. American consuls had reported that Mexican troops had little chance of capturing Villa, and military observers believed that additional raids would occur "unless Villa is relentlessly pursued and his forces scattered." Within a short while, towns such as El Paso, Bisbee, Nogales, and Tucson appealed for protection, and political leaders demanded it.[16] Spokesmen for both major parties in the Congress called for the use of military force. Senator Henry F. Ashurst, a Democrat from Arizona, disparagingly recalled former Secretary Bryan's teetotaling and pacifist proclivities, proclaiming that he preferred the use of "grape shot" to that of "grape juice."[17]

When the cabinet assembled on the morning of 10 March, the members had no good alternatives. To do nothing could invite similar raids and would expose the administration to partisan attack in an election year. Border security and political exigencies militated in favor of assertive measures. Nevertheless, an excessively zealous response could provoke unwanted trouble with Carranza at a time when European questions occasioned ever greater concern. To ease the dilemma, leaders in the administration took a middle course, opting for a punitive expedition on grounds that such a response could safeguard the frontier and quiet critics at home while averting the risks of actual intervention. They also hoped that Carranza would acquiesce, perhaps even cooperate, in the undertaking.[18]

The official announcement on 10 March asserted strictly limited goals:

> An adequate force will be sent at once in pursuit of Villa with the single object of capturing him and putting a stop to his forays. This can and will be done in entirely friendly aid of the constituted authorities of Mexico and with scrupulous regard for the sovereignty of that Republic.

Secretary of War Baker reiterated the point in a statement to the press, affirming that American troops would withdraw as soon as "the forces of the *de facto* government can take control of the situation." When the War Department instructed Brigadier General John J. Pershing to organize "an adequate military force" for the task, the directive stipulated that the Americans would retire "as soon as the de facto government of Mexico is able to relieve them" or when "Villa's band or bands are known to be broken up."[19] No one anticipated a protracted expedition.

Nevertheless, Mexicans prepared for eventualities. Arredondo looked "depressed" when he learned the news. Carranza thought relations "very delicate." On 10 March he urged "every precaution" to defend Veracruz and also instructed General Luis Gutiérrez to apprehend Villa.[20] Initially he hoped to head off a punitive expedition by claiming that his government possessed effective control. Foreign Secretary Jesús Acuña explained unconvincingly that "the fact that Villa and his forces have entered United States territory is evidence of the strength of the de facto Government's forces." Carranza similarly insisted that he could cope with "the bandits" and insure against further "deplorable" incidents. He also proposed cooperative measures to police the border, invoking a precedent established in the 1880s in response to Indian raids. Carranza asked that Mexican forces engaged in "hot pursuit" have the right to enter American territory "upon the understanding that, reciprocally, the forces of the United States may cross into Mexican territory." But he conditioned the proposal on the contingency that another raid take place. Lacking such an occurrence, Pershing could not enter Mexico with Carranza's sanction.[21]

The first chief counted on delay. Arredondo had reported that Wilson wanted to avert a war. Probably the president would lose interest in a punitive expedition once the Congress quieted down and Mexican soldiers arrived in force. Nevertheless, Carranza put his commanders on alert. On 11 March he told them of his desire "to avoid a break with the United States," but "for the sake of what could happen," he placed General Gutiérrez in charge of operations against the Americans "in case they declare war."[22] He also warned Lansing explicitly: If the United States sent military forces into Mexico without first agreeing to reciprocal terms, the de facto government would regard it as "an invasion of national territory." To emphasize the point, he instructed the Mexican people to prepare "for any emergency."[23]

American leaders nevertheless forced the issue. Lansing would not take Carranza seriously, reasoning that he intended his words "for home consumption." Secretary of the Interior Franklin K. Lane believed that a failure to capture Villa "would ruin us in the eyes of all Latin Americans," especially Mexicans whom he compared with "children" in that they "pile insult upon insult if they are not stopped when the first insult is given." On 13 March the State Department accepted Carranza's proposals and deliberately misconstrued them, announcing that the agreement had taken force and that each government could exercise "reciprocal privileges . . . without further interchange of views."[24]

Initially it appeared that Mexico might give way. Without understanding the full import of the State Department's position, Foreign Secretary Acuña believed that the Americans had relieved a "very delicate situation." Carranza in contrast withheld his endorsement, and the optimism dissipated quickly in Washington. General Hugh L. Scott, now the army chief of staff, cautioned that Mexican factions might "combine against any American force" and "cut through our thin lines on the border and commit depredations." Further, General Gabriel Gavira, the commander of the Mexican garrison at Palomas, a short way south of Columbus, intimated that he would resist the entry of a punitive expedition into Mexico unless he received orders from Carranza to the contrary.[25] The uncertainty threw Woodrow Wilson into indecision.

The president hesitated to run the risk. If intervention and war would result, he preferred not to send troops into Mexico. Nevertheless, Joseph P. Tumulty, his private secretary, Albert S. Burleson, the postmaster general, David F. Houston, the secretary of agriculture, and others advised perseverance. Tumulty feared that a retreat "would be disastrous to our party . . . humiliation to the country . . . destructive to our influence in international affairs and make it forever impossible to deal in any effective way with Mexican affairs." Although Colonel House reasoned that inaction would ruin Wilson at home and in Europe, he speculated that the president's "determination not to allow Germany to force him into intervention could account for his actions."[26] The relationship between Mexico and Europe had become incalculable. If Wilson submitted to the Columbus raid, he could damage American credibility elsewhere. Conversely, if he provoked unwanted difficulties with Carranza, he could weaken the United States vis-à-vis the Allies and the Central Powers. Before a decision, he wanted some assurance that Carranza would accept a punitive expedition.

Angling for a sign, the State Department on 15 March asked Special Agent John W. Belt to ascertain whether Carranza had ordered his commanders to resist. Before Belt replied, John W. Silliman, another special agent, reported that members of the Mexican cabinet had conveyed to him an attitude "of approval and acquiescence." Ambivalence also had beset the Mexican government. Indeed, the issue contributed to a shake-up in the cabinet which made General Cándido Aguilar, Carranza's future son-in-law, the secretary of foreign relations. Since Arredondo had warned that "enemies" in the United States wanted to provoke a war, Carranza perhaps chose to deny them the opportunity by accommodating his stance, assuming further that the punitive expedition would remain in Mexico only a short while. In any case he insisted that a reciprocal agreement specify terms and conditions.[27]

On the understanding that the de facto government would "tolerate" a punitive expedition into Mexico, the War Department on 15 March authorized General Pershing to proceed. In the event of resistance, he should await new orders. The first units crossed the border later that day without opposition. Two days later the United States Congress resolved jointly to sanction "the use of the armed forces of the United States for the purpose of apprehending and punishing Villa's band."[28]

The punitive expedition, comprised of 192 officers and 4800 enlisted men, included infantry, field artillery, quartermaster units, signal corps, a small squadron of airplanes, and four regiments of cavalry, the main strike force. Since Villa had a seven-day advantage, Pershing intended to track him through the deserts of Chihuahua with small, fast, mobile columns. Various impediments hindered him, including the resentment and obstruction of Mexican people. The War Department, anticipating possible friction, instructed Pershing to cooperate with Mexican forces and to avoid any appearance of hostility toward "the integrity or dignity of the Republic of Mexico." If Americans came under attack, they could defend themselves but "in no event" should become "the aggressor." Wilson insisted that the undertaking remain "a mere expedition," not an invasion.[29] Pershing and his officers chafed under such restrictions throughout the grueling experience.

Carranza never accepted the punitive expedition as legitimate. He immediately invoked the State Department's refusal to define reciprocal terms and conditions beforehand as grounds for quick withdrawal. On 18 March Eliseo Arredondo protested the point, but Frank L. Polk, the counselor of the State Department, told him that the United States had acted in good faith. Later Arredondo tried to limit the privilege of crossing the border in a draft protocol. It provided that military forces engaged in "hot pursuit" should number no more than 1000 men, enter foreign territory by no more than sixty kilometers, and remain no more than five days. Polk assured Arredondo that the United States would try "to conform in general" with such restrictions but would not apply them to "this particular expedition."[30] The State Department, though ready to agree "in principle," wanted the protocol to sanction Pershing's presence. On 27 March Arredondo proposed another draft which allowed military forces to remain in foreign territory for fifteen days. After a week, Robert Lansing consented to it but exempted the Pershing expedition from its terms. Arredondo then abandoned the effort, thinking that Wilson would not retire the force quickly and risk embarrassment in an election year.[31]

Arredondo correctly perceived that the Wilson administration acted in part for political reasons. Republicans eagerly exploited issues in foreign policy and subjected the Mexican question to fierce attack. During the furor over the Columbus raid, Theodore Roosevelt urged that "every American citizen" support "America first" and "no other country even second." Senator Henry Cabot Lodge of Massachusetts later asserted that, with the exception of President Buchanan, "no administration" ever had subjected the United States to so much injury "at home and abroad."[32] Albert Bacon Fall, after a 450-mile automobile trip along the border, predicted a Republican victory in November and characterized Woodrow Wilson as "a pedagogue elevated to the Presidential chair" who "has dealt with every crisis in a weak, mollycoddle, namby-pamby way that might be expected from a school teacher." Wilson's Mexican policy "has been one mistake after another" and "has increased the contempt of Mexicans for us." Fall observed, "They can't fight. Take a look at those stupid little peons. After one glimpse at them you wonder no longer why Carranza soldiers have never caught Villa."[33]

The exigencies of presidential politics constricted the president's range of choice in 1916. Although Wilson consented to send a punitive expedition, he attempted to establish a sharp distinction between it and intervention. Indeed, Colonel House related that Wilson went "so far as to say that he will address Congress demanding that in no circumstances shall we intervene at this particular time because of the foreign situation and because the enemies of the US so ardently desire it." Such a position exposed him to partisan attack. Carranza, of course, shared with Wilson an inability to separate diplomacy from politics. Late in March Washington learned that Mexican leaders might "request withdrawal of our troops in a short time in the event of failure to capture Villa soon. . . . They fear political effect if no such action taken."[34]

The crisis in German-American relations produced by the sinking of the French passenger liner *Sussex* preoccupied the president and his advisers during the first week of April. They also considered the withdrawal of Pershing but could not calculate the effect on European concerns. Baker and Burleson reasoned that an impending breach with Germany required that they give up the Mexican chase. But Houston, Lane, and House believed that such a retreat would ruin the credibility of Wilson's threat to break relations with Germany. Although Lansing anticipated that another provocation in Mexico could force intervention at a time of crisis with Germany, he denied "positively" on 6 April that the United States would retire the punitive force.[35] Six days later an incident at Parral, Chihuahua, nearly fulfilled his worst expectation.

Mexican Reaction

The effects of Mexican pique worried American leaders from the outset. Although General Hugh Scott had urged the importance of convincing Mexicans "of our justice and humanity," General Pershing found it difficult to achieve such a goal. His forces confronted the consequences at Parral on 12 April. That morning Major Frank Tompkins and units of the Thirteenth Cavalry Regiment violated Mexican warnings by entering the town in search of supplies. When the inhabitants took offense, General Ismael Lozano, the local commander, advised a quick departure; Tompkins consented, as long as he secured provisions. But before his men moved out, a riot started. Gunfire compelled a disorderly retreat, and a skirmish ensued.[36] Carranza promptly blamed the incident upon "the imprudence of the American officer who entered Parral without permission, contrary to the orders of the Government, which prohibit the entry of American forces into towns." Further, he held that the episode demonstrated "the impossibility of any longer keeping American forces in our territory," since "even more serious results" could follow. A formal protest to the State Department on the next day emphasized "the necessity of retiring American forces from Mexico."[37]

General Pershing interpreted "the outbreak in Parral" as "undoubtedly premeditated." He complained that Mexican authorities had impeded his efforts at every turn, and he anticipated an attack. Indeed, he looked "with grave suspicion" on the movement of additional Mexican forces into Chihuahua. To safeguard the punitive expedition, he wanted "to assume complete possession" of the city and state of Chihuahua. But his superiors rejected such an alternative as unduly provocative. Pershing then aligned his men in a defensive posture. After establishing a main base near Namiquipa, he divided the region under occupation into five districts and tried to police them with small cavalry detachments moving "swiftly and secretly."[38]

Leaders moved to calm the crisis. When officials in Mexico City intimated that a conference might address military questions, Secretary Lansing arranged for Generals Hugh Scott and Frederick Funston to meet with General Alvaro Obregón at the border. Lansing hoped they could "prevent misunderstanding and make possible real cooperation between the forces of the two Governments."[39] But Mexico and the United States defined their immediate goals in conflicting terms. The Americans wanted "harmonious cooperation" with Mexican forces. If Obregón should press for military withdrawal, then Scott and Funston should refer the matter to the State Department as "a diplomatic question." Carranza, in contrast, instructed Obregón to insist upon "the retirement of American forces from our territory."[40]

When the Scott-Obregón conference convened in the "Green Room" of the customs house at Ciudad Juárez on the afternoon of 30 April, the negotiations immediately became locked in stalemate. As Scott and Funston observed, "We evidently came to discuss one question, Obregon [sic] another." Secretary of War Baker on the same day affirmed his readiness "to make all possible concessions" and "to retire our forces" gradually toward the border. But, as a prerequisite, he demanded assurance for "the safety of our borders from further aggression." On the following day Scott reported that "an ultimatum to retire immediately from Mexican soil was only avoided by diplomatic adjournment."[41] Rumors of an impending attack to cut off the punitive expedition heightened his concern. To acquire defensive capability and bargaining leverage, Scott and Funston urged the deployment of additional forces along the border. Funston told Pershing, "Situation very tense. . . . Take all possible precautions. . . . No hope of being allowed to strike first blow." If it came to an open break, the message "send them at once" would move the War Department into action.[42]

Obregón also despaired of a quick solution. Indeed, he suggested the termination of the conference, but Carranza chose to persist, displaying some willingness to moderate his position. If the Americans rejected unconditional withdrawal, he would concede the necessity of safeguarding the border while striving for a graduated pullback within fifteen days.[43] Such instructions to Obregón opened the way to a tentative agreement. A different setting for negotiation also facilitated.

General Scott had found it "impossible . . . to accomplish satisfactory diplomatic results meeting in a formal way before a hostile audience which General Obregon [sic] must satisfy and carry with him." From time to time, "mutual friends" had assured Obregón of the Americans' "complete sincerity." One of them, A. J. McQuatters, the president of the Alvarado Mining Company in Parral, served as intermediary. He arranged a private session between Scott and Obregón on 2 May at the Hotel Paso del Norte in El Paso. Scott described it as a "continuous struggle" of twelve hours which "was not equaled by any similar struggle with the wildest and most exasperated Indian heretofore." In the end, the two men devised a draft agreement which Scott thought "unsatisfactory" in some respects but "the best" he could obtain. It provided for phased withdrawal and military cooperation in the interim.[44] But such an arrangement violated Carranza's instructions by failing to establish a fifteen-day limitation.

Secretary Lansing regarded the draft "in general" as "satisfactory." He hoped it would allow more regular relations and suggested that "Mr. Fletcher proceed at once to his post." President Wilson also approved, anticipating that Carranza would do similarly, but again the first chief defied American expectations. He objected because the protocol specified no date for the departure of American forces and allowed them to remain if additional raids into the United States should occur.[45] Shortly thereafter another incident seemed to corroborate his fear that "enemies" might exploit such conditions to his embarrassment. On 5 May a band of marauders, possibly Villistas, assaulted settlements at Glen Springs and Boquillas, Texas. Two days later a contingent of United States cavalry undertook "hot pursuit" into Mexico. Again Carranza alerted his commanders, cautioning that "our situation is delicate." On 8 May he rejected the proposed protocol.[46]

American leaders now contemplated the worst. Lansing advised Americans in Mexico of impending danger, and General Funston notified General Pershing, "War with De Facto Government almost inevitable. You are liable to be attacked at any time." On 9 May President Wilson called out the National Guard in Texas, New Mexico, and Arizona.[47] Nevertheless, Carranza chose to move "with calmness and without haste," calculating that "the time which passes favors us rather than prejudices us." He believed that the Wilson administration was under great pressure "to conclude the adventure and to get out of the embarrassing situation in which it finds itself." Rather than order an attack against Pershing, Carranza instructed Obregón in El Paso and Arredondo in Washington to attempt new initiatives. They should leave the question of Pershing's departure "open for further negotiation" and devise measures for "jointly controlling the border to prevent further raids." Carranza also accepted the presence of American cavalry, which entered Mexico after the raids at Glen Springs and Boquillas, but ordered his commanders to tolerate no additional incursions. His restraint persuaded General Scott that "the acute situation is over for the present . . . the Mexicans will do their best to carry out their part."[48]

Still, the punitive expedition grated on Mexican sensitivities. Arredondo wondered whether Wilson intended to maneuver Mexico into a war to assure his re-election. Mexican leaders had a deep sense of grievance which they expressed on 22 May in a long, angry note to the State Department. Carranza probably dictated much of it. The protest claimed that the United States "either precipitately or in error" had ordered the punitive expedition across the border "without the consent" of the Mexican government and thereby had placed in jeopardy "the harmony and good relations" that should exist between the two countries. Since American behavior contradicted the claim of friendship and good faith, Mexico insisted that only "real and effective acts" could end "this situation of uncertainty" and persuade the Mexican people of "the sincerity of American declarations." The punitive expedition should withdraw at once, and no additional forces should violate the border.[49]

Such frankness offended American leaders. Frank Polk thought the note "decidedly unsatisfactory and, in some places, impertinent." Robert Lansing regarded it as "insulting," "makes out the US a liar."[50] In a studied show of unconcern, he delayed a reply for nearly a month. When Arredondo queried him about it, Lansing "put him off." Arredondo told Carranza to expect a "hard" response. General Pershing meanwhile complained of the restrictions placed upon him in "the so-called punitive expedition." He told Theodore Roosevelt that the "treacherous" incident at Parral regrettably "brought us into the domain of international diplomacy." Roosevelt replied that he would like "to handle the Mexican situation . . . along the lines on which we proceeded in Cuba."[51] The tension grew steadily worse.

Threat of War

Leaders in Washington doubted Carranza's capacity to pacify the border and distrusted his intentions. General Funston held Carranza personally accountable for border troubles during the preceding year. Lansing complained that "anarchy prevails" along the international frontier, but in spite of his appeal to Mexico for vigorous measures, additional incidents took place. On the night of 11 June 1916 a small party of Mexicans set fire to bridges near Laredo, Texas, before American soldiers drove them away. Four days later a group of marauders attacked a military camp at San Ignacio, Texas, and killed three Americans. Pershing concluded that "Carranza leaders will hesitate considerably before attacking our troops," but he put little faith in local chiefs "who are only nominally controlled by Carranza Government." To guard against eventualities, General Scott asked that the War College chart new plans for an invasion of Mexico. He wanted them ready "to be put into force at once."[52]

Mexican leaders also prepared for war. On 16 June General Jacinto B. Treviño alerted General Pershing of his orders "to detain by means of force any new invasion of my country by American forces." Further, if American troops already in Mexico should move in any direction other than north, Treviño would attack them. Rumors suggested that he planned an envelopment of the punitive expedition and an assault against American border towns.[53] On 17 June another incident occurred at Mazatlán. Believing that war had already begun, Mexicans mobbed a group of American sailors from the U.S.S. *Annapolis* and killed one. Mexican authorities held the others in custody until the American consul secured their release, warning that "the affair" could assume "international significance."[54]

Washington grew apprehensive. On Saturday, 17 June, Lansing spoke with Polk about the "increasingly critical situation in Mexico." On Sunday President Wilson approved a draft in response to the Mexican note of 22 May and called out the entire National Guard for duty along the border. The units included more than 125,000 men, but confusion and disorganization impeded the mobilization. A week passed before some 16,000 ill-trained, ill-equipped militiamen were ready for action.[55] Arredondo meanwhile cautioned his superiors that the Americans wanted to goad Mexico into striking the first blow "by means of provocations." Similarly, Foreign Secretary Cándido Aguilar notified the foreign ministers of Latin America on 19 June that an "unjust and unequal" war appeared "inevitable." Nevertheless, Mexico intended to defend its "sovereignty and absolute independence" against American aggression.[56]

On 20 June Lansing replied to the Mexican note of 22 May. While expressing "surprise and regret" at its "discourteous tone and temper," he remarked with "deep concern and increasing disappointment" on "the progress of the revolution in Mexico." The United States had given "every possible encouragement to the de facto Government in the pacification and rehabilitation of Mexico." Lansing denied that Americans possessed "ulterior and improper motives" and rejected the demand for Pershing's departure. Mexico could not reasonably expect the United States to withdraw its forces and prevent their re-entry when "their presence is the only check upon further bandit outrages and the only efficient means of protecting American lives and homes." The Wilson administration would maintain "its national rights and . . . perform its full duty in preventing further invasions of the United States and . . . [remove] the peril which Americans along the international boundary have borne so long with patience and forbearance." Pershing would remain until the Mexican government fulfilled its international obligations. If Mexico should choose differently, Lansing warned of "the gravest consequences."[57]

Americans expected an attack. General Scott thought "we are verging rapidly towards war." Lansing too perceived "an increasing probability that the Mexican situation may develop into a state of war." If a conflict should occur, he advised against characterizing it as an "intervention," since such a term would embarrass Democrats, humiliate Mexicans, and offend Latin Americans. He preferred to proclaim "a state of international war without purpose on our part other than to end the conditions which menace our national peace and the safety of our citizens, and that . . . is *not* intervention with all that that word implies." President Wilson accepted the soundness of such advice, but as he typed a reply late on 21 June, he observed that "'extras' of the evening paper are being cried on the Avenue which, if true, mean that hostilities *have* begun."[58]

A clash took place earlier that day at Carrizal, Chihuahua. When a detachment of United States cavalry under Captain Charles T. Boyd rode into town, Mexican forces attacked. They inflicted several casualties and captured seventeen Americans.[59] The news set off an outcry in Washington. Senators and congressmen clamored for action. Senator J. Hamilton Lewis, a Democrat from Illinois, insisted that continuation of "this policy of extenuation" will "make us pusillanimous." On 23 June the Congress resolved jointly to authorize the use of National Guardsmen outside the boundaries of the United States. General Funston warned that Mexicans would take the offensive, and Pershing advised the seizure of Chihuahua City. But Secretary of War Baker recalled that only Washington could decide "the actual existence of a state of war."[60] President Wilson also shunned undue haste. Reflecting that "the break seems to have come. . . I am infinitely sad about it," he wondered ambivalently whether he should have withdrawn the punitive expedition but concluded that he "could [not] have done differently, holding sacred the conviction I hold in this matter." Still, the possibility of "extremist consequences" worried him; he vowed to stand against them. "Intervention," which he understood as "the rearrangement and control of Mexico's domestic affairs by the U.S.," would not occur "now or at any other time if I can prevent it."[61]

Mexican leaders feared that Americans would take the initiative. Cándido Aguilar again appealed to the nations of Latin America, affirming that "the American government, lacking a judicial or political foundation in order to declare war on Mexico, wishes to make it inevitable by means of incidents." When Argentina inquired whether Mexico wanted an offer of mediation, Carranza took it as "a sign of friendly solidarity" but first wanted firm guarantees that mediation would accomplish the withdrawal of American forces. He too blamed the United States. A note to the State Department on 24 June held American forces accountable for the incident at Carrizal, since they had violated Mexican orders by moving into the town.[62] Lansing construed this charge as "a formal avowal of deliberately hostile action . . . and of the purpose to attack [Americans] without provocation." In reply, he demanded "the immediate release of the prisoners" and "an early statement" from Mexico "as to the course of action it wishes the Government of the United States to understand it has determined upon." According to Isidro Fabela, Carranza already had ordered the release of the captives, but for some reason they remained in custody. Perhaps communications broke down, or perhaps Mexican officers wanted hostages if war should begin.[63] Whatever the explanation, the delay heightened agitation in Washington.

Wilson came under strong pressure. Leon J. Canova from the Division of Mexican Affairs favored a declaration of war. Joe Tumulty, who acknowledged that he was "an excitable person," wanted to tell Carranza, "Release those American soldiers or take the consequences." Lansing too insisted that Mexico free the captives as a condition to further discussion. The president lacked good alternatives. According to Joe Tumulty's account, perhaps apocryphal but indicative of the president's quandary, Wilson declared, ". . . there won't be any war with Mexico if I can prevent it, no matter how loud the gentlemen on the hill yell for it. . . ." Wilson intended first to exhaust "every means to keep out of this mess," because "Germany is anxious to have us at war with Mexico."[64] The exigencies of the world war militated against forcing a break, yet the president also had to take into account domestic politics and the defense of the border. Retaining his respect for the principle of self-determination, he struggled to reconcile the manifold pressures upon him.

On 26 June Wilson began work on an address to Congress in which he revealed his intentions. His draft established fine distinctions. He wanted neither a declaration of war nor an intervention. Instead, he asked for authority "to use the military and naval forces of the Government in any way that may be necessary to guard our frontier effectively, if necessary to enter Mexican soil" until Mexican authorities resumed "their full obligations to us as a neighboring and friendly state." Such a limited goal differed fundamentally in his mind from intervention, which he defined as "an attempt to determine for the Mexican people what the form, the circumstances, and the personnel of their government shall be, or upon what terms and in what manner a settlement of their disturbed affairs shall be effected." Wilson aspired neither "to interfere with the liberties of any people" nor to acquire "a single foot of Mexican territory" nor to gain "a single hour of political control."[65] He wanted only redress of American grievances.

The president completed his draft by the morning of 28 June but never had occasion to deliver it. Carranza had acted warily. Expecting the Americans to strike first, he ordered his military commanders to repel an invasion but instructed them, "Be careful in international matters and avoid actions which could have unfortunate consequences." Arredondo then alerted him that the release of the prisoners could have a good effect. Carranza's order to free them on 28 June dissipated the immediate threat of war.[66]

Defusing the Crisis

If Wilson had wanted war in June 1916, he probably could have won support. Republicans had politicized the Mexican question. Leaders such as Albert Fall and Theodore Roosevelt especially assailed Wilson's failure to establish the peace. Henry Cabot Lodge stated the Republican position succinctly:

> On our Southern border is a ruined country, the prey of predatory bands, in a condition of well-nigh complete anarchy. In a large measure that anarchy and that ruin lie at our doors. To gratify a personal animosity the only Government that had any apparent hope of success in Mexico was overthrown. . . . The man whose adherents proclaim him to have kept the peace has had a peace with Mexico marked by recurrent bloodshed and by intermittent acts of war.[67]

Before the Republican convention at Chicago in the second week of June, Fall and Roosevelt urged the endorsement of intervention but settled for less. The party platform denounced "the indefensible methods of interference employed by this Administration in the internal affairs of Mexico." Republicans condemned "with shame" Wilson's incapacity "to discharge the duty of this country," his failure "to act promptly and firmly," his support "through recognition of one of the factions responsible for . . . outrages." By unspecified means, Republicans would aid "in restoring order and maintaining peace" and would provide "adequate and absolute protection in their lives, liberty and property" for "our citizens on or near the border, and to those in Mexico, wherever they may be found." When Charles Evans Hughes of New York won the nomination, Fall and Roosevelt supported his candidacy, linking it to a settlement of the Mexican question. Fall established a Mexican bureau to distribute information and to discredit the administration's policies. Roosevelt asked the War Department for authority to raise a cavalry division in the event of war with Mexico. He later explained that "all fighting men despise the present administration so, and distrust it so deeply, that they believe it is equally powerless to do well in keeping the peace or making war."[68]

Politics influenced the president's conduct in the summer and fall. To mute Republican criticism and to safeguard the border, Wilson chose to keep the punitive expedition in Mexico until Carranza could assure effective control. The Democratic party at its convention in St. Louis in the middle of June underwrote the president's stance, affirming that "the want of a stable, responsible government in Mexico, capable of repressing and punishing marauders and bandit bands . . . has rendered it necessary temporarily to occupy, by our armed forces, a portion of the territory of that friendly state." Although the Mexico plank advised against intervention "except as a last recourse," the punitive expedition would stay "until, by the restoration of law and order . . . a repetition of such incursions is improbable."[69]

Wilson adhered to this position during the Carrizal crisis and later lashed his critics for their recklessness. While addressing the New York Press Club on 30 June, he maintained that "the easiest thing is to strike. . . . No man has to think before he takes aggressive action. . . ." Eliseo Arredondo meanwhile waited "with great anxiety" for a response to the American note of 20 June, advising that Carranza insist "serenely" upon Pershing's departure. Arredondo hoped to produce "a favorable impression" in Washington and to have sufficient latitude to negotiate.[70]

Argentina again suggested mediation once the crisis had ended, but the United States preferred a different course. On 3 July Secretary Lansing proposed the creation of a joint Mexican-American commission to study "the various questions relating to the boundary troubles and the necessary means to prevent them in the future." Nevertheless, he stipulated that

Pershing would remain until the commission had completed its labors. On the following day Mexico expressed readiness "to seek an immediate solution to the two points which constitute the real cause of controversy," that is, the insecurity of the frontier and the presence of American troops in Mexico. The note inquired whether the United States wished to pursue such questions through mediation or direct negotiations.[71] The Wilson administration opted for the latter course.

When Frank Polk and Henry Fletcher discussed the preliminaries with Eliseo Arredondo, they had difficulty defining the purview of negotiation. The Mexicans wanted to empower the joint commission with limited authority to discuss only measures for policing the border and retiring the punitive force. The Americans wanted to invest the joint commission with broad power to consider "such other matters . . . the settlement of which would tend to improve the relations of the two Governments."[72] By their insistence, the Americans probably intended to prolong the deliberations through the November election and to obtain assurances guaranteeing the protection of property, the establishment of a claims commission, and the practice of religious toleration. Such concerns had little direct bearing on the decision to send Pershing into Mexico. Nevertheless, once Carranza chose in the summer of 1916 to regularize his administration, to hold municipal elections, and to write a new constitution, the future course of the Mexican Revolution became increasingly important in determining whether Pershing should leave.

Jurisdictional questions impeded the negotiations from the beginning. When Arredondo inquired precisely what issues the United States wished to consider, Frank Polk evasively declined to specify, but he intimated that President Wilson would rather have no commission at all than one with limited authority. Later Polk assured Mexico that the United States would neither press for the cession of territory nor advance unreasonable claims. When Arredondo then suggested that the joint commission first settle the border question before turning to other matters, Carranza tentatively endorsed the formula and on 28 July the United States formally accepted the Mexican proposal to establish a joint commission. On 3 August Carranza selected Luis Cabrera, Ignacio Bonillas, and Alberto J. Pani to represent his government. Each was a civilian with close ties to the first chief. Carranza allowed them some freedom to maneuver but reserved for himself the prerogative to approve or disapprove all agreements. As the "principal object," he instructed them to devise a reciprocal border agreement and to secure American withdrawal.[73]

By the end of August, President Wilson obtained the consent of Dr. John R. Mott, a missionary and friend, George Gray, a lawyer and jurist, and Franklin K. Lane, the secretary of the interior, to serve on the joint commission. At the State Department, however, Frank Polk appraised the chances of success pessimistically. "Personally" he expected that "nothing" would come of the negotiations. Carranza was "acting more stupidly than usual" and probably would refuse "to discuss anything until the evacuation of Mexican territory . . . is disposed of." Still, Polk understood that Americans had limited choices. Either they could "deal patiently with Carranza" or "break off relations and go into Mexico." Since the later would prejudice the United States "at the most critical time in the European war," he preferred "to be patient with Carranza . . . as long as we possibly could."[74]

When the joint commission assembled on 4 September at the Hotel Biltmore in New York City, the Mexican delegates explained the condition of their country "in the fullest manner," especially their government's progress in consolidating authority. Alberto Pani recorded that the Americans had only "fragmentary knowledge" of such matters. When Luis Cabrera intimated his willingness "to go into every question which the American Commissioners thought important, provided publicity could be avoided, as . . . it would cause political trouble in Mexico," Robert Lansing took heart, regarding "the prospects" as "bright."[75] The clash of rival aims soon dissipated such optimism.

Once the deliberations began, the Mexican commissioners refused to broaden the scope until American forces actually departed from Mexico. Although General Funston previously had advised such a course, reasoning that the punitive expedition no longer served a military purpose, the American commissioners tied the question of withdrawal to other issues. General Pershing regarded "the retention of the expedition here" as "something of a club that the administration can use over the Mexican government." Indeed, Secretary of War Baker candidly asserted that "past experience does not permit us to rely upon the cooperation of the authorities of the de facto government." Hoping to bring about some movement once the conference shifted to the Hotel Griswold in New London, Connecticut, the Americans inquired on 22 September whether the Mexicans would discuss other matters while Washington passed on the details of a military pullback. But Carranza sanctioned no concession. Rather, he expressed astonishment that after two weeks the Americans had not headed northward.[76]

A resurgence of violence in northern Mexico posed further difficulty. In the middle of September a small army, reportedly composed of Villistas and "remnants" from other factions, attacked Chihuahua City. Later, when the joint commission convened at the Hotel Traymore in Atlantic City, New Jersey, the Americans insisted that they could not withdraw Pershing while such conditions prevailed. Suspecting that "our enemies work to provoke international conflict," Foreign Secretary Aguilar rebutted that the Wilson administration had lapsed in the enforcement of neutrality laws against anti-Carranza conspirators in the United States. Nevertheless,

Cabrera concluded that the Americans would not address "the primary question." Early in October the Mexicans threatened to terminate the conference unless the Americans refrained from trying to bring about "the rehabilitation" of their country.[77]

The proximity of elections in the United States further constricted Mexico's bargaining power. Cabrera understood that the administration would accept only "a successful agreement" for use in the campaign. President Wilson and others publicly reiterated their commitment to the defense of the border. Meanwhile, Republicans exploited the issue. A full-page advertisement in the *New York Times* on 26 October asked, "Has He Kept Us Out Of War?" "For months we have been conducting a border war with Mexico." But in spite of such appeals, Wilson defeated Hughes by a close margin on election day.[78] His victory relieved the political pressure and opened new approaches to Mexico.

On 17 November the Mexican delegates incorporated several compromise proposals into a draft protocol. It called for phased withdrawal within forty days and cooperative measures during the interim, including the possibility of reciprocal privileges to cross the border. The American delegates accepted the military terms but objected that the draft guaranteed no discussion of other issues. After a visit with the president, the secretary of state, and the secretary of war in Washington, Franklin K. Lane returned to Atlantic City and insisted that the United States play a role in a "larger constructive program" for Mexico. Grudgingly the Mexicans consented to tolerate the re-entry of American forces if border conditions should warrant it and also to seek the first chief's permission to discuss other issues.[79]

Alberto Pani carried the draft protocol to Mexico and met with Carranza at the city of Querétaro, where a constitutional convention soon would assemble. Characteristically the first chief bridled at the condition permitting American forces to return. Further, he wanted no commitment to broaden the scope of discussions. As the Mexicans set about the writing of a new constitution, a variety of special-interest groups, including foreign landowners and oilmen, clamored for assurance in defense of property and claims. Carranza hesitated to restrict his options. Rather than take the risk, he chose to repudiate the protocol altogether. When he inquired how the Americans would respond, Pani told him they probably would retire the punitive force. Later, at the Bellevue-Stratford Hotel in Philadelphia on 18 December, the Mexican delegates advised an explicit promise to evacuate American forces permanently. But the Americans regarded such a suggestion as "impracticable and unwise." The conference adjourned indefinitely on the following day.[80] Soon afterward the Wilson administration chose to withdraw the punitive expedition unilaterally without demanding an equivalent from Mexico.

The decision resulted more from a conviction that Pershing no longer served a useful purpose than from the imperatives of World War I. The German decision to resume unrestricted submarine warfare had not yet plunged relations with the United States into crisis. Indeed, in December 1916 President Wilson contemplated the possibility of halting the war through mediation. Nevertheless, he had reason to think that no advantage would accrue from keeping the punitive force in Mexico. Indeed, by withdrawing unconditionally he could place the burden of policing the border on Mexico and retain a free hand to act in the future as conditions might warrant. The secretary of war calculated that such a course would compel Mexico to assume "her full responsibilities as an independent government." Similarly, Henry Fletcher reasoned that "the present crisis with Mexico is diplomatic rather than military."[81]

On 3 January 1917 the joint commissioners met once again but found it "fruitless" to persist in discussion. Since they could reach no agreement "satisfactory to both parties," the Americans advised the president to withdraw unilaterally. The joint commission terminated on 15 January 1917, deadlocked to the very end. When a resolution calling for the establishment of full diplomatic relations came under consideration, the Mexicans insisted upon Pershing's recall as a condition. The Americans rejected any formal commitment; the joint commission adjourned sine die.[82]

Aims and Effects of the Punitive Expedition

The last contingents of Pershing's force departed from Mexico on the afternoon of 5 February 1917. Little fanfare awaited them. News of Wilson's decision to break relations with Germany had filled the headlines. Subsequently, some of the participants looked upon the punitive expedition as a bitter, frustrating experience. Colonel Frank Tompkins characterized the undertaking as "a hodge-podge of interference and non-intervention, of patience and petulance, of futile conferences and abortive armed invasions." Tompkins believed that a half-million men could have "cleaned-up" Mexico in short order and then could have gone to France early in 1917 as seasoned veterans. Military men often attributed the shortcomings to political restraints and civilian errors. The Wilson administration had created false expectations by proclaiming the capture of Villa as a goal. General Hugh Scott recalled that "nothing in the order" said anything "about catching Villa himself." Indeed, Pershing accomplished the primary aim "from the War Department point of view" by dispersing Villa's band, but the State Department, "by putting out erroneous information, spoiled the effect in the minds of the public." General Pershing maintained that criticism had "no basis . . . if the limitations placed upon the Expedition are taken into account."[83]

President Wilson never envisioned the punitive expedition purely in military terms. He intended it to serve a diversity of ends. Political exigencies, the security of the border, and the preservation of American credibility in Europe accounted in large part for his decision to send troops into Mexico. Later he broadened his purpose, hoping to gain influence over the course of the revolution and to shape it according to the principles of liberal capitalism. Increasingly his goals collided with the principle of self-determination and Carranza's nationalistic defense of it. As Wilson became more acutely aware of the conflict, he lost much of his sense of solidarity with Mexicans and began to perceive them as potential adversaries. For the remainder of his presidency, he struggled to reconcile the requirements of liberal capitalism with the demands of self-determination.

Chapter 4

The Question of
De Jure Recognition

The retirement of the punitive expedition left the principal issues in abeyance. American leaders intended to address them through conventional diplomacy and to reserve their liberty to act. They put little faith in Carranza. Secretary of War Newton D. Baker commented that the de facto government had not yet earned "our unlimited confidence." Nevertheless, President Wilson moved to regularize diplomatic relations by notifying the first chief on 2 February 1917 of his decision to send Henry P. Fletcher as ambassador extraordinary and plenipotentiary.[1] The difficulties encountered by Fletcher were greatly magnified by the promulgation on 5 February of a new Mexican constitution.

Constitution of 1917

The Mexican Constitution of 1917 served to legitimate the Constitutionalists' triumph and to provide a legal rationale for change. Carranza began the restoration of legal and constitutional forms in the summer of 1916 by scheduling municipal elections early in September and calling for a constituent assembly to enact reforms into law. He excluded from participation enemies who had supported other factions. In the election of 22 October 1916, only a small percentage of eligible voters turned out. In a few districts, where the government lacked real authority, no polling took place at all. Still, the victors (220 delegates and alternates) represented a fairly broad range of interests and opinions within the Constitutionalist camp. They included sixty-two lawyers, twenty-two senior military officers, nineteen farmers, eighteen teachers, sixteen engineers, sixteen physicians, fourteen journalists, seven accountants, five labor leaders, four miners, three railroad workers, two pharmacists, one actor, and thirty-one artisans, merchants, and employees. The majority, young men in their thirties and forties, lacked experience in government. Often provincial in outlook, they acted experimentally and instinctually.[2]

Beginning on 20 November 1916 at the city of Querétaro, the delegates fashioned a constitution in a little more than two months of hard labor. They addressed six issues of special concern. The political structure of the Republic, the status of labor, and the secularization of education bore mainly on Mexico's internal affairs. In contrast, the relationship between Church and State, the nature of land tenure, and the ownership of subsoil mineral resources also affected foreign interests. The participants composed three loosely connected blocs. One voted independently. The second, the so-called *liberales carrancistas,* hewed to the liberal traditions of the nine-teenth century. Taking a moderate anticlerical stance and upholding the sanctity of individual rights, they wished to change the Constitution of 1857 only slightly. Further, since they preferred that government play a limited role, they wanted to cast the constitution in general terms so that statutes subsequently could elaborate and implement its meaning. The third, the so-called *jacobinos obregonistas,* insisted upon more dramatic change. Embracing a fiercer brand of anticlericalism, they regarded government more as an instrument to promote social and economic amelioration. They stressed "societal rights over those of the individual" and wanted "detailed rather than general constitutional provisions."[3]

The participants disputed hotly over a multitude of issues, but as E. V. Niemeyer showed, their disagreements were "more of degree than of substance." Almost everyone favored "the revolution," however they might define it, characteristically in highly nationalistic terms. Further, they were divided more over questions of means than of ends. Carranza's draft on 1 December 1916 employed the Constitution of 1857 as a model and proposed few fundamental changes, but it served as a catalyst for debate.[4] In the end, delegates wrote an ideologically eclectic document, more radical than Carranza's proposals but not altogether out of keeping with his wishes.

Much as the Constitution of 1857, the Constitution of 1917 established a federal political system that provided for the separation of powers but allocated more authority to the president than to the Congress. It also guaranteed the autonomy of municipalities, insured political and civil rights for all Mexicans, and prohibited the re-election of presidents. Unlike the Constitution of 1857, the new charter assigned large responsibilities to the federal government in the social and economic affairs of Mexico. Article 123, characterized by Charles C. Cumberland as "the most enlightened statement of labor protective principles in the world to that date," sanctioned an eight-hour day, minimum wages, and restrictions on child labor. Article 3 placed public education under the control of secular authorities.

Article 130 separated the Church and the State and disallowed political activity by clergymen.[5] Through such measures, the delegates at Querétaro sought to harness governmental power to aid in creating a more equitable society.

Their efforts also impinged on foreign interests. Although anticlerical provisions angered Roman Catholics in the United States and elsewhere, Article 27 had the most volatile effect.[6] This provision addressed the question of land tenure and the ownership of mineral resources. It asserted the right to expropriate private property, a tenet long established in Mexican law, and affirmed the principle of nationalization. Under Article 27, "the ownership of lands and waters comprised within the limits of the national territory is vested originally in the Nation, which has had, and has, the right to transmit title thereof to private persons, thereby constituting private property." Although the measure permitted the expropriation of private property only "for reasons of public utility and by means of indemnification," it stipulated that "the Nation shall have at all times the right to impose on private property such limitations as the public interest may demand" and also "the right to regulate the development of natural resources."

To carry out agrarian reform, Article 27 envisioned the breakup of large landed estates, the development of small land holdings, and the establishment of new centers of rural population. To regulate extractive industries more effectively, the measure re-established in Mexican law the traditional Hispanic distinction between surface lands and subsurface resources and endowed the nation with the ownership of "all minerals or substances which in veins, layers, masses or beds constitute deposits whose nature is different from the components of the land." It further provided that "only Mexicans by birth or naturalization and Mexican companies" could obtain the right "to acquire ownership in lands, waters and their appurtenances, or to develop mines, waters or mineral fields in the Republic of Mexico." To receive such privileges, foreign residents first must agree "to be considered Mexicans in respect to such property" and to forsake "the protection of their Governments . . . under penalty, in case of breach, of forfeiture to the Nation of property so acquired."[7]

Article 27 expressly repudiated the practices of Porfirian Mexico. To encourage investment, the Díaz regime had annulled the distinction between the surface and the subsurface, permitting resident aliens to exercise exploitative privileges beneath the surface once they acquired surface lands. Consequently, foreign capitalists, especially American and British, became dominant in extractive industries. By 1910 Americans had invested an estimated $249,500,000 in Mexican mining and $15,000,000 in petroleum. By 1917 foreigners owned 90 percent of Mexico's petroleum lands;

the American stake in petroleum had reached $59,000,000; and Edward L. Doheny's Mexican Petroleum Company, together with its subsidiaries, controlled more than 600,000 acres in the Tampico and Veracruz region.[8]

The Constitutionalists based their objection on nationalistic grounds, taking the position that foreigners had prospered disproportionately at Mexico's expense. Since Mexico lacked a well-developed internal market, foreign-owned companies produced mainly for export. Constitutionalists argued that, although foreigners contributed to the Mexican economy through the payment of taxes, salaries, and rents, they took an excessive share of the profits out of Mexico. The delegates at Querétaro intended Article 27 to alleviate such inequities. They also hoped to gain political advantages and new sources of revenue. The petroleum industry invited special attention, since foreigners controlled it and since it had prospered in spite of the revolution. Production had climbed from 4,431,826 barrels in 1910 to 25,902,439 barrels in 1913 to 32,910,508 in 1915 to 55,292,770 in 1917, an amount which ranked third highest in the world behind that of the United States and Russia.[9]

Carranza initially shied away from public advocacy of nationalization. He included no such provision in his draft constitution, holding that the right of expropriation was "sufficient." Consequently, a long-established view has maintained that he accepted the more sweeping position reluctantly when "radicals" led by Alvaro Obregón and Francisco Mújica demanded it.[10] This claim has recently come under question. Possibly Carranza favored nationalization but moved warily because of foreign opposition. Since American forces still occupied Mexican territory, he may have wished to divert criticism away from himself by taking a moderate stance in public while striving for nationalization in private. The reminiscences of Pastor Rouaix, a cabinet official and an author of Article 27, support such an inference. Also, nationalization followed logically from a line of executive decrees in which the first chief required foreigners to register their property with the government and to consider themselves as Mexican for legal purposes. Americans, aided by the State Department, resisted, arguing that such stipulations violated international law and aimed at confiscation. Such obstruction perhaps encouraged Mexicans to assert the broader claim of nationalization. Carranza in all likelihood had less antipathy to the idea than some historians have supposed.[11]

Reaction to Article 27

Article 27 unsettled Americans because it threatened to place relations on an entirely new footing. By subordinating individual property rights to a conception of national rights, the Mexicans in effect repudiated the established rules of international intercourse. The challenge defied Wilson's liberal-capitalist proclivities and the entire body of assumptions implicit in American policies toward Latin America. Mexicans claimed that they merely wanted to establish juridical equality with foreigners. Americans perceived a more nefarious design.

Since Article 27 required enabling legislation to take effect, Americans could not calculate the consequences precisely. Foreigners would have to apply to Mexican authorities in the future to obtain property rights and exploitative privileges. Such a prospect distressed Americans but less so than the possibility that Article 27 would annul titles and leases acquired under previous laws. Although Article 14 forbade retroactive enforcement of congressional enactments, it placed no similar restrictions on constitutional provisions.[12] Further, although Carranza had promised to respect "legitimately acquired property," he might not regard titles and leases obtained during the Díaz and Huerta regimes as valid.

Beginning in November 1916, businessmen with a stake in Mexico contemplated the creation of a "protective association" to defend their interests. A group including H. A. Sibbett of the Richardson Construction Company, Judge Delbert Haff of the Cananea Copper Company, Frederick Kellogg of the Doheny petroleum interests, George C. Carnahan of the International Rubber Company, William Loeb of the American Smelting and Refining Company, and Frederick Watriss, the president of the Yaqui Delta Land and Cattle Company and the former law partner of Frank Polk (the State Department counselor), urged that the American delegates on the joint commission avoid any "admissions or concessions" that could jeopardize American interests. Although some suspected that Germans had encouraged Carranza in his "anti-foreign movement" and others lacked confidence in Woodrow Wilson, they resolved late in 1916 to seek the protection of their government. During the ensuing months, appeals to the State Department repeatedly charged that Article 27 had "confiscatory" intent, on occasion holding that wartime demands had rendered Mexican resources all the more vital. The critics wanted to modify the measure through diplomatic pressure.[13]

On 22 January 1917, two weeks before the promulgation of the constitution, Robert Lansing established the State Department's position. He criticized Article 27 since it afforded "no safeguards" against "unwise and arbitrary executive acts." Further, it provided no defense against retroactive enforcement and hence could result in the "confiscation of property rights vested under existing laws and treaty stipulations." Cautioning that the United States would not acquiesce "in any direct or indirect confiscation of foreign-owned properties," Lansing advised that any attempt to advance such goals could have "possible grave consequences." Addressing a related point three days later, he rejected Carranza's claim that tax levies in the extractive industries fell outside the purview of international diplomacy as acts of national sovereignty. On the contrary, Lansing insisted, "this Government . . . is amply justified in diplomatic intervention" if such taxes "are confiscatory in effect" and "are detrimental to many American citizens."[14] His posture largely fixed the administration's stance in the controversy over Article 27.

When Henry P. Fletcher reached the Mexican capital in the middle of February 1917, taxation and property rights posed immediate issues. Since Carranza was sojourning in Guadalajara, he discussed them with Foreign Secretary Aguilar, who claimed that Mexican laws would not menace properties to which foreigners held clear title. Though reassuring, such words failed to satisfy Americans who wanted guarantees.[15] Chandler P. Anderson, a distinguished specialist in international law, a former State Department counselor under Taft, and a friend of Robert Lansing, hoped to obtain them by withholding de jure recognition.

Anderson served the infant "protective association" during much of 1917 as adviser and liaison with the State Department. The possibility that Mexicans would enforce Article 27 retroactively especially worried him; he believed that Wilson had realized the danger tardily. Initially he reasoned that a treaty could provide the appropriate assurances. If Carranza would repudiate retroactive designs, the United States should extend de jure recognition. When Anderson urged such a strategem upon Robert Lansing and Frank Polk in March 1917, they responded sympathetically but hesitated to embrace it. Probably the president would object. As the crisis mounted in relations with Germany during the spring of 1917, Wilson preferred conciliation more than coercion in his approach to Carranza. Nevertheless, when Anderson drafted part of a treaty, Polk encouraged him but then grew cool. As a departmental memorandum recalled, ". . . a treaty cannot change the Constitution or be held valid if it be in violation of that instrument."[16] Such an interpretation held true in American law; in all likelihood it applied in Mexico as well.

German Courtship of Mexico

Uncertainty over relationships with Germany accounted in part for the State Department's reticence. When German leaders resumed unrestricted submarine warfare on 31 January 1917, the Americans broke diplomatic ties four days later. They expected German intrigues in Mexico. Robert Lansing believed that German influences had aided Carranza. The Zimmerman telegram (proposing a Mexican-German alliance) heightened his concern. He later recorded his impression that German agents had incited Mexican opinion against the United States and that Carranza had utilized "the popular antipathy for Americans as a political asset." Because of the world war, however, Americans had "to swallow [their] pride and maintain as good relations as possible" with "this impossible old man."[17] Such reasoning articulated a basic premise of American policy during the war years. Rather than risk diversions while engaged in Europe, leaders in the Wilson administration hoped to cultivate Carranza. Nevertheless, his advocacy of Article 27 posed a dilemma. To resist too vigorously could serve German interests by embroiling Americans with Mexicans. To submit, in contrast, could jeopardize American investments and American access to Mexican oil. The ensuing tactical difficulties often instilled a sense of ambivalence. Americans had to choose whether to court Carranza or to safeguard their interests in Mexico by other means.

Before the onset of World War I, Germany had taken only sporadic interest in Mexico. During the Díaz years, German nationals in Mexican commercial and military circles numbered only 3827 according to the 1910 census. For a time at the turn of the century, Emperor Wilhelm II contemplated the extension of large-scale military assistance programs but decided against it. Washington probably would object, and Berlin had no wish "to alienate the United States for the sake of having a strong voice within the Mexican military establishment." Occasional subsequent efforts to capitalize on the prestige of the German army accomplished comparatively little. In contrast with the British and the Americans, the Germans possessed scant influence.[18]

Once the European war had begun, German aims in Mexico became more ambitious and opportunistic. German leaders toyed with schemes to engage the United States in an intervention or a war. Either could impede the flow of money and supplies to the Allies and limit the American capacity to determine the outcome in Europe. German agents employed a variety of stratagems, such as cultivating the principal factions, encouraging the Plan of San Diego (to provoke an uprising in the American Southwest), and plotting sabotage in the Mexican oil fields.[19] The nature of German goals has become reasonably clear; the extent to which Germans actually influenced Mexican behavior has remained much less so.

Carranza initially took more interest in the Americans than in the Germans. Since the Constitutionalist revolt took precedence over the European conflict in his order of priorities, the attitude of the United States held great significance. In September 1914 Carranza declared a policy of neutrality in the European struggle. Later he avoided shows of partisanship, especially if they could embarrass him in relations with the United States. Late in 1915, when American authorities expelled attachés Karl Boy-Ed and Franz von Papen of the German Embassy for espionage and other offenses, Carranza too regarded Papen as persona non grata.[20]

The first chief's position grew more ambiguous in 1916. With the onset of the punitive expedition, the question of German relations with Mexico became even more important. Some Americans believed that German provocateurs had instigated Villa's attack on Columbus, intending to precipitate a war. Six weeks after Pershing entered Mexico, Charles B. Parker, a State Department agent in Mexico City, recounted rumors that Germany would aid Mexico if a war with the United States should occur. Although Parker tended to discount them, lacking the "slightest tangible evidence," he allowed that a German-Mexican alignment could conceivably take shape. American intelligence watched for signs, but Carranza's government acted independently. Late in May 1916 Cándido Aguilar turned down an offer by "a German subject" to deliver 150,000 rifle cartridges each month.[21]

The longer Pershing remained, the more attractive outside support became. In the fall of 1916 Carranza played Germans against Americans. In October he intimated the possibility of a submarine base if German leaders would declare publicly against American intervention. In November he proposed a new treaty of commerce and friendship, invited technological and military assistance, and again hinted about a submarine base. But German leaders responded coolly, seeing little advantage in arousing the United States against them at this juncture. Nevertheless, a submarine base held some interest, but when German agents pursued the question late in November, Carranza reportedly spurned their overtures.[22] Rumors also suggested an impending treaty between Mexico and Japan. Possibly Carranza wanted to obtain a new source of arms. The gossip was dismissed by Charles B. Parker as having "but slight foundation in fact."[23]

The coincidence of such maneuvers with the proceedings of the Mexican-American joint commission and the presidential elections in the United States suggested the nature of Carranza's motives. Probably he desired a show of international support more than an actual alliance. Such a demonstration would strengthen his hand vis-à-vis the United States, especially in securing Pershing's withdrawal. Further, if the Republicans should win the election and intervention should follow, an alignment with Germany could prove valuable. Carranza in all likelihood had less interest in an alliance after Wilson's re-election, but he continued to keep the alternative alive, anticipating eventualities if Pershing should remain.

German leaders grew more avid for an alliance once they chose early in 1917 to resume unrestricted submarine warfare. Since the decision could entail war with the United States, they regarded it as a calculated risk. They also considered the possibility of occupying the Americans elsewhere. A plan to use Mexico as a diversion impressed Foreign Minister Arthur Zimmermann.[24] On 16 January 1917 he sent a coded telegram to Count Johann von Bernstorff, the German ambassador in Washington, instructing him to communicate the contents to Heinrich von Eckhardt, the German minister in Mexico City. Since Britain had severed the German trans-Atlantic cable, Zimmermann transmitted the message by wireless and also through the facilities of the Swedish diplomatic service and the United States Department of State, which had extended the privilege as a courtesy. The Zimmermann telegram disclosed the decision to resume submarine warfare on 1 February. Zimmermann hoped that the United

States would remain neutral. Nevertheless, if Wilson should choose otherwise, Zimmermann authorized Eckhardt to propose an alliance with Mexico on these terms: "Joint conduct of war. Joint conclusion of peace. Ample financial support and an agreement on our part that Mexico shall gain back by conquest the territory lost by her at a prior period in Texas, New Mexico and Arizona." Eckhardt should make the proposition "in strict confidence" if war broke out with the United States and also should try to bring in the Japanese. Later, when the United States broke diplomatic relations, Zimmermann urged his subordinate on 5 February to act with greater haste, "provided that there is no risk of the secret being betrayed to the United States."[25]

The scheme miscarried wretchedly. Unknown to Berlin, British cryptographers had deciphered the German code. Further, British intelligence intercepted Zimmermann's three transmissions on 16 January as well as Bernstorff's relay to Eckhardt three days later. After a delay to confuse the Germans, British authorities on 23 February presented a copy of the fourth transmission to Walter Hines Page, the American ambassador at the Court of St. James. After notifying the State Department that he had information of great importance, Page forwarded the Zimmermann telegram to Washington early the next morning. When Woodrow Wilson learned of it on the following day (decoding and translation occasioned further delay), he indignantly favored immediate publication. But Frank Polk prevailed upon him to wait until Robert Lansing returned from a holiday and the authenticity of the document was established. The newspapers printed the Zimmermann telegram on 1 March.[26]

For leaders in the administration, the Zimmermann telegram confirmed suspicions of German duplicity. Though still unready to advocate war, Wilson lost "all faith" in the German government. Unsurprised by the revelation, Colonel House had believed "for a long time" that Germany wanted "to stir up all the troubles they could in order to occupy our attention." Lansing reasoned similarly but characterized Zimmermann's behavior as "a stupid piece of business." Lansing anticipated that Zimmermann would denounce the document as a forgery, since President Wilson could not reveal his source without alerting the Germans that the British had cracked their code. When Zimmermann confounded this expectation by admitting publicly his responsibility, Lansing thought it "a most astounding blunder."[27]

The episode also animated American mistrust of Mexico. Initial indications suggested that Carranza might have accepted the German offer. On 7 February 1917 American immigration authorities in San Antonio, Texas, arrested a group of aliens for entering the United States illegally, among them two young Austrians, Olga Visser and Heinrich Kolbeck. Once placed in detention, Olga Visser claimed that she and Kolbeck possessed important documents, carried at the bequest of the Austro-Hungarian Embassy in Mexico City. Failing a suicide attempt, she then produced a ciphered message, reportedly intended for a groceryman in San Antonio who headed an espionage network in the American Southwest. Allegedly, it conveyed word that Carranza had embraced Germany in an alliance. The information reached Washington on 1 March and caused further stir in official circles. Subsequent investigations by the Justice Department failed to substantiate the story, for Heinrich Kolbeck persuaded his interrogators that he had invented the tale to impress his companion. Whether this odd affair, either conspiracy or farce, revealed anything about Carranza's policy toward Germany has remained a matter of conjecture.[28]

Publication of the Zimmermann telegram prompted swift disclaimers from some Mexican officials. Ramón P. de Negri, the chargé d'affaires in Washington, expected a formal disavowal from his government. Andrés G. García, the inspector-general of Mexican consulates, testified that his countrymen had pro-Ally sentiments. Ernesto Garza Pérez, the undersecretary of foreign affairs, said he knew nothing about it. The Japanese also denied complicity. Their embassy in Washington characterized the revelation as "a very monstrous story . . . an impossible story . . . an outrageous story." Later the Foreign Office in Tokyo attributed Zimmermann's scheme to German "mental delusions." Nevertheless, suspicions lingered in the United States.[29]

On 26 February the State Department instructed Henry P. Fletcher to seek immediate clarification. Since Carranza still remained in Guadalajara, the ambassador sought out Cándido Aguilar, who professed ignorance. When Fletcher advised a formal statement on grounds that the Zimmermann telegram would create "a sensation" in the United States, Aguilar informed the first chief and awaited instructions. Carranza then called him to Guadalajara and also invited Fletcher, who seized the opportunity to size up Aguilar as "very cautious, somewhat prejudiced and of rather narrow outlook, an intense believer in the principles of the present revolution. . . . He was very guarded in his remarks about the United States."[30]

When they arrived in Guadalajara on 1 March, news of the Zimmermann telegram had preceded them. After a conference with his superior, Aguilar told Fletcher on the following day that Carranza had decided against a public statement but would receive him formally. On 3 March Fletcher presented his letter of credence but could not gain a private audience until the next day. He then broached the German question directly. Since the Zimmermann telegram could create "a false impression" in the United States about "Mexico's attitude," Fletcher asked for a statement that would leave "no doubt" about Mexico's position if war between the United States and Germany should occur. But Carranza equivocated. When asked how he would respond to an alliance offer, he avoided saying "directly" that he would reject such a proposition. Instead, he claimed that he had received no such proposal from Germany, that he wanted to keep the war from crossing the Atlantic, and that Mexico desired to remain uninvolved. He also inquired why the United States had not responded to Mexico's offer to halt the war through neutral mediation.[31]

Mexico had appealed to the warring countries on 11 February, asking that they accept the good offices of neutral nations to stop the fighting. If the belligerents should refuse, Mexico proposed an embargo on trade, which would deny access to Mexican oil. Since the United States had not replied, Carranza explained that pro-German sympathies had not inspired the note. Rather, humanitarian concerns and Mexican self-interest had inspired his wish to isolate the western hemisphere from the war. Among other things, Carranza calculated that American intervention in Europe might drag an unwilling Mexico into the conflagration.[32]

Although Carranza and Aguilar couched their utterances in guarded terms, Fletcher believed they "inclined toward Germany" in their "sentiments." Nevertheless, he reasoned that Mexico would not enter an alliance "under present circumstances." Carranza possibly withheld a "categorical statement" to that effect in order to induce the United States to endorse his call for a peace conference. Fletcher also took solace in Aguilar's observation that Mexico would behave justly and correctly with or without a formal statement.[33]

Mystery still obscures Mexico's response to the Zimmermann telegram.[34] The evidence, albeit fragmentary, suggests that Mexican leaders certainly knew of the German proposition. Many years later Cándido Aguilar claimed that Germany never proposed an alliance formally. Rather, Mexico broke the German code and learned of the plan by intercepting telegraphic communications. On another occasion he stated that German spokesmen informally intimated the possibility of an alliance to him and that he turned it down because of the risk of war with the United States. According to still another account, Carranza also knew of the proposition, discussed it with his confidants, and spurned it because of the probable consequences in relations with the Americans. He thought an actual alliance would benefit Germany far more than Mexico.[35]

Heinrich von Eckhardt's dispatches to Berlin provide partial corroboration. On 20 February Eckhardt sounded out Aguilar, who "willingly took the matter into consideration; and thereupon had a conversation, which lasted an hour and a half with [the] Japanese minister, the tenor of which is unknown to me." Eckhardt presumed that Carranza later learned of the offer. When newspapers publicized the secret on 1 March, Eckhardt, believing his career in jeopardy, informed his superiors that the betrayal had not occurred in Mexico City and also wired Aguilar in Guadalajara "to give him a line, that the affair was unknown to me." Later in the middle of April, Eckhardt reported that Carranza would "in all circumstances" remain neutral; "premature publication" had ruined the scheme for the present. Nevertheless, if Mexico should enter the European war, Eckhardt reasoned that an alliance "would become necessary at a later period." Further, since Carranza still needed money and arms, Eckhardt believed that Germany could win his sympathy. But when Germany again suggested an alliance in May 1917, Carranza rejected it outright.[36]

For Carranza, the threat of an alliance always had more utility than the actuality. Once the punitive expedition withdrew and the United States broke relations with Germany, a formal alignment with Germany became more of a liability than an asset. Indeed, an alliance might goad the United States into forceful measures, and Carranza had no assurance that Germany could or would support him effectively. After the first week of February 1917, Carranza hoped that the United States would remain neutral. By his appraisal, a war between the United States and Germany could entail the risk of becoming dependent on one or the other. Rather than make a choice, he preferred to leave his position unclear after the revelation of the Zimmermann plot. He also tried unsuccessfully to encourage American support for his peace initiative. On 16 March Robert Lansing refused to endorse it, explaining that German violations of international law had rendered any such course inadmissable. Two days later Carranza inquired whether the United States would accept Mexico's good offices to restore relations with Germany, but the offer availed nothing.[37] On 6 April 1917 the United States intervened in World War I.

American leaders tried to anticipate beforehand how Mexico might respond to a declaration of war. On 30 March Fletcher reported that "anti-American sentiment" was "very strong from the highest to the lowest in the land." He expected that Germans would exploit it. Since Mexican "sympathies" would support Germany, Fletcher wanted a commitment to sustain neutrality. He reasoned also that Mexico would try to profit from the American "preoccupation" with Germany, probably by implementing controversial provisions in the Constitution of 1917. President Wilson had similar concerns. While describing the first chief as a "pedantic ass," he lamented, "All that Carranza has said and done shows his intense resentment of this Administration." Wilson wanted a guarantee of neutrality. Two weeks after the declaration of war, he advised "very frankly" that the United States expected that Carranza would remain neutral and would prevent Mexico from becoming "a base of hostile acts."[38]

Carranza had already assuaged American misgivings. In an address to the Mexican Congress on 15 April, he affirmed his desire to maintain "the most rigorous and strict neutrality" and to cultivate relations "of friendship and harmony" with all nations. When he expressed himself similarly in a conversation with Henry Fletcher, the ambassador took heart, reporting that "Mr. Carranza fully realized the desirability and necessity of Mexico maintaining strictly its neutrality." Fletcher characterized his attitude as "frank, cordial, and rather encouraging."[39]

Nevertheless, the likelihood of German intrigues in Mexico worried Americans. In trying "to foresee what might happen," Colonel Frank R. McCoy, the American military attaché who directed intelligence in Mexico in the spring of 1917, regarded sabotage in the oil fields as "the first danger." He also expected that Germany would try "to involve the Mexican government with us," probably by instigating "breaches of neutrality" and border troubles. Still, he judged that German machinations had been "greatly exagerated [*sic*] in the United States, as well as their influence with the De Facto Government." Carranza would try "to keep every body guessing" but was "to [*sic*] canny to invite any break with us," since he understood his "absolute dependence for money, supplies, etc." General John Pershing also thought it unlikely that Mexicans would enter a war against the United States. Although "some of them might be led by German influence and perhaps by German money . . . and might indulge in border raids or otherwise make trouble for us," he believed that "matters in Mexico seem to be shaping themselves rather favorably." Similarly, General Hugh Scott observed that "the German situation in Mexico seems to be solving itself. . . ." Although trouble might reach "annoying proportions," he did not regard it as "dangerous." In striking contrast, Robert Lansing reasoned pessimistically that the dominant political factions were "intensely pro-German or at least anti-American," and that Carranza, "whatever his personal views," would not "be strong enough to resist the pressure of the element hostile to us." Since German propagandists had distorted Mexican perceptions of the war, Lansing prepared for all "eventualities."[40]

Other Americans shared his apprehension. Throughout the war, diplomats, consuls, and agents of the Justice Department, the Army, and the Navy watched for signs of German intrigue but had difficulty judging accurately. Spy stories cropped up repeatedly. One informant asserted that German agents in Milwaukee shipped beer to Yucatán with secret messages inside the labels. Another claimed that Germans in the legation at Mexico City sent ciphered communications in packages of dirty laundry.[41] More reliable evidence suggested that Germans intended sabotage in the oil fields, that wireless stations in Mexico tried to aid German submarines in attacking American shipping, and that German propagandists preyed upon Mexican antipathies toward the United States. For example, the Verband Deutscher Reichsangehöriger (Union of Subjects of the German Empire), a propaganda agency with offices in Mexico City and branches elsewhere, subsidized Mexican newspapers and marshaled support for the German cause.[42]

Americans speculated endlessly on whether a German-Mexican alignment would take shape. Some observers claimed that Germany still wanted to bring Mexico and possibly Japan into an alliance against the United States. Agents of Navy Intelligence affirmed in November 1917 that Mexico had special importance as "the center of all German intrigues in America" and "the last stronghold . . . in the American continent" from which Germans "can still communicate directly with Asia and Japan." Reportedly, the Japanese had assisted the Germans in preparing "an uprising in Mexico against the United States." Additional information in May 1918 held that Germany had arranged to ship arms to Mexico through Japan in order "to foment revolutionary disorders."[43] When serious ones failed to materialize, Americans surmised that Germans wanted more to strengthen their economic position in Mexico after the war than to instigate an attack against the United States. Similar conjecture persisted into the postwar years. R. M. Campbell, the military attaché in Mexico City, claimed in December 1919 that he had seen "a great mass of Mexican official documents" which demonstrated that Mexican authorities had permitted Germans to operate wireless stations in return for military assistance. Campbell conceded that "these documents may not be considered absolute proof of the existence of a Carranza-German understanding," but he regarded them "certainly" as "strong corroborative evidence taken in connection with other information in possession of our government.[44]

Carranza probably angled for German assistance during the war, but no known evidence substantiates the claim that he was subservient to German influence. Still, a sequence of incidents animated American mistrust. In August 1917 Mexicans hissed the American flag at the "best theater" in Guadalajara. In December 1917 the Mexican Senate rejected a resolution calling for a policy of benevolent neutrality toward the Allies. In August 1918 Boaz Long, the chief of the Division of Latin-American Affairs in the State Department, affirmed his suspicion that "every high Carranza official is surrounded by the influence of one or more Germans, who are provided with ample funds and guided by directing hands from Berlin." Long believed that such circumstances accounted "in no small degree for the continuation of disturbed conditions throughout Mexico" and prevented that country from conducting its relations with the United States in an unprejudiced manner."[45]

To counter German aims, the United States utilized espionage and propaganda. In 1917 such functions centered in the American Embassy under the direction of Colonel Frank R. McCoy, the military attaché. Later they proliferated to new agencies. By the spring of 1918 American intelligence monitored the communications of Mexican consulates and the Mexican embassy in the United States.[46] Also George Creel's Committee on Public Information subsidized "some pro-Ally papers in Mexico, so as to counteract the effect of German propaganda." In March 1918 the Committee on Public Information opened the "Mexico Section" with Robert H. Murray as chief. Formerly a *New York World* correspondent with wide experience in Mexico, Murray later recalled, "With the possible exception of Spain, in no other country outside Mexico did the German propaganda attain such vigor and proportion and nowhere was it waged with more determination and vicious mendacity." Mexicans "reacted favorably" to the "specious and insidious endeavors of the Germans to deceive them," readily believing that an Allied triumph would mean "menace and disaster" for them, while a German victory "would ensure . . . every manner of political and economic benefits." Murray recorded that Germans failed because they delivered "a propaganda of lies." The Americans in contrast dealt "exclusively in truth," a "fact" which accounted for their success. The "Mexico Section" employed a variety of techniques, including pamphlets, motion pictures, news releases, and subsidies to friendly papers. By the summer of 1918 Murray calculated, "We are getting our German friends on the run a bit."[47]

Difficulties with Mexico during the war years were not solely the result of German machinations. Henry Fletcher cautioned repeatedly against attributing all manifestations of anti-American sentiment to German wiles. In August 1917 he reported that he had no particular "fear" of "official German influence or activity here." His talks with Carranza and others had convinced him that Mexican leaders understood "the danger of a German connection even should Germany win the war." Nevertheless, "the great weight and influence of the United States" alarmed Mexicans, who "naturally" looked toward Germany "for a counterbalance." Fletcher believed that a "German victory would probably not cause great shedding of tears in Mexico." In March 1918 he concluded that "fear" of "American influence" was "the master-key of Mexico's present attitude to the great war." Carranza desired "correct rather than cordial relations with the United States" and hoped "to find in the victory or non-defeat of Germany . . . a defense or counterbalance of the moral and economic influence of the United States in Mexico."[48]

Diplomatic Reactions

Fletcher's insight revealed a great deal about Mexican foreign policy. Once the United States intervened in World War I, Carranza tried to exploit the American preoccupation with Europe. In the spring of 1917 he initiated a series of moves to bring about the consolidation of his regime, the establishment of more regular relations with the United States, and the implementation of the Constitution of 1917. In the national elections called for 11 March 1917, Carranza's candidacy for the presidency had no opposition. To insure a friendly Congress, the first chief selected official candidates in most states but usually stopped short of outright imposition. To represent Mexico as ambassador in Washington, he chose Ignacio Bonillas, a Constitutionalist from Sonora. Though Bonillas had little diplomatic experience, his assets included experience as a cabinet member and education as an engineer in the United States.[49]

Carranza also moved against foreign enterprise. A decree on 13 April 1917 levied heavier taxes on foreign-owned petroleum companies. Carranza justified the measure as an attempt to constitute "a source of income for the Federal Treasury" in "just relation to the great profits of the industry." By exempting commodities consumed in Mexico from payment, the decree placed the main burden on corporations engaged in the export trade. Another decree on 24 April 1917 denied special privileges to foreigners in the extractive industries. It also defined the procedures for obtaining exploitative concessions in the future, requiring that resident aliens consider themselves as Mexican for legal purposes. Until foreigners renounced their right to seek the protection of their governments, they could obtain no new concessions.[50]

Americans appraised Carranza's intentions with uncertainty. Fletcher pointed to the influence of "the pro-German factor" and noted that "radical anticapitalistic, therefore anti-British and anti-American proclivities" had animated "the triumphant revolutionary party." Nevertheless, he attributed the tax ordinance to Carranza's "urgent need" for funds and advised no response to the second decree until the Mexican Congress had devised enabling legislation for Article 27.[51] That body would assemble on 1 May. Carranza's inauguration as president on the same day posed another perplexity. Since Mexicans might construe Fletcher's presence at the ceremony as de jure recognition, thereby implying an endorsement of Article 27, Secretary Lansing urged care to avoid a false impression. Although he thought it perhaps "impossible" to accept constitutional provisions "which are in contravention of the international obligations of Mexico," he wanted "for reasons of high policy" to avoid forcing an issue, preferring to meet such questions "when they arise." Fletcher should attend the festivities, seeking "to hold the confidence and friendship of Carranza," but should "say or do nothing that would indicate a recognition of his government as de jure in character."[52]

The edicts of March 1917 also dismayed Chandler P. Anderson. Previously he had advised a treaty to modify Article 27; he now concluded that such a course entailed "almost insurmountable difficulties." To negotiate a treaty would amount to de jure recognition. Since Article 27 had "the undoubted purpose" of confiscating foreign-owned property and since Americans needed Mexican oil more than ever after the declaration of war, he argued that conditional recognition could safeguard American "rights." If the State Department would inform Carranza that it interpreted the constitution to have non-retroactive effect, the Wilson administration could reserve its liberty to act. Anderson also hoped to capitalize on Mexico's financial duress. Since Carranza wanted money and arms in addition to de jure recognition, the United States should make them available as a *quid pro quo,* seeking thereby to bring him to terms on the question of Article 27. Indeed, Anderson and his clients pondered the possibility of bringing Mexico into the war through such devices. In the interim, Anderson called for a note of protest to counter "the hostile policy" upon which Mexico had embarked.[53]

Anderson participated in drafting a strong admonishment. The note recalled prior assurances in defense of legitimate property rights and warned against retroactivity, charging further that exorbitant tax rates threatened "the confiscation of American rights." Again, officers in the State Department affirmed that they would not acquiesce "in the direct or indirect confiscation of American properties." Nevertheless, Lansing hesitated to force an issue. On forwarding the note to Fletcher on 6 June, Lansing conveyed confidentially his intention "to initiate a discussion and to delay action which is of the utmost importance."[54]

Fletcher questioned the tactical wisdom of the note, anticipating that "representations along these lines now" would "prove fruitless and possibly harmful." Indeed, Carranza might refuse to discuss the question "on the usual Mexican ground that it is interference in a purely domestic matter." Since the Mexican Congress had recently asked the president to draft a petroleum law based on Article 27, the ambassador preferred to await the outcome. He also reasoned that Mexican leaders had no compelling wish to alienate American property owners. Conversations with Venustiano Carranza, Alvaro Obregón, Pablo González, and others had convinced him that Mexicans might respond more generously if the United States would lift the arms embargo and provide financial assistance. Conciliatory gestures in his view had more utility than forceful protest.[55]

The State Department on this occasion allowed him his discretion, although Chandler Anderson grumbled, wondering how an ambassador could overrule the secretary of state. On Fletcher's instruction, George T. Summerlin, the secretary of the embassy, read the note to someone at the Mexican Foreign Office but left no copy.[56] The ploy permitted Fletcher to make the point without directly confronting the consequences. The Wilson administration meanwhile experimented with conciliation. When Ambassador Ignacio Bonillas on 12 June presented formal notification of Carranza's election as president, Secretary Lansing instructed that the American ambassador henceforth omit the phrase "de facto" in official reference to the Mexican government.[57] A short while later, Fletcher returned home to be married. He took the occasion to confer with Chandler Anderson, who suspected that he was not "thoroughly informed as to the rights of American owners and the effect of the new constitution." Anderson still wanted a formal protest. On 17 July when he arranged a meeting with some of his associates, including William Loeb, George Carnahan,

Frederick Kellogg, and Frederick Watriss, he found Fletcher's replies "far from satisfactory." Anderson complained that Fletcher thought it more important "to support and save the Carranza Government" than "to protect American interests." Indeed, "our Government was not dealing with the root of the trouble . . . but was trying to tide over the present critical situation without making an issue with Carranza."[58]

Tactical questions more than fundamental issues set leaders in the administration apart from Anderson and his clients. Both groups wanted to safeguard material interests. They differed over means. Fletcher and Anderson both had affirmed the utility of a loan. Further, a relaxation of export restrictions might assist. Recently American authorities had detained at the border 2,700,000 rounds of ammunition purchased by Mexicans. Fletcher had firsthand knowledge of the effect of the arms embargo. When he returned to Mexico late in July with his bride aboard "The Honeymoon Special," Mexicans at the border fired a salute with five cannons instead of the customary nineteen, and guards on the train had no bullets in their guns.[59]

The *démarche* culminated in September with de jure recognition. On Fletcher's recommendation, the State Department secured a temporary relaxation of the arms embargo in the middle of July. Fletcher later addressed the question of a loan. In a conversation with Carranza on 2 August, he learned that American bankers already had broached the subject. Indeed, Carranza anticipated satisfactory terms if Washington placed no obstacles in the way. Although Fletcher regarded official interference as unlikely, he cautioned that the mistrust of American businessmen could impede the transaction, especially if the Mexican Congress enacted injurious petroleum legislation. When Carranza replied that Americans had no reason for alarm, Fletcher gained the impression that Mexico would not take over property "now in exploitation." Early in September, Carranza initiated work on a "conservative" petroleum law with non-retroactive features.[60] Meanwhile, the United States extended de jure recognition.

Aims and Effects of De Jure Recognition

Contrary to the wishes of Chandler P. Anderson and his clients, the United States bestowed de jure recognition without conditions or reservations. On 31 August President Wilson addressed a formal letter which affirmed his wish for "friendly relations" with Mexico and acknowledged Carranza's election as president. When Fletcher presented the letter on 26 September, the United States in effect sanctioned the legitimacy of the Carranza regime.[61] The decision exasperated Anderson and his associates. Harold Walker of the Mexican Petroleum Company and others were "very much up in the air about it." Some wanted to organize "a publicity bureau" to dramatize conditions in Mexico and to agitate for tougher policies. But Anderson suspected that such an undertaking would have little influence on President Wilson and might provoke the Mexicans to take reprisals. After lunching with Robert Lansing, Anderson speculated that the administration might try to induce Carranza to join the war against Germany by offering a loan while seeking simultaneously to impose "such terms and conditions as were necessary to secure the full protection of American and foreign owned properties in Mexico."[62] But such a course had little chance of success, and Robert Lansing knew it.

Leaders in the Wilson administration made no serious effort to bring Mexico into the war. Rather, they employed de jure recognition as an all-purpose device to ward off the threat of German imperialism, to facilitate Mexican neutrality, and to blunt the effect of Article 27. They understood that American participation in the world war somewhat weakened their hand in Mexico. De jure recognition encouraged accommodation and lessened the possibility of a German-Mexican alliance. Nevertheless, as a tactical expedient, the decision signaled no readiness to sacrifice American property. Rather, Americans hoped that Carranza would respond with concessions. The gambit accomplished less than they hoped. Burgeoning Mexican nationalism and the imperatives of Mexican politics precluded a settlement on American terms. Carranza would neither modify Article 27 nor provide ironclad guarantees in defense of property, and Americans lacked the means to bring them about. When it proved impossible to parlay de jure recognition into a modus vivendi, American leaders utilized diplomatic interposition against the Constitution of 1917, seeking to defer a settlement until the end of the European struggle.

Chapter 5

Bandits, Rebels, and Oil

*The world war and its consequences submerged the
Mexican question after 6 April 1917. Although President
Wilson retained the ultimate decision-making power, the
day-by-day conduct of Mexican policy fell largely to officials
of the second rank. They tried to insure that Mexico neither
divert the United States from Europe nor impede the American capacity to prosecute the war effectively. Their efforts
were complicated by American need for Mexican oil and by
dangers to American citizens in Mexico and along the border.*

Anti-Carranza Forces

Carranza never mastered all of Mexico. Although his government dominated the central portions, the Constitutionalists lacked authority on the
periphery. Banditry was common; also anti-Carranza rebels posed a challenge. Emiliano Zapata controlled most of Morelos and Guerrero. In Veracruz, Oaxaca, and Chiapas, Félix Díaz headed an insurgent movement. In
the Huasteca region south of Tampico, Manuel Peláez cultivated ties with
American oilmen. In Chihuahua, Francisco Villa still endured, and in Baja
California, Esteban Cantú established an autonomous regime. In the spring
of 1917 George C. Carothers, a special agent of the State Department, believed that Mexico was "teeming" with revolution. Although "little or no
connection" yet existed among the various movements, they might coalesce.
Carothers perceived "no solution of it all, until the collapse of the present
government occurs, and the American government is free to act as the occasion requires us."[1]

Anti-Carranza leaders presented themselves as alternatives to the established regime in efforts to win American favor. When Félix Díaz, the nephew
of the former dictator, abandoned his exile in the United States and mounted
a rebellion in February 1916, he appealed indirectly for American support.

The Plan of Tierra Colorado called for national reconstruction through gradual change. Though ready to sanction expropriation to bring about land reform, Díaz rejected confiscation as illegal and unconstitutional and promised just treatment to foreigners. Later his adherents attacked the Constitution of 1917 as a fraudulent derogation of the Constitution of 1857 and the liberalism of Benito Juárez (president from 1857 to 1872). Rebels in exile also exploited foreign mistrust of Article 27. The Díaz group in the United States under Pedro del Villar depicted Carranza as a German sympathizer and a despoiler of private property. The Alianza Legalista Mexicana, which developed from a New York junta with Villista connections, also upheld a commitment to the Constitution of 1857.[2]

The possibility that Americans might repudiate Carranza in favor of his enemies worried Mexican authorities. An episode early in 1917 heightened their concern by suggesting that Senator Albert B. Fall of New Mexico had conspired against them. Fall had associations with a variety of entrepreneurs who had Mexican interests, among them Charles F. Hunt of El Paso, Texas. On 17 January 1917 Hunt dispatched an intriguing proposition in a letter to Francisco Villa, intimating that Fall and "some of his friends" would support the creation of an independent republic in northern Mexico if the rebel leader would guarantee the sanctity of American lives and property. Hunt later informed Fall that "everything seems to be progressing fine." George C. Carothers meanwhile intercepted the communication and threatened to publish it in the newspapers. Although Fall disclaimed responsibility on 21 February, Hunt repeated the proposal a few days later in another letter to Villa, which fell into the hands of a Mexican secret service agent. Fall then protested his innocence before the secretary of state, explaining that Hunt had initiated the scheme on his own. Mexican leaders, however, took the matter seriously.[3]

To keep watch, Mexico employed an espionage network in the United States, composed of secret agents and private detectives. They provided large amounts of information, some of which lacked veracity. Jesús M. Arriola, the chief of the Mexican secret service in the United States, was dismissed from his post when subordinates denounced him in the summer of 1917 as a triple agent, allegedly in league with "reactionaries" and the United States Department of Justice; then, a year later he received an appointment in the consular service, apparently absolved of wrongdoing. Charles E. Jones, an American investigator employed by the Mexican government, infiltrated the Díaz organization in New Orleans in the summer of 1918 but may have acted as a double agent.[4] Multiple loyalties sometimes impaired Mexican intelligence. A succession of difficulties over the border, the oil fields, and Article 27 augmented the concern that Americans might prefer the rebels to Carranza.

Border Incidents

The departure of the punitive expedition left the question of policing the border unresolved. Since bandits and rebels operated in close proximity to the United States and sometimes entered American territory to loot and pillage, Secretary of War Baker on 16 February 1917 advised the continuance of practicing "hot pursuit." Other observers anticipated additional difficulties. Albert Fall, Zachary Cobb, and George Carothers warned of a German-backed invasion across the border in the spring of 1917. American residents in Mexico later complained of forced loans and other impositions, even though the Mexican military took matters more in hand. American consular reports in the spring and summer of 1917 often remarked on improved conditions.[5] They deteriorated in the fall, as "looting bands" multiplied in number and Villa mustered sufficient strength to seize the border town of Ojinaga in November. Consul Thomas Edwards at Ciudad Juárez attributed the upsurge to "the practical abandonment" of Chihuahua by Constitutionalist forces.[6]

Border violations repeatedly occasioned diplomatic exchanges. Since anti-Carranza rebels sometimes staged forays into Mexico from the United States, Ambassador Ignacio Bonillas filed a series of protests, asking that the United States prevent "evildoers" from entering Mexico "to commit lawless acts." The State Department similarly complained that Mexican marauders crossed into the United States to rob and steal. When American border guards heightened their vigilance, Bonillas charged that they harassed innocent people and sometimes shot at Mexican civilians. He objected further to the American practice of "hot pursuit" as a violation of Mexican sovereignty.[7] On 11 February 1918 he protested specifically that a cavalry detachment had trespassed into Mexico and had murdered a Mexican citizen. If other such unprovoked outrages should occur, he warned, Mexican toops would "beat back" such American forces "as may tread the territory of the Republic." His "discourteous" language offended Robert Lansing, who refused to accept the note, insisting upon terms "more consonant with diplomatic usage in the correspondence between friendly nations."[8] Nevertheless, he had no wish to press the issue too vigorously, as he displayed during an uprising by Yaqui Indians in Sonora.

The Yaquis of Sonora had resisted encroachments through four centuries while engaging Mexicans in chronic warfare. Porfirio Díaz had forced many into slavery on henequen plantations in Yucatán. During the revolution, Yaquis served in the armies of Villa and Obregón. Others fought independently. To bring them under control, the government of Sonora promised land and provisions in the autumn of 1916 in return for peace. About 1500 Yaquis accepted the terms, taking quarters near Lencho, a small village in southwestern Sonora, but soon grew disenchanted. Charg-

ng that the government had reneged on commitments, some joined with
other Yaquis who had not accepted the peace. In the summer and fall of
1917, small bands waged guerrilla war against army patrols and military
outposts. Fierce and relentless fighters, the Indians provoked Governor
Plutarco Elías Calles to proclaim a campaign of extermination in October
1917.[9]

Americans came under attack on 6 December 1917, when Yaquis attacked the town of Esperanza, the residence of forty Americans and the
headquarters of the Richardson Construction Company, an affiliate of the
American-owned Yaqui-Delta Land and Water Company. One American
died. When other Americans appealed for help, Frederick Simpich, the
American consul at Guaymas, advised the dispatch of a naval vessel. Lansing, thinking it unwise, agreed only to ask the Mexican government for
additional forces.[10] On 2 January 1918 Yaquis attacked a train and killed
thirty-six people, among them three Americans. Calling it an "unspeakable
massacre," Simpich again requested a naval vessel and also the landing
of troops at Guaymas and Empalme. But Lansing hesitated to create an
"embarrassing situation." He consented only to facilitate the export of arms to
American residents and to consider stronger measures if they should encounter "dire distress."[11] The immediate danger then passed away. For
Americans, the Yaquis posed more an irritation than a menace. For Mexicans, the guerrilla war became one of the issues which set Sonorans against
Carranza and precipitated the rebellion against him in the spring of 1920.

Elsewhere, border difficulties became ever more acute in the spring
of 1918. Bonillas protested a multitude of grievances, complaining that the
Wilson administration had failed to enforce neutrality statutes against anti-
Carranza conspirators, had permitted the sale of arms to Yaqui Indians,
had conscripted Mexican nationals into the United States Army, had tol-
erated the killing of Mexican civilians by border guards, Texas Rangers,
and vigilantes, had sanctioned the entry of United States forces into Mexico, and had allowed American soldiers to fire small arms across the border
at Mexicans. Cándido Aguilar served similar complaints on Henry Fletcher
on 10 April, maintaining that "hot pursuit" had violated Mexican territory
and that American citizens, most notably oilmen, had supported the enemies
of his government.[12]

In April 1918 Mexico re-enforced military garrisons in the North and
took a conciliatory diplomatic stance. Bonillas explained that he had not
intended his note of 11 February to injure American "susceptibilities."
Aguilar wanted no quarrel. Since his government had forbidden Mexican
forces from shooting across the international frontier, he wondered if
Washington would reciprocate.[13] Although Leon J. Canova, the chief of
the Division of Mexican Affairs, wanted to station at least 50,000 soldiers
along the border and to pursue marauders into Mexico without restraint,

the War Department disapproved. Since more than 30,000 troops already occupied positions along the border, additional allocations of manpower would serve German interests. Lansing also opposed. The arrival of Mexican re-enforcements persuaded him that the United States could rely less on "hot pursuit" and also could seek the elimination of gunfire across the border. When the president and the secretary of war concurred late in April, Lansing placed the responsibility for halting border raids on Mexican authorities, urging that they exercise greater vigilance.[14]

Americans employed different devices to encourage order in the Northern District of Baja California. In this region Colonel Esteban Cantú had established an autonomous regime. After seizing power in 1915, Cantú had taken a neutral position in the struggle between Villa and Carranza. Although Carranza later acknowledged his de facto authority in December 1915 and recognized him as governor in May 1917, Cantú pursued an independent course, maintaining himself in part by licensing gambling, prostitution, and other such commercial vices. Trouble impended early in the summer of 1917 when Carranza asserted his authority to designate customs collectors. Presumably he contemplated the ouster of Cantú.[15]

Such moves unsettled Americans, who preferred Cantú. Thomas E. Gibbon, an attorney for the Richardson Construction Company who later anathematized Carranza in a polemical tract, maintained that Cantú alone was the "exception to the rule of looting American property."[16] Further, the prospect of military operations was worrisome. Fighting could endanger irrigation facilities in the Colorado River Valley, upon which the livelihood of the Imperial Valley in Alta California depended, and also the interests of the California-Mexico Land and Cattle Company, a Mexican subsidiary of the Colorado River Land Company owned by General Harrison Gray Otis, the tough Republican publisher of the *Los Angeles Times*, and his son-in-law Harry Chandler. Rather than sanction such effects, Canova advised in September 1917 that Fletcher restrain Carranza "unofficially" from using force.[17]

Cantú also had ties with Germans. His German father-in-law, Paul Dato, reportedly had intimate connections with espionage. To guard against eventualities, Americans devised an impromptu understanding in the spring of 1918. When Dave Gershon, an agent of the Justice Department, cautioned that Germans could commit "depredations" by sabotaging the irrigation works and "inciting" the Mexicans, intelligence agents and middle-ranking officers in the State Department arranged a "gentlemen's agreement" late in May to provide "appropriate protection." American authorities consented to relax restrictions on exports to Baja California if Cantú would assure the defense of American property and the suppression of German intrigues. Polk and Fletcher approved but insisted that "the arrangement is temporary, informal, no record will be kept, and . . . either side may withdraw therefrom at any time." Cantú nevertheless mistook it as a sign of American favor, boasting that he might secede from Mexico or lead a new revolution with American support. Later his enthusiasm cooled when he understood American aims more fully. Cantú remained in power until the summer of 1920.[18]

In spite of such expedients, trouble persisted along the border. Early in July 1918 Lansing remarked that he had difficulty answering all the complaints of the Mexican ambassador. An incident at Nogales, Arizona, late in August occasioned further exchanges, when the shooting of a Mexican civilian by American guards provoked a gunfight and a small invasion of the United States. Nevertheless, the level of violence diminished. In June 1918 General W. A. Holbrook, the commander of the Southern Department, reported that he required "no additional troops . . . to maintain relatively good order and to prevent raids of a serious character." Holbrook attributed the reduction of tension to the establishment of "friendly relations" with Mexican commanders. Consular dispatches corroborated the view that Mexican authorities had exerted more effective influence and noted also that export controls, food card systems, and visa and passport restrictions had contributed by reducing the incidence of border traffic. Conditions so improved that Henry Fletcher observed late in October 1918 that protests over isolated episodes would serve no useful purpose.[19]

Dangers to American Oil Interests

The oil question during World War I caused more concern than any other issue. American investments in Mexican oil reached an estimated $15,000,000 in 1917. Further, Mexico produced 55,292,770 barrels of crude oil in 1917 and 64,605,422 in 1918, the third highest amount in the world, and exported nearly half to the United States. Americans often regarded Mexican oil as a necessary complement to their domestic sources of supply. After the declaration of war against Germany, Robert Lansing thought it vital.[20]

A multitude of dangers threatened American access to Mexican oil during the war years. Violence, disorder, and Article 27 could impede production. Further, Robert Lansing feared that Carranza might enforce a strict neutrality and forbid the sale of oil to the Allies. The question posed a difficult problem which repeatedly raised the possibility of using force. Soon after the United States entered the war, Leon J. Canova proposed the creation of a 6000-man mobile force at Corpus Christi or Galveston, ready to take quick possession of the oil fields if necessary. Similarly, Robert Lansing reasoned that "we cannot respect Mexican neutrality so far as Tampico is concerned." But President Wilson hesitated to embrace the idea, holding that the United States, "the leading champion of the right of self-determination and of political independence everywhere," could not afford to be too "practical." Only "the most extraordinary circumstance of arbitrary injustice" would justify the seizure of the oil fields. Nevertheless, he suggested that Britain perhaps could exercise "an influence there which anti-American sentiment in Mexico for the time prevents our exercising."[21]

Peculiar circumstances rendered the difficulty even more perplexing. The Mexican government controlled the cities of Tampico and Tuxpan, the principal terminals for export, but not the outlying regions. In the oil fields, General Manuel Peláez wielded the dominant influence and cultivated a special relationship with oil producers. "Fortunately," Lansing recalled, "he was able to give them the protection which they required, and the shipment of oil from Tampico continued without interruption."[22]

Peláez, a landowner who had political connections with Félix Díaz, had mounted a rebellion against the Constitutionalists early in 1914. Later he financed the movement by selling protection to foreign oilmen. Beginning in January 1916 Edward L. Doheny's Huasteca Petroleum Company paid about $1500 each month as tribute. The Texas Company, the Mexican Gulf Oil Company, the International Petroleum Company, the Penn-Mex Fuel Company, and others also contributed. Oilmen maintained they had no choice. If they withheld the tribute, Peláez would burn the wells, cut the pipelines, and drive away the workers. Critics in contrast claimed that Peláez served oilmen by keeping Carranza at bay.[23]

The relationship offended Mexican authorities, but they could do little about it. If Peláez disrupted production, he would deprive them of vital revenues. In effect, Peláez taxed production, Carranza distribution. On occasion the government permitted oilmen to deduct tribute payments from their tax obligations.[24] The United States government also consented tacitly. Edward L. Doheny affirmed that officials in the State Department approved the payments to Peláez "so far as they could, without giving it in writing." Levi Smith of the Penn-Mex Fuel Company recounted that Frank Polk told him, ". . . you are helpless. You cannot do otherwise than pay it." Nevertheless, when Peláez proposed a more formal arrangement in the summer of 1916, the State Department withheld its sanction. It took the position that tribute payments concerned only the producers, as long as Peláez remained friendly and caused the United States no embarrassment. In March 1917 Robert Lansing raised no objection when oilmen suggested the utility of providing the rebel leader with arms.[25]

Lawlessness and disorder posed repeated dangers. According to Claude I. Dawson, the American consul in Tampico, banditry became "so rife" that it was accepted "as part of each day's experience." The possibility of military operations in the oil fields also distressed him. When the Mexican government assembled 2000 troops at Tuxpan in August 1917, Dawson forecast that a change in the status quo would render conditions "intolerable" and "a possible source of international complications." Similarly, Harold Walker of the Mexican Petroleum Company characterized Peláez as a "valiant friend" and an "interested protector." He urged that the United States preserve the existing circumstance.[26]

When Henry Fletcher advised restraint, seeking "to prevent action which might endanger oil exports," he found it an "exceedingly delicate" matter. Mexican leaders believed that Peláez had enlisted oilmen in an alliance against them. Luis Cabrera, the minister of finance, told Fletcher that the government had to stop the disaffection from spreading. Later Cabrera elaborated in an address before the Chamber of Deputies on 17 October 1917, holding that the oil producers had engaged anti-Carranza leaders in a plot to bring Mexico under foreign domination and to place enemies of the revolution in power.[27]

Although Cabrera probably inflated his case, other observers corroborated the essentials of his charge. An American oilman, unnamed but described as "one of the biggest, most aggressive and most unscrupulous," told Louis Richardson, the commander of the U.S.S. *Annapolis* stationed off Tampico, that "local Mexicans" would launch a new revolution and create "an Oil Republic" if they had assurance of American support. Other informants recounted that Manuel Peláez and Félix Díaz intended to establish Tampico as "the center of an independent government." When Mexican forces initiated dilatory operations in the oil fields, Fletcher lamented that he had tried to dissuade the government "indirectly and unofficially" but could do nothing after Cabrera's speech. Robert Lansing and Josephus Daniels then contemplated the creation of a mobile force for quick action in Tampico.[28]

The government offensive against Peláez had little effect. The opposing forces pondered each other "from a safe distance." Neither interfered with oil production. Possibly the expectation of American intervention served as a restraint. In Mexico City, *El Demócrata,* a newspaper unfriendly to the United States, warned of it. Early in 1918 the Mexican government suggested a negotiated settlement, offering Peláez amnesty in return for submission, but the rebel rejected such terms. Instead, he proclaimed his determination to unify the anti-Carranza forces and to overthrow the regime.[29] In Washington, officers in the State Department arranged "to throw out a danger signal" to Bonillas late in January. In the middle of February, they complained of "chaotic conditions in and around Tampico," asking that Mexico "take steps necessary to protect American properties and the shipment of oil."[30] The question became more acute when Carranza tried to implement the Constitution of 1917.

Interpretation of Article 27

The actual effect of Article 27 was still uncertain at the beginning of 1918. When Frank Polk inquired late in January whether the measure would prohibit foreign companies from gaining access to Mexican resources, Alberto J. Pani, the secretary of commerce, industry and labor, replied that it merely required foreign capitalists to organize as Mexican companies, subject to Mexican law.[31] President Carranza then designated the procedures in an executive decree on 19 February 1918.

Cast as a fiscal device, this complicated provision established additional taxes on the oil industry and specified the methods for validating petroleum rights acquired before the Constitution took effect on 1 May 1917. First, the decree levied new taxes on titled surface lands, on rental fees, and on royalties, a practice that could entail a double tax on land and production. Second, the decree required that landowners and concession holders register their property within three months by submitting titles and leases to the Department of Industry, Commerce and Labor for verification; then they should file formal claim to their holdings. Otherwise, the Mexican government would regard existing rights as void.[32]

The decree touched off a furor. In Mexico City, conservative newspapers ran editorials against it, arguing that inequitable taxes would drive foreign investors out of the petroleum industry. One journalist compared the effect with killing the goose that laid golden eggs. Mexican landowners near Tampico marshaled resistance, and Americans joined in. Edward L. Doheny later claimed that if Americans had complied with the decree, they would have acknowledged "the confiscation of their own properties," a course he regarded as inadmissible, since "the future welfare and prosperity of the United States" depended upon "the uninterrupted operation and control of the oil fields in Mexico."[33] Most American oilmen disobeyed the decree. Some drew nearer Manuel Peláez, who asked for additional funds. When Harold Walker of the Mexican Petroleum Company told the State Department of Peláez's request for $50,000 to buy arms, Gordon Auchincloss, the son-in-law of Colonel House who replaced Canova at the Mexico desk, replied that he would not give advice in such matters. But if payment would facilitate protection, the oilmen knew their own best interests.[34]

Henry Fletcher characterized the decree as a radical triumph. Since it would raise "the whole question of Article 27" and could place Allied oil shipments "in serious jeopardy," he urged that his superiors decide "how far" they would go to support the oilmen. Lansing feared that an oil shortage would impede wartime production and interfere with naval operations. On the secretary's instructions, Fletcher requested a thirty-day suspension while the United States examined the probable consequences, but the ambassador received little satisfaction. Cándido Aguilar was "vague and noncommittal." According to Pastor Rouaix, the secretary of *fomento* (development), Article 27 had restored "the absolute ownership of petroleum" to Mexico, a statement that Fletcher interpreted to portend the annulment of "all private property rights to petroleum." Lansing then set forth his objections on 19 March, authorizing the presentation of a formal protest if "prudent and necessary."[35]

When Fletcher presented the note as a protest on 2 April 1918, he complained that the decree of 19 February implied "an intention" to separate ownership of surface lands from mineral resources beneath the surface. It also allowed owners of surface lands "a mere preference" in the right to exploit subsurface resources and required exorbitant taxes. Americans would neither obstruct expropriation "for sound reasons of public utility," if "just compensation" was provided, nor seek to evade their fair share of tax burdens. But they could not acquiesce "in any procedure ostensibly or nominally in the form of taxation or the exercise of eminent domain, but really resulting in confiscation of private property and arbitrary deprivation of vested rights." Since the decree of 19 February suggested "a trend in that direction," Fletcher emphasized "the necessity" which may impel the United States "to protect the property of its citizens in Mexico divested or injuriously affected."[36]

Although Fletcher in the past had felt sure that he could prevent Mexico "from distracting our attention and efforts from the Great War," he now pessimistically anticipated that his protest would have little "deterrent effect." Foreigners had become identified with the Díaz regime. He expected that Mexico would "force the issue." Indeed, "the whole trend of recent events" implied an attempt "to annul or abrogate foreign property rights." Nevertheless, Carranza moderated his position slightly, agreeing under pressure to extend the deadline for registration until 31 July 1918.[37] Meanwhile, American oilmen petitioned the Mexican government for additional change.

To constitute "a united front," the principal corporations formed the Oil Producers Association with Edward L. Doheny as chairman and commissioned James R. Garfield and Nelson Rhoades, Jr., to represent them before the Mexican government. Both experienced Mexico hands, Garfield and Rhoades had formed a partnership early in 1918 and enlisted among their clients twenty-seven petroleum companies, including major producers such as the Mexican Petroleum Company, the Huasteca Petroleum Company, the Texas Company, the Penn-Mex Company, Standard Oil of New Jersey, and the British-owned Compañia Mexicana de Petroleo "El Aguila."[38]

When Garfield and Rhoades traveled to Mexico City, Carranza received them in an "extremely gracious" fashion on 20 May but denied their charge that the petroleum decrees had confiscatory intent. Carranza described the one of 19 February as an attempt to distribute the tax burden more equally among Mexicans and foreigners. In subsequent discussions, Alberto Pani, the secretary of commerce, industry and labor, and Rafael Nieto, the undersecretary of the treasury, maintained that the measure simply facilitated the procedures for validating rights obtained under a nullified law. Seeking further accommodation, Pani described the decree essentially as a tax measure in which questions of title and retroactivity should not figure prominently. Garfield and Rhoades took heart, suspended the talks, and returned home to confer with their clients. Garfield hoped for a "satisfactory conclusion."[39]

Crisis in the Oil Industry

Tactical questions preoccupied leaders in the Wilson administration during the spring and summer. When German submarines appeared off the Mexican coast early in June, Gordon Auchincloss at the Mexico desk again suggested the concentration of 6000 marines at Galveston. Lansing and Baker favored it, concurring in the need "to preserve that absolutely necessary supply of oil for us and our Allies." But President Wilson demurred. He hesitated to disturb "the peace of Latin America" unless "very pressing and unusual circumstances" required it. Daniels' warning that seizure of the oil fields would amount to "an act of war against Mexico" especially impressed him.[40] Wilson preferred a different course, opting once again to court Carranza.

On 7 June 1918 Wilson addressed a group of Mexican newspaper editors who had come to the United States at the bequest of the Committee on Public Information. He affirmed his "sincere friendship" for Mexico, "not merely the sort of friendship which prompts one not to do his neighbor any harm, but the sort of friendship which earnestly desires to do his neighbor service." By his account, he had acted consistently on the principle that "the internal settlement of the affairs of Mexico was none of our business. . . . When we sent troops into Mexico, our sincere desire was nothing else than to assist you to get rid of the man who was making the settlement of your affairs for the time being impossible." He also exhorted Mexico to support a favorite project, a Pan-American treaty, which he described as "a common guaranty, that all of us will sign, of political independence and territorial integrity."[41]

Fletcher first reported a favorable response, then an adverse one. On 13 June newspapers in the Mexican capital published the American protest of 2 April, comparing it critically with Wilson's statement of 7 June. *El Demócrata* regarded the inconsistency as proof of cynicism and duplicity. *El Pueblo* maintained that "each gives the lie to the other," holding that the United States had no right to protest acts of national sovereignty. *El Pueblo* later attacked Wilson's idea of Pan-Americanism, proclaiming that the Carranza Doctrine had supplanted the Monroe Doctrine. The Carranza Doctrine asserted nonintervention and equality among states as absolute principles.[42]

Henry Fletcher and Robert H. Murray, the chief of the "Mexico section," believed that Carranza had inspired the attacks "to offset the president's speech" and "to tie the U.S. Government's hands." Under "the shibboleth of this new Carranza Doctrine," Mexico would try to enforce Article 27 and to justify "its disregard for the elemental principles of justice and fair dealings." Although Fletcher volunteered to take "full responsibility" and "retire without a word" if the protest of 2 April should prove a "stumbling block," he preferred a firm stand.[43]

Officers in the State Department refused to repudiate the protest but still desired "some concrete and tangible means . . . to translate into action [Wilson's] expressions of friendship." A relaxation of export restrictions and the possibility of a loan impressed them as viable methods. When Fletcher broached the subject on 28 June, Carranza bridled at the implied threat of intervention in the note of 2 April. He responded more favorably when Fletcher explained his government's wish to transform "friendly sentiments" into "concrete acts" and, further, its readiness to regard Article 27 as a "juridical" question to be settled in the Mexican courts. Fletcher believed that proper incentives might dissuade Carranza until the end of the European war.[44]

When the State Department ascertained that the Food Administration had a surplus of some products and also that Mexico had a commercial credit balance of $24,000,000, Robert Lansing sanctioned the export of foodstuffs and other commodities "which we can spare." On 6 July Fletcher was instructed to announce "a more liberal policy" toward export licenses. In return, the United States would count on Mexico "to allow the exportation to this country of such commodities as were not imperatively needed by her."[45] Two days later, Carranza promulgated two executive decrees. They brought the petroleum controversy to crisis stage.

The first decree of 8 July 1918 imposed additional taxes on petroleum lands; the second elaborated procedures for validating petroleum concessions and threatened to revoke exploitative privileges unless producers complied with the terms of 19 February no later than 1 August. Fletcher immediately took alarm, declaring that "the petroleum difficulty" had become "so formidable an obstacle to good understanding" that it would "render futile all attempt at cordial friendship." He perceived "no indication" that Mexico would "recede" from Article 27 and speculated that Carranza aimed "not only at the elimination of the financial, economic and political influence of the United States in Mexico" but intended "by alliance with a strong European or Asiatic power and treaties with other Latin-American States, to isolate the United States and destroy its influence in the hemisphere." The administration could avoid "endless trouble and difficulty" only "by standing firmly on the principles which the Department has already laid down."[46]

Oilmen similarly believed that "the expected crisis had come." In Washington, the Oil Producers Association appealed for assistance through a six-man committee consisting of Harold Walker of the Mexican Petroleum Company, Frederick Proctor of the Gulf Oil Refining Company, Frederick C. Watriss of the International Petroleum Company, Amos L. Beaty of the Texas Company, and A. E. Watt and J. W. Zevely, both of the Sinclair Petroleum Company. They conferred on 19 July with James Garfield's brother, Harry Garfield, the head of the United States Fuel Administration, and Mark L. Requa, the chief of the Oil Division. Requa preferred to support them strongly rather than tolerate oil shortages.[47]

On the following day, Harold Walker explained to Frank Polk that oil companies wanted "to exhaust" their legal remedies but had encountered a dilemma. The only available corrective, the *juicio de amparo,* had no exact counterpart in American law. It allowed recourse "in all cases and by all persons to the Federal courts for relief and redress against any act of any authority, judicial or administrative, which is deemed by the appellant to be a violation of individual guaranties or the rights of man." As Walker explained, if oilmen disobeyed Carranza's decrees while filing an *amparo,* they might forfeit their land. On the other hand, if they registered titles and leases even under protest, Mexican authorities might construe the act as acceptance of the decree and hold the oilmen ineligible for an *amparo.* Walker wondered whether the State Department would offer advice and support.[48]

Oilmen in Washington wanted strong measures. On 20 July, Walker, Watriss, and Proctor put Gordon Auchincloss through "a strenuous grinding day," seeking in his view "to force our hand." Auchincloss did not propose "to let them get away with it," although he conceded that "the oil situation" was "undoubtedly in a bad mess." Four days later when Walker and his five companions urged the use of force, Auchincloss recorded, "This we will not do unless we have to, inasmuch as it would amount to a violation of the sovereignty of Mexico." Nevertheless, he contemplated assembling "an adequate force of marines" at Galveston "in the event of trouble."[49]

James Garfield and Nelson Rhoades, now representing forty-seven petroleum companies, meanwhile resumed conversations in Mexico City, but could not budge the Mexican government. When Alberto Pani explained that the decree of 19 February had no confiscatory aims and insisted further that oilmen abide by the designated procedures, Garfield and Rhoades acquiesced reluctantly. In effect, they accepted the principle of nationalization. In return, Carranza reduced taxes slightly and extended the deadline for registration until 15 August. Nevertheless, the arrangement dissatisfied the members of the Oil Producers Association. Rather than endorse the principle of nationalization, they repudiated the work of Garfield and Rhoades. William F. Buckley, an independent operator, later denounced the two emissaries as "notoriously and pitifully incompetent."[50]

Oil producers again asked their government for help. On 4 August Walker and his five colleagues warned of disastrous consequences unless the United States provided aid "immediately to protect us in possession of our oil properties." They persuasively used the language of wartime necessity. Few leaders in the Wilson administration wanted to sacrifice Mexican oil and the American stake in it. The war provided an immediate justification for resisting Article 27. Some also looked beyond. Mark L. Requa, the chief of the Oil Division, characterized the Mexican oil fields as "perhaps the greatest industrial prize in the world."[51] He believed it necessary to protect American companies. The question was means. Officers in the State Department hesitated to use military force except as a last resort, since among other things such a course would embroil the United States with Mexico at a critical time in the European war. Fletcher advised the utility of another protest in combination with accommodating gestures. His superiors also favored diplomatic means. On 6 August Auchincloss told Harold Walker that oilmen should submit titles and leases under protest and the State Department would intercede in their behalf, reserving "all rights" possessed by the companies under international law. But the oilmen resisted. When James Garfield and Frederick Proctor explained their objections in a "very long-winded" fashion on 8 August, Gordon Auchincloss arranged a meeting for the following day with Josephus Daniels, Harry Garfield, Mark Requa, and Bernard Baruch of the War Industries Board.[52]

Some oilmen urged the use of force. Frederick Watriss claimed that precedents could justify the seizure of the oil fields "for the protection of the rights of [American] citizens" and that such an action "would not mean war any more than did the occupation of Vera Cruz, or the Pershing Expedition, each of which was undertaken for a specific purpose." In Daniels' office on the morning of 9 August, James Garfield and Frederick Proctor also gave preference to intervention over acquiescence. Requa supported them in such a view, but Daniels and Baruch opposed it. That afternoon they confronted the president with the question. Wilson had no stomach for intervention to defend oil properties. Auchincloss recorded Wilson's assertion that "if we could not get the oil in a peaceful manner from Mexico, we would simply have to do without." Baruch later recalled that Wilson had compared intervention in the oil fields with the German invasion of Belgium and affirmed, "We cannot do the same thing." Daniels put it succinctly: "We . . . decided that oil men could not stampede us . . . what they wanted amounted to a declaration of war."[53]

Wilson ruled out the use of force but sanctioned diplomacy. He advised another protest. The State Department took a tough stance. On 10 August Boaz W. Long, the chief of the Division of Latin-American Affairs, affirmed a set of common assumptions. Since the European war commanded "our first attention," all other issues held secondary importance. Accordingly, "international expediency" required "a policy of temporization" in Mexico. Nevertheless, Long regarded "the rehabilitation of Mexico" as "an American problem" and anticipated "a settlement . . . immediately after the conclusion of the European peace." Further, he remarked that the American dependency on Mexican oil "may force us at any moment to possess ourselves of the oil fields."[54]

Lansing implied as much on 12 August in his instructions to Fletcher. Presented as a protest on the following day, they warned of "grave apprehension" over "the possible effect" of Mexican decrees and of "the necessity which may arise to impel the United States to protect the property of American citizens in Mexico." Carranza took offense, claiming as usual that acts of national sovereignty afforded no grounds for diplomatic interposition, but later he accommodated his position. Carranza, too, hesitated to force a showdown. On the evening of 13 August he and his staff prepared another decree, antedated by one day. The measure forbade oilmen from sinking new wells on unworked land unless the Mexican government expressly approved. It also abandoned the demand for immediate registration of oil properties and left the question in abeyance until the Mexican Congress formulated enabling legislation for Article 27. Fletcher reported that Carranza's retreat "at the eleventh hour" had "relieved the situation and removed the danger of arbitrary proceedings."[55] Americans retained access to Mexican oil for the duration of World War I.

Mexico Neutralized

American diplomacy during the world war succeeded to an extent in neutralizing the Mexican question. As Fletcher remarked with satisfaction, ". . . during the war my job was to keep Mexico quiet, and it was done."[56] Still, fundamental issues divided Americans from Mexicans. The Constitution of 1917 and Carranza's incapacity to insure order still threatened the liberal-capitalist ethos of President Wilson. During the war, he tried to adjust diplomatic tactics to the exigencies of global conflict. His hesitancy to dissipate resources away from Europe accounted in part for his reluctance to use force in Mexico. His growing consciousness of the divergence between liberal capitalism and self-determination also contributed. Wilson's categories of thought had come into conflict. Ideological imperatives no longer ran parallel with economic interests. Lacking justification derived from a sense of common purpose with Mexicans, he spurned intervention. Whether similar calculations would hold at the conclusion of World War I was uncertain. Wilson's difficulty lay in deciding whether the exercise of self-determination outside the bounds of liberal capitalism had legitimacy. The question became ever more urgent in 1919.

Chapter 6

The Question of Intervention

*The peace conference and the treaty fight absorbed
Woodrow Wilson after the European armistice on 11 November 1918. Three weeks later he departed for Europe,
leaving the conduct of Mexican policy to his subordinates.
During his absence, a coalition of critics in the United States
began to agitate for a change in the established policy,
arguing that the conclusion of World War I had freed the
Wilson administration to adopt a tougher stance.*

Opposition to Wilson's Policy

Carranza's concession to American oil interests in August 1918 relieved the most pressing difficulty. Early in September Gordon Auchincloss observed that since "the mess" over Article 27 had "drifted over,"
officers in the State Department were "not concerned with it much these
days." Henry Fletcher later urged that Carranza embrace "some solution"
which would "amply" insure Mexican sovereignty and also recognize "private rights acquired honestly and in good faith."[1] The draft of a petroleum
law early in November 1918 alleviated some objections. It acknowledged
the validity of titles and leases if landholders had invested capital for ex-
ploration or exploitation before 1 May 1917 and further bestowed prefer-
ential rights if they had done so after that date. But the draft also required
that landholders pay the specified taxes and comply with "the applicable
prescriptions of the law relative to titled claims." The implications distressed members of the Oil Producers Association. James Garfield wondered
whether Mexican leaders would place "an unreasonable construction" on
such provisions to obtain "an excuse" for depriving Americans of their
property. Although Frank Polk and others in the State Department thought
the proposal "a decided advance," remarking that they could not assume
"in advance" that it would serve as "an instrument of injustice," oilmen
perceived the measure as "a trap" to force acceptance of nationalization.
According to Frederick Watriss, the legislation "did not differ materially
from previous suggestions except that the same joker was a little more
artfully concealed."[2]

[87]

When Carranza transmitted the draft to the Mexican Congress, the State Department placed such misgivings on record. A note on 13 December commended Mexico for choosing "to conciliate foreign interests" but rejected the claim that petroleum decrees were exempt from "diplomatic interposition" as acts of national sovereignty. Under international law, all nations had "certain minimum duties" to foreigners, including the protection of "vested property rights." Asking no more than "equal and just treatment" for "legitimately acquired rights," the State Department reserved the prerogative to take further action "in this important and serious matter."[3]

The oil question remained crucial in 1919, in part because of expected oil shortages in the United States. In the spring of 1919, the United States Geological Survey predicted the exhaustion of American reserves within ten years. Subsequently, American oilmen sought new sources of supply in Latin America and the Middle East, asking that their government support them energetically.[4] Such concerns had important consequences for Mexico. Among other things, they contributed to Mexico's exclusion from the Paris Peace Conference and the League of Nations.

Leaders in the Wilson administration preferred to include Mexico. They suggested in the preliminaries at Paris that each neutral have one delegate. But the European powers demurred, insisting that only the nations which had declared war or severed relations with the Central Powers should write the treaty. Later the neutrals could participate in creating the League of Nations, but Mexico, an exception among them, never received an invitation.[5] Carranza nevertheless authorized Alberto J. Pani, an experienced diplomat, to attend the conference as envoy extraordinary and minister plenipotentiary. Early in January 1919, he traveled to France aboard the *George Washington* with members of the American delegation but encountered a rude reception in Paris. The English and the French would not receive him. Pani attributed their slights to resentment over Article 27, Carranza's alleged pro-German sympathies, and Mexico's failure to make good on foreign debts. Still, he remained as an unofficial observer, alerting Carranza that Edward L. Doheny had come to request measures in defense of petroleum rights in Mexico.[6]

Investors and financiers had a similar interest but favored different means. Before the European armistice, a group of New York bankers, most notably J. P. Morgan and Company, considered the establishment of an International Bankers Committee, including "prominent financial institutions" in the United States, Britain, and France, to oversee future financial transactions with Mexico.[7] Early in October 1918, the State Department gave its unofficial approval. In the following month, Henry Fletcher tried to expedite the plan in Mexico City, reporting that Thomas P. Honey, a "leading English banker," had proposed "a reconstruction loan" of $150,000,000 conditioned on the settlement of the petroleum question, the recognition of the Huerta bonds, and the acceptance of foreign claims. When Carranza learned of it, he reportedly "flatly refused" and objected further when bankers in New York proposed similar terms in January 1919.[8]

Fletcher nevertheless believed that a loan might obtain bargaining leverage. He also advised more demanding policies. Early in January 1919, the State Department recalled him for temporary assignment with the Divisions of Latin-American and of Mexican Affairs. Since President Wilson had returned home for a short stay, Fletcher drew his attention to Mexican perplexities in a confidential memorandum on 1 March. Although Fletcher acknowledged that the Mexican government had "practical, if not unchallenged control of the country," he questioned its good faith and intentions. Carranza functioned "virtually" as "a dictator," presiding over a "pro-German" party "entirely out of sympathy with our ideals and struggle." Further, "the spirit" of the regime was "intensely, archaically nationalistic." Mexicans regarded foreign rights and interests "as privileges" and respected them "grudgingly — if at all." Indeed, Carranza considered himself "the bulwark of Latin America" against the United States. Without "external pressure," Americans could expect little "substantial improvement." Although the United States could "let matters drift in their present unsatisfactory condition" and "confront the clamor at home and abroad," Fletcher preferred to call upon Mexico either "to perform its duties" or "to confess its inability so to do and accept disinterested assistance from the United States or of an international commission to restore order and credit."[9] A coalition of critics in the United States took a similar stance in the spring and summer of 1919.

Congressional Discontent

Republican leaders found a common cause with American entrepreneurs in opposition to Wilson's Mexican policy. After winning control of the Congress in the fall of 1918, Republicans anticipated a victory in the presidential campaign of 1920. They assailed the incumbent on a variety of fronts. Differences over the treaty, the League, and other questions heightened political partisanship. By filibustering appropriations bills at the end of the short session in March 1919, Republicans in Congress compelled the president to summon a special session in May, enabling them to take command of important committees. As chairman of the Senate Committee on Foreign Relations, Henry Cabot Lodge of Massachusetts especially challenged the wisdom of Woodrow Wilson.

Business leaders meanwhile created the National Association for the Protection of American Rights in Mexico (see Table), with Charles H. Boynton, a New York banker and stockbroker, as executive secretary and with a twelve-man executive committee. The organization comprised a variety of commercial and financial institutions, land and cattle companies,

MEMBERS OF THE NATIONAL ASSOCIATION
FOR THE PROTECTION OF AMERICAN RIGHTS IN MEXICO

OFFICERS

Executive director: Charles H. Boynton, president, Consolidated Copper Mines Co.
Secretary: Frank J. Silsbee.
Treasurer: W. E. Stetson, vice president, Guaranty Trust Co. of New York.

EXECUTIVE COMMITTEE

J. S. Alexander, president, National Bank of Commerce in New York;
Amos L. Beaty, general counsel of the Texas Co.;
George H. Carnahan, president, Inter-Continental Rubber Co.;
Edward L. Doheny, president, the Pan-American Petroleum and Transport Co.;
C. F. Kelly, vice-president, Greene Cananea Copper Co.;
Thomas W. Lamont, J. P. Morgan and Co.;
Charles H. Sabin, president, Guaranty Trust Co. of New York;
Chester O. Swain, general counsel of the Standard Oil Co. of New Jersey;
Frederick N. Watriss, counsel, Yaqui Delta Land and Water Co.

GROUP MEMBERS

PETROLEUM GROUP	REPRESENTED BY:
Pan-American Petroleum and Transport Co.	E. L. Doheny
Mexican Petroleum Co., Ltd. of Del.	E. L. Doheny
Huasteca Petroleum Co.	E. L. Doheny
Mexican Petroleum Corp.	Chester O. Swain
Tuxpan Petroleum Corp.	Chester O. Swain
Tamiahua Petroleum Corp.	Chester O. Swain
Standard Oil of New Jersey	Chester O. Swain
The Texas Co.	Amos L. Beaty
Continental Mexican Petroleum Co.	Frederick N. Watriss
Freeport & Mexican Petroleum Co.	A. E. Watts
Southern Oil and Transport Corp.	Charles F. de Ganahl
Snowden and McSweeney	Frank H. Hitchcock
Oilfields of Mexico Co.	Arthur Payne
National Oil Co.	F. Straith-Millet
Port Lobos Petroleum Corp.	
Burton W. Wilson	Burton W. Wilson
Atlantic Refining Co.	
Mexican Gulf Oil Co.	
Frederick R. Kellogg	Frederick R. Kellogg
Panuco Boston Oil Co.	

MINING AND SMELTING GROUP	
Greene Cananea Copper Co.	C. F. Kelly
Montezuma Copper Co.	Walter Douglas
Joseph S. Qualey	Joseph S. Qualey
George W. Bryant	George W. Bryant
Joseph B. Cotton	Joseph B. Cotton

AGRICULTURE GROUP

Yaqui Delta Land & Water Co.   Frederick N. Watriss
Hacienda Ramona Co.
Rancho Fertile Co.

LAND AND CATTLE GROUP

California-Mexican Land and Cattle Co.   Thomas E. Gibbon
Sonora Land & Investment Co.

BANKERS AND SECURITY HOLDERS GROUP

Guaranty Trust Co. of New York   Charles H. Sabin
The National City Bank of New York   F. A. Vanderlip
J. M. Wallace   J. M. Wallace
J. P. Morgan and Co.   Thomas W. Lamont
First National Bank of New York   Francis L. Hine
Mechanics and Metals National Bank   G. W. McGarrah
National Bank of Commerce in New York   J. S. Alexander
Chase National Bank   Eugene V. Thayer
Bankers Trust Co.   Seward Prosser

INDUSTRIAL GROUP

Inter-Continental Rubber Co.   George H. Carnahan

---

and mining and petroleum enterprises, among them influential members of the Oil Producers Association. Designed to disseminate propaganda and to exert pressure, the National Association alerted the American people to "true conditions" in Mexico.[10]

Senator Albert B. Fall of New Mexico served as liaison between Republicans and other critics. Tough, wily, and partisan, Fall had a long career in the borderlands as an entrepreneur and politico. As a young man, he cultivated an enduring friendship with Edward L. Doheny (both were later disgraced in the Teapot Dome affair). Fall's association with William C. Greene, "the copper king of Cananea," later sparked his interest in Mexican mining and other speculations. Although Fall claimed to possess no personal stake, having liquidated his Mexican holdings in 1910, he embraced Americans in Mexico as his special constituents during the revolution.[11]

As a member of the Senate Committee on Foreign Relations, Fall engineered the assault in 1919. The failure of the administration's attempt to unseat him in the election of the previous year perhaps encouraged him. So did the appeals of American businessmen. Fall responded energetically when Harold Walker of the Mexican Petroleum Company asked for assistance in February 1919. Recalling Theodore Roosevelt's observation that Mexico had succumbed to "a condition as hideous as that of the Balkan Peninsula under Turkish rule," largely because of "Mr. Wilson's able assistance," Walker urged Fall to speak out. Since Roosevelt's death, only Fall could provide the necessary "dramatic presentation." In this instance, Fall's concern for American enterprise complemented personal political interests and those of his party.[12] Fall tried during the next year to bring Carranza into disrepute and to reorient the goals of American policy.

Democrats often attributed ulterior motives to their critics. Robert Lansing believed that Republicans wished "to mortify the President, to humiliate him, to prove to everyone that he is distrusted at home and is unworthy of regard abroad."[13] Others outside the administration shared such suspicions. Early in 1919 the League of Free Nations Association, a peace organization founded soon after the European armistice, established a special committee on Mexico. Directed by Dr. Samuel Guy Inman, a missionary, a scholar, and an authority on Latin America, it urged friendly cooperation with Mexico and warned that oilmen had tried to manipulate foreign policy for selfish purposes. In addition, journalists of more radical bent, such as John Kenneth Turner, Leander J. De Bekker, and Arthur Thomson, charged that "the interests" had undertaken "a plot" to bring about military intervention in Mexico.[14] The possibility became ever more likely as difficulties mounted.

Increased Opposition to Carranza

Resurgent opposition to Carranza in Mexico contributed to worsening relations. At the end of World War I, anti-Carranza groups, such as the Alianza Legalista Mexicana, anticipated the likelihood of intervention and urged the rehabilitation of the country before the United States could act. In December 1918 General Felipe Angeles, a founder of the Alianza, returned to Mexico from the United States, calling for the restoration of the Constitution of 1857 and the overthrow of tyrants. He struck an agreement with Francisco Villa to coordinate guerrilla warfare until a larger offensive could begin.[15]

Anti-Carranza factions elsewhere also maneuvered to construct a united front. In February 1919 Emiliano Zapata invited Villa and Peláez to embrace Francisco Vázquez Gómez, a one-time Madero supporter, as the "Supreme Chieftain" of a new revolutionary coalition. Striving similarly, the adherents of Félix Díaz appealed to the United States. On 5 February 1919, the second anniversary of the Mexican constitution, Pedro del Villar, the head of the Díaz organization in the United States, addressed a manifesto to leaders in the Wilson administration in which he denounced Carranza as a bolshevik and advised the recognition of Félix Díaz as a belligerent. Other Felicistas such as Roberto Gayón circulated petitions calling for such action among Mexican residents in the United States.[16]

These bids for American support distressed leaders in the Mexican government, who worried that an alliance between rebels and oilmen might ersuade the Wilson administration to repudiate Carranza. Such concerns probably encouraged the Constitutionalists in the plot to assassinate Emiliano Zapata on 10 April 1919. Ambassador Ignacio Bonillas advised care to void any appearance of hostility toward Americans and hoped that the United States would enforce neutrality laws against anti-Carranza conspirators. When American authorities arrested Roberto Gayón for attempting to send troops into Mexico from the United States, the Mexican consul in New York urged similar measures against Pedro del Villar and others. To aid n pacification, Mexican officials wanted to purchase additional arms in the United States.[17] But new difficulties in the petroleum dispute impeded their effort to secure less restrictive export policies.

In the spring Mexico charged that oil producers had violated executive decrees by drilling new wells without permission and threatened on 2 March to punish transgressors by revoking exploitative concessions. The State Department replied that Mexico had denied drilling permits to compel acceptance of Article 27. On 11 April George T. Summerlin, the chargé d'affaires during Fletcher's absence, was instructed to protest. Nonetheless, Frank Polk, the acting secretary of state, hoped that the issuance of provisional permits would resolve the matter. Fletcher similarly told Bonillas that a refusal to grant them could obstruct "more liberal treatment" in the shipment of arms to Mexico. Mexican leaders still resisted, holding that the Congress might enact new petroleum legislation at any time. When the State Department then learned that concession seekers had claimed petroleum lands unregistered by Americans, another protest on 16 April alleged that Mexico had tried to coerce Americans into accepting the Mexican position.[18] Mexico's exclusion from the Paris Peace Conference heightened the dispute.

Alberto Pani, Mexico's unofficial observer, anticipated that the Treaty of Versailles would prejudice small powers. He objected especially to Article 21, which sanctioned the Monroe Doctrine. Such a provision would serve to perpetuate the American hegemony in the western hemisphere. Further, if the Republicans should triumph in the election of 1920, they might invoke it to justify intervention in Mexico. Later in April Ignacio Bonillas informed the State Department that Mexico would not recognize any such doctrine "which attacks the sovereignty and independence of Mexico." Carranza expressly repudiated the Monroe Doctrine in a newspaper interview on 8 May, describing it as "a species of tutelage" and "an arbitrary measure" which imposed "a protectorate" on independent countries. He proposed to substitute in its place the principles of nonintervention and equality among nations.[19]

American diplomats meanwhile could not obtain provisional drilling permits. Late in May Ernesto Garza Pérez, the acting secretary of foreign relations, blamed the oilmen themselves for the trouble. If they had registered their property, then concession seekers could not file claims. The

question remained unsettled in the middle of June when Bonillas took leav
for home. Fletcher suspected it had "some relation" to his own "long con
tinued absence."[20]

Francisco Villa exacerbated the difficulty. His revival augured a unioi
of factions. Early in June at Agua Florida, San Luis Potosí, representative
of Villa, Angeles, Peláez, and lesser leaders agreed to harass the govern
ment with a concerted campaign. Since Villa had an army estimated a
7000, the likelihood of an assault against border towns worried Americans
Following a discussion in the cabinet on 10 June, Secretary of War Bake
authorized American military commanders to enter Mexico if the defens
of life and property required it but forbade "any invasion or occupation."
The State Department meanwhile arranged to permit the export of 150,000
rounds of ammunition to the Mexican commander at Ciudad Juárez.[21]

Villa's attack against Ciudad Juárez early on 15 June produced ai
immediate response. When gunfire threatened El Paso, American troop
crossed the border and participated in repelling the assault. By noon o
the following day, most of the force had returned, but the possibility o
diplomatic complications lingered. On 17 June Mexico regarded the in
cursion as "a violation of Mexican sovereignty" and hoped for a satisfactory
adjustment. Another statement on the following day uncharacteristically
considered the incident as closed.[22]

The likelihood of a change in American policy probably accounted
for such equanimity. Mexican leaders had no wish to risk a reversal throug
undue provocation. General Heriberto Jara already had cautioned tha
rebels had exploited Carranza's criticism of the Monroe Doctrine in the
United States. Cándido Aguilar also urged prudence. Recently commis
sioned as a special ambassador to the United States and Europe, Aguilai
traveled to Washington early in June to discuss petroleum and a loan. Ini
tially he gained the impression that Wilson's Mexican policy had inspirec
"indignation among the parties and the press." Wilson "goes from one
blunder to another and shows each day more clearly that he is a perfectly
incompetent person." Indeed, Aguilar perceived "a criminal intention to
intervene," Later he modified his judgment. If the Republicans won ir
1920, intervention might occur, but Wilson and the Democrats stood against it
Aguilar hoped for a solution but understood the dilemma. To declare Article
27 inapplicable to petroleum would impede other reforms; conversely, tc
carry out a "radical" program would bring "foreign pressure" and "per
haps conflict."[23]

Pressure on the Wilson administration intensified in the summer.
Leaders in the House of Representatives inquired briefly into the Mexican
question, summoning Frank Polk and Henry Fletcher for testimony.[24] Crit
ics proposed a variety of solutions. One plan called for cooperation with
"the better Mexicans" who would "rehabilitate the country with our aid.'
Other schemes suggested the utility of diplomatic pressure, culminating

if necessary, in the use of force. Late in June Frederick Watriss affirmed that "the time for some action has arrived." The United States should withhold all favors "until Mexico does the right thing." On 1 July the National Association published the first edition of the *Bulletin,* which proclaimed the purpose of "arousing, organizing and leading a public sentiment" to sustain the United States "in taking without further delay whatever steps may be necessary to secure . . . protection for the lives and property of Americans in Mexico."[25]

President Wilson's return from Paris heightened speculation. On 9 July spokesmen for the National Association and the Oil Producers Association urged tough measures upon Frank Polk and Henry Fletcher. Polk told them, ". . . we would back them up as far as we could" but "we could go just so far and then it would become intervention." Still, the administration took a harder position, imposing an arms embargo and sanctioning the prudent use of "hot pursuit." Further, on 17 July Polk informed Bonillas "very frankly" that "something had to be done." Otherwise, the president might withdraw recognition.[26]

On 21 July Mexico consented to provisional drilling permits, provided that oilmen accepted "legislative regulations that may be enacted in the future." On the same day the State Department lodged another protest, this time over the murder of Peter Catron, an American shot to death by bandits in San Luis Potosí. Mincing no words, the note warned that if Americans suffered because of "the unwillingness or inability of the Mexican Government to afford adequate protection," the United States "may be forced to adopt a radical change in its policy."[27] Such a contingency came under serious discussion in the following weeks.

Amidst speculation in the Mexican press that intervention impended, the Foreign Office replied on 28 July that Mexico "always" tried to provide "full security." The United States could not properly hold the government accountable, since foreigners often brought "offenses" upon themselves by venturing into dangerous regions through ignorance, imprudence, or rash eagerness for profit. Mexican leaders displayed more concern in private. Cándido Aguilar wondered whether the British and French had encouraged Americans to collect foreign claims. General Pablo González cautioned that "the present hour" was "grave."[28] Some Americans shared his impression. Franklin D. Roosevelt, the acting secretary of the navy, and Paul H. Foster, the consul in Veracruz, both requested "ample notice" in case of intervention.[29]

In Washington Henry Fletcher approved the warning of 21 July, reasoning that it would keep Mexican leaders "alive" to their responsibilities. Unless they understood "the seriousness of the present situation. . . matters will drift from bad to worse." On 4 August President Wilson asked for Fletcher's views. Since the president had carried the confidential memorandum of 1 March to Paris and returned without reading it, he wondered whether the ambassador would still make the same recommendations. Fletcher's position had not changed. The United States still had "the responsibility . . . of making every effort to secure relief . . . from the almost intolerable conditions existing in Mexico." Otherwise, he anticipated "a gradual drifting" until "some sudden emergency" might compel intervention. Fletcher thought it imperative to impress upon the Mexican government its "grave responsibility." If such a "last effort" should fail, the United States, "alone or in conjunction with other governments," should take measures "to restore orderly conditions in Mexico."[30]

Fletcher supported his view with evidence of "Carranza's attitude of hostility to the United States and its citizens." It consisted of correspondence in which the Mexican president urged Hermila Galindo to make haste in completing *La Doctrina Carranza,* a volume which upheld Pan-Hispanicism as an ideal and castigated the northern colossus for its pretensions of hegemony in the western hemisphere. Carranza advised a lively discussion of "the tortuosity of American policy . . . causing the figure of Wilson to stand well out as the director of that policy." He also planned to publish a "Bluebook" to justify his government's "hostility towards foreign speculators." Fletcher believed that Carranza intended "to launch an active, perhaps secret anti-American campaign throughout Latin America."[31] Indeed, he tendered his resignation, convinced that "further effort" on his part "to bring about friendly relations" was "useless." Rather than accept it, Wilson inquired whether Fletcher should return "at once" to Mexico City. Regarding the issue as "exceedingly serious," Wilson reasoned that Carranza lacked "sufficient restraining influence" during Fletcher's absence and hence felt free "to express publicly this outrageous attitude."[32] Meanwhile, the United States Senate initiated an inquiry into the question.

Plot against Mexico

A resolution on 8 August 1919 authorized an investigation of Mexican affairs by a subcommittee of the Senate Committee on Foreign Relations. A month later, Albert B. Fall, the chairman, Frank B. Brandegee, a Republican from Connecticut, and Marcus Smith, a Democrat from Arizona, initiated hearings. During the next nine months, they summoned 257 witnesses, of which fifty-two appeared in executive sessions, and they compiled more than 3000 pages of published testimony. Senator Fall dominated the undertaking. Brandegee and Smith shared his wish for a more stringent policy and usually deferred to him. Although Fall professed disinterested friendship for Mexico and denied any personal stake, his partisan conduct of the investigation provided critics of Wilson and Carranza with a forum.

Witnesses fell into three broad groups. The majority offered no explicit recommendations for American policy. A small minority defended the Mexican government and American policy toward it. Another minority attacked the Mexican Revolution and Woodrow Wilson's response to it.[33]

The first group of witnesses before the subcommittee functioned as apologists for Carranza and the Constitutionalists. They included Dr. James G. McDonald, the president of the League of Free Nations Association, Dr. Samuel Guy Inman, the chairman of the committee on Mexico, George B. Winton, a missionary, John Lind, the one-time special executive agent, Leander J. De Bekker, a reporter for the New York *Tribune,* and Arthur Thomson, a free-lance journalist. According to them, the Mexican government, whatever its shortcomings, had tried to alleviate injustice and to keep faith with the United States. They argued further that oil corporations and other businesses had sought to influence foreign policy to their special advantage. De Bekker and Thomson charged more emphatically that Fall and the oilmen had undertaken a "plot" to provoke military intervention.[34]

Such witnesses sometimes failed to defend their position effectively. Senator Fall badgered, bullied, and baited them. He demanded proof, not vague allegations, and when they could not provide it, he undermined their credibility. De Bekker was not intimidated. In contrast, Inman argued that oilmen had supported Peláez to keep Carranza away but could not explain the distinction between the Oil Producers Association and the National Association for the Protection of American Rights in Mexico. When Arthur Thomson expounded the thesis of his booklet, *The Conspiracy against Mexico,* and confessed that Mexican consulates in the United States had aided him in distributing it, Fall made him appear as a fool acting as a Mexican agent: "It is a wheel within a wheel. You get something from Mr. De Bekker . . . and you swing it around, and then Mr. De Bekker gets something from you, and he swings it around, and that is the way it goes on." Fall then referred Thomson to some historical works on Mexico to alleviate his ignorance.[35]

Fall responded more generously to witnesses such as Edward L. Doheny, the president of the Mexican Petroleum Company and the chairman of the Oil Producers Association, Charles H. Boynton, the executive secretary of the National Association, Frederick Kellogg, an attorney of the National Association, Amos L. Beaty of the Texas Company, William F. Buckley, an independent oilman, Henry Lane Wilson, the former ambassador, and Nelson O'Shaughnessy, the former chargé d'affaires. Such critics argued that Carranza always had taken a hostile attitude toward foreign interests and that Wilson had erred repeatedly. They proposed a variety of solutions, ranging from the seizure of Mexican customs houses to the establishment of an American protectorate, but most claimed to oppose intervention except as a last resort.[36] Most would have concurred with George Agnew Chamberlain, the former American consul-general in Mexico, who advised graduated pressure. While preserving the option of cooperating with Carranza's rivals, the United States should revoke recognition, break diplomatic ties, institute an economic embargo, and utilize naval demonstrations before employing military force.[37]

Senator Fall favored a similar strategem. The "plot" against Mexico, irregular and informal as it was, revolved around him. Only his presence brought a degree of unity of purpose to the otherwise disconnected efforts of American property owners, dissident officials in the United States government, and anti-Carranza rebel leaders. Fall preferred to overthrow Carranza by indirect means. He anticipated that a diplomatic break could precipitate an anti-Carranza rebellion, resulting in the creation of a new, more sympathetic government. Such a scheme could achieve the desired goal without the costs of intervention. To bring it about, Fall courted anti-Carranza leaders and stigmatized the Mexican president.[38]

Fall reasoned that anti-Carranza factions could coalesce into a solid phalanx of opposition if the United States would repudiate the established regime. The extent of rebel activity buoyed his hopes. His contacts with Pedro del Villar and the Díaz clique further encouraged him. In a memorandum to the Fall committee early in August, Villar depicted Carranza as a "bolshevik" but advised against intervention. Mexicans would misunderstand the motives; recognition of Díaz as a belligerent would have more utility. Early in September the principal factional leaders overcame some of their differences and issued a joint "Manifesto to the President and People of the United States." Félix Díaz, Francisco Villa, Manuel Peláez, and Gilardo Magaña, the new head of the Zapatistas, promised "to unite in the formation of a provisional administration" if the United States would aid them in their "great work of reconstruction."[39]

To encourage such a course, Fall tried to discredit Carranza by linking him with allegedly radical and subversive elements in the United States. On 13 November he alerted Robert Lansing that Carranza had fostered sedition by permitting Mexican consulates to disseminate Arthur Thomson's *The Conspiracy against Mexico,* which Fall described as "a Bolsheviki appeal to labor elements in the United States." He also regarded Carranza's collaboration with Hermila Galindo in preparing *La Doctrina Carranza* as evidence of nefarious design. Members of the subcommittee later charged that the Mexican government had ties with "left wing organizations" in the United States, such as the American Federation of Labor, and had attempted to foment revolution by plotting an uprising among Mexicans in the American Southwest.[40] Presumably Carranza intended to eliminate the threat of interference in Mexico by stirring trouble for Americans at home.

Such allegations had special potency during the era of the great Red Scare. In the autumn, R. M. Campbell, the American military attaché in Mexico City, claimed that Mexican agents had incited recent race riots in Washington and Chicago. "The spread of Bolshevism in the United States" and "the tendency toward Communistic ideas" also alarmed Robert Lansing.[41] Fall sought to exploit America's postwar paranoia by establishing a connection with the revolution in Mexico.

Mexicans anticipated the possibility of intervention. Ramón P. de Negri, the Mexican consul in New York, believed that oilmen and rebels had undertaken a conspiracy against Carranza. Mexican newspapers warned repeatedly of the danger. To counter it, the government reportedly planned a propaganda campaign, showing that violence in the United States actually exceeded that in Mexico. Rumors also intimated that Mexican agents had hired thugs to assassinate Senator Fall.[42] When at last a crisis developed, a breakdown had stricken the American president.

The Jenkins Affair: Concessions by Carranza

President Wilson stumped the country for three exhausting weeks in September 1919, seeking to marshal support for the treaty and the League. After a collapse at Pueblo, Colorado, on 25 September, he agreed reluctantly to cancel the tour. Upon his return to Washington, he suffered a cerebral thrombosis on 2 October. The attack prostrated him for nearly a month and incapacitated him for several more. While he recuperated, Edith Bolling Wilson, his wife, Joe Tumulty, his private secretary, and Dr. Cary T. Grayson, his personal physician, established a kind of regency. They governed access to the president and transacted the most pressing business. Robert Lansing tried to provide executive leadership in the cabinet, while the bureaucracy functioned autonomously according to established policies and procedures.[43] For an administration already crippled by the president's disability, the Jenkins affair then produced a crisis.

On the night of 19 October a band of insurgents under Federico Córdoba, possibly under orders from Manuel Peláez, abducted William O. Jenkins, an American consular agent in the city of Puebla. Hoping to embarrass the Mexican president before the United States, the kidnappers demanded a ransom of 300,000 pesos, payable only by the Mexican government. The scheme went awry when Jenkins fell ill. Rather than risk his death, the rebels accepted a ransom from private sources and released the victim on 26 October. Officials in the state of Puebla then arrested Jenkins, charging that he had testified falsely and had arranged his abduction in collusion with Córdoba. Witnesses supported the allegation with testimony later proven false, while Jenkins professed innocence, refusing to post bail.[44] While Jenkins languished in confinement, new reports reached Washington that Mexican authorities again had interfered with drilling operations in the oil fields. Relations with Mexico degenerated rapidly.[45]

When Robert Lansing took charge, he came under strong pressure to act decisively. Henry Fletcher and Boaz Long in the State Department advised "a strong position." Senator Fall took a similar stance. Lansing hoped to win support for a tough policy but responded ambivalently to the use of force. Once assured that Fall and his committee would "play the game," Lansing decided to lay "all the cards on the table."[46] When he brought the issue before the cabinet on 18 November, Burleson and Lane wanted "drastic measures," apparently ready "to go into Mexico," but the others resisted. On the same day the State Department asked that Mexico refrain from interfering with drilling operations. Fletcher meanwhile prepared an ultimatum which threatened a break in relations unless Jenkins was released within forty-eight hours. But Lansing told him "to can it," preferring to couch a warning in less explicit language.[47]

Lansing's note to the Mexican government on 23 November characterized the "unwarranted" arrest of Jenkins as "an arbitrary exercise of public authority." It asked for the "immediate release" of the prisoner and cautioned that a refusal would have "a very serious effect." Mexico spurned the request three days later, denying that Jenkins' incarceration had resulted from injustice. The United States had "no legal foundation" to support its "demand." Further, a presidential order to release Jenkins would violate the prerogatives of the judiciary and the autonomy of a state. Possibly political concerns influenced the decision. In anticipation of forthcoming presidential elections, Carranza may have wished to bolster the nationalist image of his regime.[48] In any case, his position displeased Robert Lansing.

On the morning of 28 November the secretary of state called the Mexican ambassador to account for the "insolence" of his government. Lansing maintained that the American people had displayed a "spirit of friendship and forbearance" while suffering "indignity after indignity." Their patience was "nearly exhausted." Indeed, "the tide of indignation . . . might overwhelm and prevent further diplomatic discussion and force a break in our relations" which "almost inevitably" would mean war. Such words "manifestly offended" Bonillas, who promised nevertheless to report them and then stalked out "white with rage." On the next day another note to Mexico City stated Lansing's refusal to engage in "a juridical discussion of irrelevant matters" and accused the Mexican government of "wilful indifference to the feelings of the American people." Lansing again asked for the "immediate release" of the captive.[49]

By his own account, Lansing desired a peaceful solution, but he placed the responsibility on Mexico. Reasoning that "the numerous and flagrant violations of American rights" were "really at the bottom of the present excitement," he expected "a climax" unless "the Mexican Government changes its policy." Lansing wished to avert "an open rupture," hoping that "sense and decency would finally penetrate the thick skull of President Carranza," but he worried that Mexican obstinacy already had rendered his effort "apparently useless." He conceived of the interview with Bonillas as "a last resort to get the Mexicans to change their policy and prevent an explosion in Congress and the adoption of drastic demand for action." He intended his "bellicose . . . manner and language . . . to prevent war."[50] Uncertain yet determined, he suspected nevertheless that war might result.

His refusal to lay the matter before the cabinet aroused suspicion. Lansing reportedly remarked that a conflict with Mexico could achieve solidarity among the public in the United States. Newton Baker thought he was spoiling for a fight; Josephus Daniels believed that he had joined with the proponents of intervention.[51] Lansing nevertheless cooperated with Democratic leaders in seeking "to hold down" the Senate in case of "a flare-up." He also sought diplomatic accommodation. On 1 December the Mexican ambassador inquired what might come of "this tempest in a teapot over Jenkins?" When Henry Fletcher told him that Mexico had committed "a great blunder" in its handling of the case, Bonillas intimated that his government probably would release the consular agent. Lansing then sought to settle the Jenkins affair independently of other issues, refusing to complicate the immediate question by pressing for provisional drilling permits.[52]

Lansing hoped to maintain control. He expressed satisfaction that "All Congress" had lined up in support of his policy. Although he doubted that President Wilson "will like it when he learns of it," he insisted that "I am right, so I don't care." Others agreed. Franklin K. Lane wanted to give Lansing "a free hand in the matter." Characterizing Mexicans as "naughty children who are exercising all the privileges and rights of grown ups," Lane thought they required "a stiff hand, an authoritative hand." Senator Fall also persuaded Lansing of his readiness to aid "in every way to keep waters quiet as to Mexico." Lansing designated Fletcher to serve as liaison with him and responded with chagrin upon learning that Fall intended to force an issue.[53]

On the morning of 3 December the senator proposed a concurrent resolution which supported the State Department's stand in the Jenkins case and called for a break in diplomatic relations. Lansing thought it "bad business," especially since the second portion could compound the crisis and tie his hands. Fall in all likelihood calculated that the repudiation of

Carranza would galvanize the rebels into a united front. W. E. D. Stokes, an adherent of Félix Díaz, implied as much on 28 November, when he alerted Fall that he was "absolutely authorized" to propose an alliance for General Díaz and "the parties who stand behind him." If the United States would support the anti-Carranza rebels, the latter would sanction the practice of "hot pursuit," deed Baja California to the United States, and permit Americans to take "full control" in the oil fields.[54]

Lansing had decided "to give Republicans all the rope they wanted about going to war with Mexico." Still, Fall's move threatened to outflank him. To counter, he instructed Fletcher on the morning of 4 December to ask that the Committee on Foreign Relations defer a decision on recognition. That afternoon Lansing too went before the committee, requesting an endorsement of his handling of the Jenkins case but advising against a break in relations. When he admitted under questioning that he had not apprised the president, he inadvertently heightened speculation about Wilson's capacity to perform his duties. At Fall's bequest, the senators called for an inquiry and arranged an audience on the following day for Gilbert M. Hitchcock, a Democrat from Nebraska, and Albert Fall.[55]

Although Lansing had alerted the White House to "false intimations" that he had inspired the Fall resolution, he had not provided additional information. He did not want Mrs. Wilson and Tumulty "to decide our policy," since they opposed "a strong stand with Mexico." But Fall had forced his hand. On the morning of 5 December Lansing explained to the president that he had not "troubled" him, since the Jenkins affair in itself could not warrant intervention. Still, the Fall committee might exploit "the whole series of outrages and wrongs" by demanding "drastic action." Seeking "to treat the matter with proper deliberation," he had tried "to divert attention" to the Jenkins case which "could not possibly result in a rupture between the two Governments." Lansing wanted Wilson to know that "the real question" was "Carranza's past record of hostility." He was sure that the State Department could manage it "without endangering our relations with Mexico."[56]

When the visitation took place on the afternoon of 5 December, Wilson rejected a break with Mexico. Edith Bolling Wilson recorded the encounter with animus. Senator Fall "entered the room looking like a regular Uriah Heap, 'washing his hands with invisible soap in imperceptible water.'" When he remarked, "Well, Mr. President, we have all been praying for you," Wilson inquired, "Which way, Senator?" Mrs. Wilson believed that Fall and the Republicans intended to drive the president from office by discovering evidence of mental disability. If such was the case, Wilson disappointed his adversaries. Cheerful, alert, scarcely the mindless lunatic conjured by rumor, he persuaded Fall of his fitness. Further, the inquisitors witnessed the denouement of the Jenkins affair. Dr. Cary Grayson rushed in with the news: The Mexican president had chosen to release the consular agent.[57]

Carranza's concession relieved the immediate crisis, but the petroleum question still pended. Also, critics in Congress and elsewhere still wanted a change in policy. When Wilson asked Fall for his recommendation, the senator held that Carranza's record justified a break. Other Republicans on the Foreign Relations Committee hesitated to act without the president's sanction. When Wilson stated his position on 8 December, he couched his objection in constitutional terms. Since "the Executive, and . . . the Executive only" had "the initiative in directing the relations of our Government with foreign governments," it would "gravely" concern him "to see any such resolution pass the Congress."[58]

Still, the clamor persisted. Henry Cabot Lodge perceived no escape from intervention and "the creation of a government . . . which we should sustain." William Jennings Bryan contemplated the seizure of the oil fields and also Baja California to insure the payment of American claims. In the State Department, Boaz Long regarded a break as "the most effective way, short of armed intervention, of conveying to the Mexicans that we mean what we have said," and Henry Fletcher urged "a definite statement of policy." Since the Mexican refusal to permit drilling had created "a desperate situation," he wanted to lay "the matter . . . before the President for decision." On 12 December Fletcher and Long advised Lansing that Carranza had proven "his inability to clean up Mexico" and "to observe her international obligations." Although military intervention would provide "the surest way" to accomplish a "clean-up," the United States should give "the Mexicans one more chance . . . select the most likely available Mexican to do the job; then back him morally and physically if need be. . . ." If "honorable Mexicans" should fail to alleviate "the present chaos," the United States should resort to strong measures.[59]

The question still divided the cabinet. Only Lane and Burleson urged the use of "strong arms." Unable to reach a decision, Lansing asked the president on 19 December for "directions," cautioning that Carranza would go to "the point of a definite break . . . before abandoning the policy which he has adopted." On 3 January 1920 Lansing again entreated the president, suggesting the utility of an arbitration scheme devised by Fletcher. An ambassador should return to Mexico and insist upon the protection of American "lives, rights and property," a commitment "to adjudicate all claims," and an agreement to submit the question of property rights under the Constitution of 1917 to the Hague Tribunal. If Carranza failed to endorse such proposals within "a reasonable time, say four weeks," the United States should rescind recognition and sever relations. Such a course in

Lansing's view would not necessarily presage intervention. Rather, it could "check" Mexican hostility and might eliminate President Carranza "by the actions of the Mexicans themselves." Elections were scheduled for the following June. Once a new government took power, the United States could renew diplomatic ties "upon an entirely just basis and upon such conditions and assurances as may be deemed advisable."[60]

No evidence reveals Wilson's response. Possibly the memoranda never reached him, and Lansing despaired, recording his impression that "the President's failure to act on the most important questions and his apparent resentment that I dare to advise him are producing a practically impossible situation." At his "wits' end," Lansing anticipated retirement from his post. Similarly disenchanted, Fletcher resigned "with the greatest regret" on 20 January, "convinced that . . . further effort" on his part "to bring about friendly relations" was "useless."[61]

Meanwhile, tension eased in the petroleum dispute. On 13 January 1920 the Oil Producers Association appealed for "just and equitable treatment," promising "to abide by all lawful regulations" provided that their applications for provisional drilling permits implied no repudiation of "pre-existing rights." Carranza seized the opportunity to arrange a modus vivendi. On 17 January he authorized provisional drilling rights until the Mexican Congress should enact an organic petroleum law, stipulating that the decision jeopardized in no way the claims of the Mexican government. His second concession in two months accommodated the Mexican position with American demands and "practically" settled "the present acute phase of the oil controversy."[62]

The Mexican crisis had continued effects within the Wilson administration. Franklin K. Lane, a proponent of forceful policies, left the cabinet on 5 February. Two days later Wilson called Robert Lansing to account for his conduct, inquiring whether the secretary had summoned unauthorized cabinet meetings. When Lansing confessed, Wilson rebuked him for usurping authority and asked him to resign. Although Lansing denied improprieties, he complied with the president's wish. Differences over the treaty and the League accounted in part for the rift. Further, Lansing's independence during the Mexican crisis impressed the president as disloyalty.[63] His departure eliminated still another critic of Mexican policy.

Liberal Capitalism versus Self-Determination

The Mexican question in 1919 posed a fundamental difficulty for Woodrow Wilson. Ironically, just as he extended a liberal-capitalist vision of international order to encompass the world, Mexico refused to adhere. Carranza's nationalistic stance in effect required that Wilson decide whether the exercise of self-determination outside the bounds of liberal capitalism had legitimacy and, if not, what measures to employ against it. The congruence among components in Wilson's thinking had broken down. The tension had become acute.

Wilson relied on diplomatic interposition during the war years to safeguard material interests in Mexico. At the conclusion of the conflict, the release of American forces from Europe could have occasioned a drastic change in policy, but the president shunned such a course. Political animosities arising from the treaty fight accounted in part for his reluctance. Also, following his collapse in the autumn, his isolation in the White House contributed further to the immobilization of Mexican policy. The seizure distorted Wilson's perceptions and heightened his intransigence. Beleaguered and assailed, he construed criticism as personal affront. Senator Fall's advocacy of strong measures in December was in itself a deterrent.

More importantly, Wilson lacked justification. Mexico's right to self-determination had clashed particularly with the economic requirements of liberal capitalism, and Wilson lacked the ideological means to reconcile them. In the past he had acted most dramatically when convinced that he shared common goals with the Constitutionalists. Deprived of a sense of higher purpose to serve Mexico, he could not sanction a drastic departure from the established policy. In this instance, his definition of American aims in self-interested terms militated against intervention. Instead, he capitalized on Carranza's proclivity to make opportune concessions and sought accommodation through diplomatic interposition. His response to the revolt against Carranza in the spring of 1920 demonstrated how much his position had changed since 1913.

Chapter 7

The Overthrow of Carranza

*Carranza appeared ready to make further concessions
to American oil interests in Mexico, and Wilson was hope-
ful of better relations. The hopes of both men were disappointed. In the spring of 1920 a rebellion triggered by the
Mexican presidential campaign ended all immediate prospects of accommodation between Mexico and the United
States.*

Rebellion in Mexico

Wilson restored his administration early in 1920. Late in February he
selected a secretary of state. Bainbridge Colby, a prominent lawyer and
politician from New York, lacked diplomatic experience, but, as a former
Progressive Republican turned Democrat, he shared an affinity for the treaty
and the League. Colby seldom challenged Wilson on policy questions.[1] The
president also sought reconciliation with Mexico. When Henry Morgenthau, a veteran diplomat, volunteered for the post, Wilson made ready to
appoint an ambassador. A variety of issues still pended. Mark L. Requa,
the chief of the Oil Division, regarded the petroleum question as the most
crucial. Warning of "an industrial crisis" unless federal authorities and private corporations cooperated closely to secure petroleum supplies, he expected that "the new form of title" in Mexico would have an "extremely
detrimental" effect upon "the interests of American oil companies" and
"the national welfare of the American people."[2] In addition, William Jenkins
still faced criminal charges for rebellion, perjury, attempted bribery, and
contempt for judicial authority. Anti-Carranza factions still opposed the
government, and Senator Fall persisted in his investigation, in spite of Mexican complaints that he had established "a tribunal to judge the Mexican
Republic."[3]

Mexico countered in the spring with a propaganda campaign to justify
petroleum decrees in the United States. Carranza hoped to ease the ten-

sion. Early in February he conveyed his readiness to discuss the creation of a claims commission. Later in March he authorized new petroleum concessions for periods of ten years but stipulated that recipients must comply with Mexican laws.[4] Still, the opposition in the United States remained strong. When Wilson sent Henry Morgenthau's nomination to the Senate for confirmation on 23 March, the Foreign Relations Committee refused to act. Senator Fall thought it "ridiculous" to send an ambassador, since "the whole country" was in ferment. The Mexican consul in New York charged that Fall intended his obstruction to aid Carranza's enemies in bringing about the overthrow of the regime.[5]

The presidential campaign in Mexico had divided the Constitutionalist coalition.[6] High prices, unemployment, the tardy pace of land and labor reform, allegations of corruption in official circles, and dissatisfaction with the accomplishments of the revolution placed Carranza on the defensive. His determination to designate a successor and a rift with Alvaro Obregón, "the hero of Celaya," compounded the difficulty. Obregón had returned to his ranch in Sonora after resigning his post as secretary of war in May 1917, but he remained in close touch with politics. He considered himself Carranza's heir and won wide acclaim as such. In all likelihood he hoped for the president's endorsement but never received it. Seeking to silence speculation over the presidential succession, Carranza warned in January 1919 against surging factionalism, calling for unity to sustain his government. Contrary to his intention, the statement aroused suspicion that he planned to impose his successor. Without consulting Carranza, Obregón announced his candidacy on 1 June 1919, explicitly stating his aversion to an official nominee. While urging cooperation among "true revolutionaries," he demanded that the people choose freely and offered himself as the leader of a new "liberal" coalition to achieve the promise of the revolution. Infuriated, Carranza vowed to withhold his support.[7]

Obregón successfully capitalized on his reputation as a folk hero. He quickly gained a mass following, especially with organized labor, and effectively exploited disenchantment with the shortcomings of the Mexican Revolution. On occasion he criticized Carranza's conduct of foreign relations, intimating that he would ease chronic tension in relations with the United States by acknowledging "legitimately acquired" foreign rights. Meanwhile, General Pablo González, a long-time Carranza loyalist and the division commander who had engineered the assassination of Emiliano Zapata, also mounted a drive for the presidency. Although less successful in the campaign than Obregón, González won support from *hacendados* and businessmen.[8]

Once two generals had taken the field, Carranza feared a disastrous military struggle to determine the outcome. He asked that each withdraw. When they refused, he cast the issue as a contest between military and civilian rule and then unveiled his candidate. Ignacio Bonillas, the ambassador to the United States, was an odd choice. Almost unknown in Mexico, Bonillas lacked popularity and standing. Carranza probably regarded him as a figurehead to perpetuate his own influence. Further, Carranza's antipathy to generals in positions of political authority may have influenced his decision, as he recalled his earlier struggles against Huerta and Villa. Possibly Carranza calculated that Obregón and González would neutralize one another, allowing Bonillas to prevail.[9] The president undoubtedly conceived the Bonillas candidacy as a signal to the United States. He remarked on one occasion that "we should not elect a military man but a civilian, and he must be a man of culture, of ample preparation, able to resolve the great diplomatic problems with which we shall be faced."[10] Presumably, with Bonillas in the presidency, the conduct of diplomacy would reside in experienced hands.

Bonillas had misgivings at the outset. Although the Carranza party had touted him since November 1919, he remained in Washington, insisting that he would accept the nomination only if the Mexican people wanted him. When at last he returned to Mexico and announced his availability on 18 March 1920, he appealed to civilian bureaucrats and entrepreneurs around the president but otherwise encountered apathy and abuse. Critics called him "Mister" Bonillas, alleging that he had forgotten Spanish during his residence in the United States. An editorial in *El Universal* under the headline *"El Rey de Burlas"* compared him with Sancho Panza. Obregón characterized him as "an excellent person . . . serious, honest, and hardworking. The world has lost a magnificent bookkeeper."[11] By supporting Bonillas, Carranza committed the worst error of his political career. Mexico still lacked the mechanism for transferring political power peaceably.

Carranza's feud with Sonora, Obregón's home state and a hotbed of enthusiasm in his support, ignited the rebellion. Relations deteriorated immediately once Obregón became a candidate. Ten days later on 11 June 1919 the president declared the waters of the Sonora River federal property, perhaps in reprisal, and thus outraged Sonorans who protested the violation of their state's autonomy. The Yaqui Indian question exacerbated the dispute. When Adolfo de la Huerta became governor of Sonora in September 1919, he set out to pacify the Indians. With Carranza's consent, he arranged a peace settlement while promising land, food, and equipment. But Carranza rejected it. In an ironic reversal of his own circumstance in 1913, Carranza anticipated the possibility of a revolt and seized upon the persistence of Indian troubles as an excuse to order federal troops into Sonora late in March 1920.[12] He also struck against Obregón, summoning him to Mexico City on 2 April to appear as a witness in the treason trial of General Roberto Cejudo. Although lieutenants advised against it, Obregón went to the capital, where detectives shadowed him and then placed him under house arrest. Obregón expected imprisonment and possibly execution. When he then learned that Sonora had broken with the federal government, he eluded his captors and escaped to Guerrero, where he called for revolution to rectify Carranza's transgressions. In the Plan of Agua Prieta on 23 April 1920, Obregón and the Sonorans repudiated the president, urged the creation of a provisional government, and designated Adolfo de la Huerta as supreme military commander.[13]

The insurgents triumphed quickly. Pablo González, most commanders in the federal army, and a variety of anti-Carranza factions supported the uprising. Lacking the means to sustain himself, Carranza withdrew from the capital on 7 May, seeking to make his way to Veracruz, his refuge after the break with Villa in 1914. Hard pressed yet determined, he told his nephew, General Alberto Salinas Carranza, as he departed his home on Calle Lerma, "I will not flee as Porfirio Díaz nor resign as Señor Madero. I am the president of the Republic, and I will return to my house triumphant or dead."[14]

The Wilson administration had ample forewarning but responded uncertainly. Throughout the early months of 1920, American diplomats in Mexico cautioned that the presidential contest could result in violence. Nevertheless, President Wilson ignored such contingencies. In the middle of April, he wondered whether he should receive a new ambassador from Mexico.[15] As relations between Sonora and the federal government worsened in the spring, Bartley F. Yost, the American consul in Guaymas, requested a naval vessel, but the State Department demurred until the break actually occurred in April. The secretary of state then instructed Matthew E. Hanna, the chargé d'affaires in Mexico City, to aid the rebels in no way, and Wilbur J. Carr, the director of the Consular Service, advised his subordinates to act with "the utmost discretion."[16]

Although the Wilson administration maintained its legal obligations to Carranza, the adjacency of Sonora to the border posed a special problem. The uprising immediately occasioned rumors that Obregón had won American favor. Private citizens in the United States reportedly supported the insurgents with money and arms. Early in April the Mexican consul at Douglas, Arizona, claimed that the Phelps Dodge Corporation had supplied the Sonorans with 200,000 rounds of ammunition.[17] Further, Obregón partisans appealed for equal treatment and urged that American officials spurn any bid by Carranza to transport Mexican troops through American territory. Some allegations held that Carranza sought such privileges, only to suffer rejection, but the State Department repeatedly denied ever receiving such a request "formally."[18] Reports of official favoritism, largely unfounded, probably originated when twenty Carranza loyalists asked permission to flee from Sonora into the United States, hoping to return to Mexico City by way of El Paso. Although the State Department granted the request, rumors of an anti-Carranza bias within the administration persisted.[19]

Improvisation and prudence characterized the American response. On 23 April Secretary Colby alerted the president that conditions had entered "an acute stage." Colby anticipated "the possibility of rapid and significant developments" and asked that the Navy Department order warships to principal Mexican ports. American authorities also stepped up vigilance along the border, seeking to police illegal traffic in contraband more effectively. On 1 May the State Department reiterated the ruling that trade in military provisions required individual export licenses. A short while later the collapse of Carranza's government obviated any need to develop a more coherent policy. On 7 May Colby reported that "the revolutionary element" controlled one-third of Mexico. He expected the Mexican president to relinquish power.[20]

When Carranza and a party of loyalists retreated from Mexico City by railroad convoy, rebels harrassed the refugees with sporadic attacks and finally halted the trains by destroying the tracks. Carranza then fled on horseback into the mountains of Puebla. On 20 May he took refuge at San Antonio Tlaxcalantongo. That night horsemen rode into the village and shot Venustiano Carranza to death.[21]

Recognition Considered

The insurgents quickly consolidated their triumph. With very little disorder, a provisional government under Adolfo de la Huerta took power and scheduled elections for September. Obregón disclaimed responsibility for Carranza's death. Reportedly the assassination had little effect on "the strength and prestige of the new revolutionary movement."[22] Although a few Carranza loyalists still resisted, the provisional government eliminated most rivals by bringing them into the administration or retiring them from politics. Manuel Peláez accepted the new regime. Spokesmen for the Zapatistas affirmed their loyalty. Francisco Villa withdrew from the arena in return for a subsidy, and Félix Díaz took refuge in exile.[23]

The new regime courted the United States through emissaries and intermediaries. Late in April General Salvador Alvarado appeared in Washington as an agent of the Sonora government. Later Luis Morones, an influential labor leader, represented the provisional government, while Colonel Myron M. Parker, an attorney of the Oil Producers Association, advised de facto recognition, reasoning that Obregón and his allies would deal fairly with petroleum companies. Early in May Provisional President Adolfo de la Huerta persuaded Francis J. Dyer, the American consul in Nogales, Sonora, that his government intended as a principal priority "to cultivate friendly relations with the United States."[24]

The Wilson administration responded cautiously, in part because of uncertainty over "the shifting Mexican situation." Charles M. Johnston, the chief of the Mexican Affairs Division, cautioned against "precipitous action," and the State Department instructed its personnel "to take no steps" which might imply recognition.[25] Domestic politics also contributed. Late in May 1920 Senator Fall and his subcommittee concluded the investigation of Mexican affairs, advising against recognition unless Mexico agreed in a treaty to respect American rights and to exempt American property from Article 27. To prevent future violations, the United States should reserve the prerogative of intervention.[26]

Late in May Dr. Alvaro Torre Díaz, another emissary, pressed for recognition. Later the State Department learned that Fernando Iglesias Calderón soon would present his credentials as ambassador to the United States.[27] The administration in response asserted no test of "constitutional legitimacy." Such a criterion had little point in 1920. President Wilson much preferred accommodation with the new regime but insisted, nevertheless, that Mexican leaders accept his conditions. Wilson now defined the American stake in Mexico almost exclusively in material terms. He possessed no sense of common ideological purpose with Obregón and the insurgents; he had no compelling wish to make common cause with them in extending the area of liberty. Rather, he intended to insure respect for American rights in Mexico. The State Department established bases for recognition on the assumption that Obregón would take office as president after the election in September. Charles M. Johnston of the Mexican Affairs Division advised informal conversations with Iglesias Calderón to determine whether the new government had "a sincere desire to reverse the foreign policy of its predecessor." If Mexico would consent to a claims commission and the recognition of American rights, then Johnston believed de facto recognition justifiable.[28]

When Fernando Iglesias Calderón arrived in Washington late in June, he conferred unofficially with Undersecretary of State Norman H. Davis, since Secretary Colby was attending the Democratic convention in San Francisco. Calderón affirmed his government's determination to establish cordial relations, to compensate foreigners for damages, and to defend life, liberty and property.[29] Despite this conciliatory pose, officers in the State Department held back, insisting upon additional assurances. The petroleum question deterred quick recognition. When Adolfo de la Huerta tried to enforce Carranza's decrees later in the summer, the State Department protested new restrictions on drilling privileges.[30] The possibility of further disorder also impeded a decision. When rumors suggested that General Pablo González might revolt, the provisional government arrested him early in July. Later in the month, when Esteban Cantú, the governor of Baja Cali-

fornia, proclaimed the independence of his government, de la Huerta compelled him to capitulate by threatening the use of armed force.[31]

Meanwhile, American politics engulfed the Mexican question. Both
major parties addressed it as the presidential election process began. At
the convention in Chicago early in June, the Republicans endorsed the
essentials of Senator Fall's position. The Mexico plank, written largely by
Fall, characterized the Republican party as "a sincere friend of the Mexican people" and pledged "a consistent, firm and effective policy." Recognition would depend on "sufficient guarantees that the lives and property
of American citizens are respected and protected; that wrongs are promptly
corrected and just compensation will be made for injury sustained." Later
Warren G. Harding, the Republican nominee, characterized Wilson's policy as "vacillating and un-American." Although Harding had no intention
of telling the Mexicans "who should govern there," he adhered to the
tenets of the Republican platform. The Democrats also insisted that Mexicans prove their willingness to uphold law and order, to fulfill international
obligations, and to implement "just laws under which foreign investors shall
have rights as well as duties." Although James M. Cox, the Democratic
candidate, later repudiated intervention, refusing to send American troops
into a "hornet's nest," tactical questions more than basic goals set him
apart from Harding.[32]

Although Wilson failed to win his party's endorsement for a third term,
he had not precluded a settlement of the Mexican question before he left
office. Diplomatic sparring persisted in Washington. Late in August Norman Davis informed Iglesias Calderón that recognition required specific
acts in defense of property. Davis particularly wanted an abandonment of
Carranza's petroleum decrees. The Mexican emissary first protested the
irregularity of such conditions but then moderated his position. His government intended to remove all obstacles. Still, American leaders would
not let him present his credentials unofficially to the president, wary that
even an informal gesture might signify recognition.[33] The provisional government recalled Iglesias Calderón a short while later. As he departed late
in September, he blamed the failure of his mission on unreasonable American demands, to which Norman Davis replied that Wilson would grant recognition when circumstances should warrant it.[34]

On 5 September 1920 Alvaro Obregón won election as president of
Mexico to a term beginning on 1 December. Soon afterward he stated his
desire for "harmonious relations," and Woodrow Wilson again contemplated recognition. Public opinion exerted some pressure. A variety of civil
and commercial groups in the border states and the governors of Texas,
Arizona, and New Mexico urged it.[35] Also, the proximity of presidential
elections in the United States early in November encouraged it. Wilson

regarded recognition as personal vindication and as a *fait accompli* with which to present the electorate. Consequently, when Roberto V. Pesqueira, the Mexican financial agent, claimed on 23 September that the president-elect wanted to adjust all issues and would go "to practically any extreme" to settle the petroleum wrangle, Norman Davis told him that "general principles" rather than a single issue would determine the decision. Davis demanded "fair and equitable treatment" for Americans but specified no exact terms, holding that "it was entirely within the control of Mexico to bring about conditions and a situation" to justify recognition. Four days later President Wilson consented to it if Mexico would act upon Pesqueira's intimations.[36]

Other intermediaries conveyed word of Mexico's readiness. In October George Creel, formerly the chief of the Committee on Public Information, traveled to Mexico in a private capacity but at Wilson's bequest. He learned from the provisional president that Mexico would not construe Article 27 retroactively and, further, that Roberto V. Pesqueira had the authority to pursue additional discussions in Washington. With Creel's encouragement, Pesqueira alerted Bainbridge Colby on 26 October that Mexico would accept a protocol providing for the creation of a claims commission and the defense of legitimate property rights. He emphasized that Article 27 "must not be interpreted as retroactive or violative of valid property rights."[37] The State Department responded favorably. On 28 October Colby apprised the president that "the material conditions, on which we have a right to insist, are satisfactorily set forth" and have established "a basis on which the preliminaries of recognition can proceed." When Wilson agreed, Colby informed the press on the following day that the Mexican government had displayed sufficient "stability, sincerity and creditable sensitiveness to its duties" to justify recognition.[38]

The arrangement then collapsed precipitously. On 5 November Adolfo de la Huerta repudiated the proposed protocol, claiming that Pesqueira had exceeded his authority and had acted independently.[39] The regime spurned recognition conditioned by terms and stipulations. To do otherwise would subvert the integrity of the revolution. The Wilson administration then suspended discussions. Suspicion of incipient radicalism in the Obregón regime discouraged new initiatives. Finally, the Democratic defeat at the polls concluded all hope. Since Obregón would have to come to terms with the Republicans, he disdained recognition by a lame-duck president, and Wilson hesitated to commit his successor. At the State Department's instruction, George T. Summerlin, the chargé d'affaires, stayed away from the new president's inauguration on 1 December.[40] Three months later Woodrow Wilson left the White House with the question of recognition as unsettled as it had been when he took office.

Breakdown of the Wilson Paradigm

Woodrow Wilson's attempt to circumscribe the Mexican Revolution within the bounds of liberal capitalism ended inconclusively. Although his utilization of diplomatic interposition blunted the effect of Article 27 on American interests, the larger conflict between the principles of liberal capitalism and the nationalistic affirmations of the Mexican Revolution was unresolved. Wilson's inability to decide the question of recognition on his terms before leaving office symbolized the breakdown of his orderly, integrated conception of hemispheric unity.

At the outset Wilson presumed a fundamental congruence of interest and aspiration with Latin Americans. He premised his messianic vision on a belief in the universality of liberal capitalism and simultaneously asserted a commitment to the principle of self-determination. Such a position developed from his view of history as a process expanding the area of human liberty. But his formulation retained internal coherence only to the extent that Wilson could empathize with Latin Americans and identify his goals with theirs — that is, cast himself as the champion of self-determination. It was in the crusade against Victoriano Huerta that anti-militarist and anti-imperialist prejudices first aroused Wilson. Later he perceived the Huerta regime as a violation of Mexico's right to self-determination and linked his own purposes with those of the larger body of Mexicans in the decision to intervene. The imperatives of liberal capitalism in this instance strengthened and re-enforced the requirement of self-determination.

Nationalistic outrage induced by the seizure of Veracruz shocked Wilson, but he failed to grasp the full implication. Neither Huerta nor Carranza would let him act in Mexico's behalf; yet the president persisted. After the breakup of the Constitutionalist coalition, he tried abortively to forge a liberal-capitalist party through the reconciliation of factions. When at last he abandoned such a strategem and opted for Carranza, he naively expected Villa and Zapata to acquiesce in his decision. The consequences again shocked him.

Growing disparities of purpose and intention became even more evident during the punitive expedition. Initially, Carranza's obstruction worried him; later, the future course of the revolution. Although the latter concern had little direct bearing on the decision to send Pershing into Mexico, it figured prominently in the deliberations on whether to withdraw him. Carranza's continued inability to insure order and his departure from liberal-capitalist standards in the Constitution of 1917 posed difficult tactical questions. The American intervention in World War I rendered them all the more perplexing.

Anomalies in the Wilson position became ever more difficult during the war years. After April 1917 Wilson lost all sense of common purpose with Carranza and the Constitutionalists. Article 27 menaced important economic interests in ways compounded by the possibility of an alignment between Germany and Mexico. Paradoxically, imperialism and revolution threatened to unite in common opposition to liberal capitalism on the Mexican front. The breakdown of Wilson's position resulted in part from the intransigence of Carranza's nationalism. Lacking justification derived from a sense of ideological affinity with the Constituionalists, Wilson could not bludgeon Mexico into line through the use of military force. His reliance on diplomatic interposition from 1917 through 1920 served to bridge disparities but not to mend them. The internal coherence of his position collapsed with the divergence of ideological and material components in his thinking. As his commitment to human liberty became even more incompatible with the need to safeguard material interests in Mexico, the president experienced a kind of intellectual paralysis. He needed to act yet could not justify the kind of measures wanted by vested interest groups. Their ill will complicated domestic politics for him in the fight over the treaty and the League.

Wilson attempted to devise policies that would uphold his ideological commitments, safeguard material interests, and convey a modicum of respect for Mexican self-determination. The difficulty of sustaining such goals became evident in the range of criticism leveled against him. In the opinion of many oilmen and Republicans, Wilson had scant regard for national interests, seeking instead to pursue abstract visions of moral uprightness. For Mexicans, in contrast, the Wilson position always implied an unacceptable degree of dependency. Such disparate perceptions have contributed to the ongoing debate over the motives and consequences of Wilson's policies and have on occasion obscured the linkage between intentions, actions, and effects.

Karl R. Popper has remarked that students of human affairs above all should explore "the unintended social repercussions of intentional human actions."[41] Such a recommendation assists in the study of Woodrow Wilson. Wilson amalgamated learned traditions and concrete interests into a liberal-capitalist synthesis which shaped his response to the Mexican Revolution. Although the balance between these components in his thinking shifted situationally, sometimes favoring ideology, sometimes material concerns, the president never abandoned the formulation. His effort to mediate between the demands of economic interest groups in the United States and the insistence of Mexicans on self-determination repeatedly had unanticipated consequences. Indisputably, his use of diplomacy served the economic needs of the American nation state. He intended his position, however, to differ substantively from overt imperialism. Indisputably, his use of diplomacy blunted the demands of Mexican nationalism. He intended, however, to establish a community of interest and purpose with Mexicans. For him, anti-imperialism of the liberal-capitalist variety seemed a viable alternative to the extremes of imperialism and revolution. For critics with other perceptions, his position appeared either to abandon American interests or to perpetuate Mexican dependency. The chasm perhaps was unbridgeable. Whatever Wilson's intentions, the consequences mattered more to his critics.

Bibliographic Essay

The study of Mexican-United States diplomatic relations during the Wilson-Carranza era encompasses a large body of literature in Spanish and in English. Notes to the chapters provide specific direction to research materials. This essay, cast as a select bibliography, includes primary and secondary sources of particular importance. Additional bibliographical information is contained in the two-volume, revised edition of *Harvard Guide to American History,* edited by Frank Freidel (Cambridge: Belknap Press of Harvard University Press, 1974); in *A Bibliography of United States-Latin American Relations Since 1910, A Selected List of Eleven Thousand Published References,* edited by David F. Trask, Michael C. Meyer, and Roger R. Trask (Lincoln: University of Nebraska Press, 1968); in *Cuestiones Internacionales de México, Una Bibliografía,* edited by Daniel Cosío Villegas (Mexico: Secretaría de Relaciones Exteriores, 1966); in the second edition of *Bibliografía de la Revolución Mexicana,* edited by Roberto Ramos (Mexico: Biblioteca de Instituto Nacional de Estudios de la Revolución Mexicana, 1959); in the three-volume *Fuentes de la Historia Contemporánea de México, Libros y Folletos* (Mexico: Colegio de México, 1961-62); and in the *Handbook of Latin American Studies* (Cambridge: Harvard University Press; Gainesville: University of Florida Press, 1936 ff.).

Primary Sources

The most important documentation for understanding the development of United States policy is located at the National Archives, Washington, D.C. Records of the Department of State Relating to Internal Affairs of Mexico, 1910-1929 [Record Group 59, Microcopy 274 (1959)], and Records of the Department of State Relating to Political Relations between the United States and Mexico, 1910-1929 [Record Group 59, Microcopy 314 (1960)] contain dispatches, instructions, memoranda, and a variety of other papers. Records of the Department of War, the Adjutant General's

Office, Record Group 94; Records of the Department of War, the General Staff, War College Division, Record Group 165; Records of the Department of the Navy, the Records of the Office of Naval Intelligence, Record Group 38; and Records of the Department of the Navy, the Office of Naval Records and Library, Record Group 45, hold intelligence reports on conditions in Mexico and bear on issues such as politics, the border, the oil fields, and Article 27.

Personal papers further illuminate the decision-making process among leaders in the Wilson administration, especially the Papers of Newton D. Baker, Bainbridge Colby, George Creel, Josephus Daniels, Norman H. Davis, Henry P. Fletcher, Robert Lansing, William Gibbs McAdoo, Frank R. McCoy, John J. Pershing, Hugh L. Scott, and Woodrow Wilson at the Library of Congress, Washington, D.C.; and the Papers of Gordon Auchincloss, Edward M. House, and Frank L. Polk at Yale University, New Haven, Connecticut. Other collections pertain to questions of petroleum, recognition, and intervention, especially the Papers of Chandler P. Anderson, Harry A. Garfield, James R. Garfield, and Samuel Guy Inman at the Library of Congress, Washington, D.C.; the Papers of Albert B. Fall (microfilm copy), University of Nebraska, Lincoln; the Papers of Henry Cabot Lodge, Massachusetts Historical Society, Boston; the Papers of William F. Buckley, University of Texas, Austin; the Papers of John Lind, Minnesota Historical Society, St. Paul; and the Papers of Mark L. Requa, University of Wyoming, Laramie.

Primary sources in Mexico on the whole are less complete and less revealing than those in the United States. Official government records do not permit close scrutiny of decision-making in foreign policy, yet they convey important insights. For the study of Carranza's foreign policy, the Archivo de la Secretaría de Relaciones Exteriores, México, D.F., holds the most important collections. Revolución Mexicana durante los Años 1910 a 1920, Informaciones Diversas de la República y de las Oficinas de México en el Exterior (Expediente H. 513″910-20/1, L-E-610R-868R), comprises 259 bound volumes composed mainly of reports to the Mexican Foreign Ministry. *Revolución Mexicana 1910-1920* by Berta Ulloa (Mexico: Secretaría de Relaciones Exteriores, 1963) is a guide and index. Reglamentación de la Ley de Petróleo Mexicano 1914-1928, Controversia entre México y los Estados Unidos de A. con motivo de la Fracción I del Artículo 27 Constitucional (Expediente III/628(010)/1, L-E-533-544), focuses on the 1920s. The *expedientes personales* of Cándido Aguilar (L-E-896-897), Ignacio Bonillas (L-E-1351), Venustiano Carranza (L-E-1441-1445), Salvador Diego Fernández (L-E-894-895), Hilario Medina (L-E-903-904), and Alberto J. Pani (L-E-911-912) consist mainly of routine communications but provide some understanding of the workings of the Mexican Foreign Ministry.

The Archivo de Venustiano Carranza, a large, well-organized collection at the Centro de Estudios de Historia de México, Departamento Cultural de Condumex, S.A., México, D.F., contains significant research materials but reveals disappointingly little about foreign policy. This fine repository also possesses the Archivo de Francisco de la Barra. Through the courtesy of Alicia Reyes and my friend Anthony Bryan, I was permitted to use the Archivo de Bernardo Reyes in the "Capilla Alfonsina," México, D.F. The Latin American Collection of the University of Texas, Austin, houses the Archivo de Lázaro de la Garza Vidaurri, which includes a small amount of Francisco Villa's papers, and a microfilm copy of the Archivo de Pablo González, which pertains largely to military affairs and also contains some of Félix Díaz's papers. Mexican newspapers and periodicals are available at the Hemeroteca Nacional, México, D.F. *Fuentes de la Historia Contemporánea de México, Periódicos y Revistas,* edited by Stanley R. Ross (Mexico: Colegio de México, 1965-67) is a helpful guide in two volumes.

Published collections of documents and papers include the following volumes: Ray Stannard Baker and William E. Dodd, eds., *The Public Papers of Woodrow Wilson,* 4 vols. (New York: Harper & Brothers, 1926-27); Ray Stannard Baker, ed., *Woodrow Wilson, Life and Letters,* 8 vols. (Garden City, N.Y.: Doubleday, Doran & Co., 1927-1939); U.S. Department of State, *Papers Relating to the Foreign Relations of the United States, 1913-1921* (Washington, D.C.: Government Printing Office, 1920-36), including *The Lansing Papers,* 2 vols. (1939-40); and U.S. Congress, Senate, *Investigation of Mexican Affairs,* 66th Cong., 2d Sess., Document 285, 2 vols. (Washington, D.C.: Government Printing Office, 1920).

The following published diaries and memoirs are of special utility: George Creel, *How We Advertised America* (New York: Harper & Row, 1920); E. David Cronon, ed., *The Cabinet Diaries of Josephus Daniels, 1913-1921* (Lincoln: University of Nebraska Press, 1963); Josephus Daniels, *The Wilson Years,* 2 vols. (Chapel Hill: University of North Carolina Press, 1946); David H. Stratton, ed., *The Memoirs of Albert B. Fall,* vol. 4, no. 3, monograph 15, *Southwestern Studies* (El Paso: Texas Western Press, 1966); *War Memoirs of Robert Lansing, Secretary of State* (New York: Bobbs-Merrill Co., 1935); Hugh L. Scott, *Some Memories of a Soldier* (New York: Century Co., 1928); Colonel Frank Tompkins, *Chasing Villa; The Story behind the Story of Pershing's Expedition into Mexico* (Harrisburg, Pa.: Military Service Publishing Co., 1934); Joseph P. Tumulty, *Woodrow Wilson As I Know Him* (Garden City, N.Y.: Doubleday, Page & Co., 1921); Edith Bolling Wilson, *My Memoir* (New York: Bobbs-Merrill Co., 1938); and Henry Lane Wilson, *Diplomatic Episodes in Mexico, Belgium and Chile* (Port Washington, N.Y.: Kennikat Press, 1971).

Printed Mexican records are indispensable supplements to manuscript collections. *Labor Internacional de la Revolución Constitucionalista de México (Libro Rojo)* (Mexico: n.p., 1960, first published, 1919); and *Documentos Relacionados con la Legislación Petrolera Mexicana,* by the Secretaría de Industria, Comercio, y Trabajo (Mexico: Poder Ejecutivo Federal, 1919) are basic sources. The two-volume *Diario de los Debates del Congreso Constituyente of the Cámara de Diputados* (México, D.F.: Imprenta de la Cámara de Diputados, 1922) records the deliberations at the Querétaro convention. Isidro Fabela and his co-editors have collected a wealth of materials in *Documentos Históricos de la Revolución Mexicana* (México, D.F.: Fondo de Cultura Económica, Editorial Jus, 1960 ff.), a most significant series; volumes 12 and 13, *Expedición Punitiva* (1967-68), and volume 20, *Las Relaciones Internacionales en la Revolución y Régimen Constitucionalista y la Cuestión Petrolero, 1913-1919* (2 tomos; 1970-71), have special importance for this study.

Significant Mexican memoirs are *Historia del Ejército y de la Revolución Constitucional,* 2 volumes, by Juan Barragán Rodríguez (Mexico: Talleres de la Editorial Stylo, 1946); *México Revolucionario,* by Alfredo Breceda (Mexico: Ediciones Botas, 1941); *Ocho Mil Kilómetros en Campaña,* by Alvaro Obregón, volume 5 of *Fuentes para la Historia de la Revolución Mexicana,* edited by Manuel González Ramírez (Mexico: Fondo de Cultura Económica, 1959); and *Mi Contribución al Nuevo Régimen,* by Alberto J. Pani (Mexico: Editorial Cultural, 1936).

Secondary Sources

Published accounts form a rich, diverse literature written from a variety of perspectives. Among the studies focusing on Woodrow Wilson, most proceed from an "idealist" or a "materialist" model of explanation. Examples of the idealist model are *The United States and Pancho Villa: A Study in Unconventional Diplomacy,* by Clarence C. Clendenen (Ithaca, N.Y.: Cornell University Press, 1961); *The United States and Mexico,* revised edition, by Howard F. Cline (New York: Atheneum, 1963), in which the chapters on Wilson are adapted from "The Mexican Policy of Woodrow Wilson," by Philip Holt Lowry (Ph.D. diss., Yale University, 1949); *The United States and Huerta,* by Kenneth J. Grieb (Lincoln: University of Nebraska Press, 1969); *Revolution and Intervention: The Diplomacy of Taft and Wilson with Mexico, 1910-1917,* by P. Edward Haley (Cambridge, Mass.: The MIT Press, 1970), a volume flawed by its failure to take Mexican sources into account; *Wilson,* 5 volumes, by Arthur S. Link (Princeton, N.J.: Princeton University Press, 1947-65), a magnificent biography; and *The Origins of the Foreign Policy of Woodrow Wilson,* by Harley Notter (Baltimore, Md.: Johns Hopkins Press, 1937). Examples of the materialist model are *La Revolución Mexicana de 1910-1917 y la Política de los Estados Unidos,* by Moises S. Alperovich and Boris T. Rudenko, translated by Makedonio Garza y Armén Ohanián *et al.* (Mexico: Fondo de Cultura Popular, 1960); *Righteous Conquest, Woodrow Wilson and the Evolution of the New Diplomacy,* by Sidney Bell (Port Washington, N.Y.: Kennikat Press, 1972); *The Economic Thought of Woodrow Wilson,* by William Diamond, volume 61, number 4, of *The Johns Hopkins University Studies in Historical and Political Science* (Baltimore, Md.: 1943); *Wilson versus Lenin, Political Origins of the New Diplomacy, 1917-1918,* by Arno Mayer (New York: Meridian Books, 1964); *Dollar Diplomacy: A Study in American Imperialism,* by Scott Nearing and Joseph Freeman (New York: B. W. Huebsch, 1925); "Woodrow Wilson and the Political Economy of Modern United States Liberalism," by Martin Sklar, in *For a New America, Essays in History and Politics from Studies on the Left, 1959-1967,* edited by James Weinstein and David W. Eakins (New York: Random House, 1970); *The United States and Revolutionary Nationalism in Mexico, 1916-1932,* by Robert Freeman Smith (Chicago, Ill.: University of Chicago Press, 1972); and *The Tragedy of American Diplomacy,* 2d edition revised, by William A. Williams (New York: Dell Publishing Co., Delta Books, 1972).

These books explain a great deal about Woodrow Wilson and his approach to foreign policy. Nevertheless, to adhere too rigidly to either model can entail the reductionist fallacy of artificial dualities, forcing scholars to choose whether to uphold ideological abstractions or material interests as the chief determinants of Wilson's policies. My efforts to moderate the ensuing conceptual dilemma have benefited immensely from the work of N. Gordon Levin, Jr., *Woodrow Wilson and World Politics, America's Response to War and Revolution* (New York: Oxford University Press, 1968). By depicting Wilson as a "liberal capitalist," this provocative, insightful book suggests conceptual apparatus by which the ideal and material components in Wilson's thinking can be understood as acting and reacting dialectically one on the other.

Another conceptual difficulty followed from my belief that students of human affairs should develop explanations by establishing connections between motives, actions, and consequences. As Karl M. Popper remarked, they should examine above all the unintended consequences of conscious human actions. Popper's observation heightened my awareness that the proponents of one model of explanation often do not address directly the issues raised by the proponents of the other. Scholars working with the idealist model seem more concerned to explain Wilson's motives and intentions than to explain the consequences of his acts. Similarly, scholars using the materialist model appear more intent upon scrutinizing the effects of Wilson's behavior than upon ascertaining the motives that gave rise to it. The "idealists" thus can attribute the president's actions to ideology, while the "materialists" can argue that his behavior served the political and economic needs of the American state. In those few instances in which scholars lost track of such distinctions, all attempts to devise valid explanatory forms broke down.

My effort to establish linkages among motives, acts, and consequences relies on a strategy of "situational analysis." My understanding of this methodological approach improved greatly after reading *A Behavioral Approach to Historical Analysis,* by Robert F. Berkhofer, Jr. (New York: Free Press, 1969); and *American Historical Explanations, A Strategy for Grounded Inquiry,* by Gene Wise (Homewood, Ill.: Dorsey Press, 1973). Of course, I cannot attribute responsibility to Professors Levin, Popper, Berkhofer, and Wise for any travesties that I may have committed upon their thoughts.

Much in the fashion of Woodrow Wilson, Venustiano Carranza and his role in the Mexican Revolution have provoked sharp controversy. Mexican writers have employed two quite different perspectives. The first, highly critical, holds that Carranza, far from serving the cause of revolution, actually obstructed it. As a champion of order, he posed as a reformer to heighten his appeal, and he sacrificed Mexican interests to obtain United States support. A somewhat idiosyncratic example is Ignacio Muñoz's *Verdad y Mito de la Revolución Mexicana (Relatada Por un Protagonista),* 4 volumes (Mexico: Ediciones Populares, S.A., 1960). A more sophisticated version by a North American scholar is suggested by James D. Cockcroft in *Intellectual Precursors of the Mexican Revolution, 1900-1913* (Austin: University of Texas Press, 1968). A second perspective, closer to the position expressed in this study, views Carranza as a liberal reformer who desired to promote moderate change through paternalistic means and as a strong nationalist who stood against American interference. Manuel González Ramírez, in *La Revolución Social de México,* volume 1, *Las Ideas — La Violencia* (México: Fondo de Cultural Económica, 1960), develops a cogent statement. My essay, "Carranza and the Decision to Revolt, 1913: A Problem in Historical Interpretation," *The Americas,* 33 (Oct. 1976), pp. 298-310, provides some historiographical commentary.

The most thorough single volume concerning the Carranza ascendancy is *Mexican Revolution, The Constitutionalist Years,* by Charles C. Cumberland (Austin: University of Texas Press, 1972), published posthumously with David C. Bailey's assistance. The first chief still lacks a first-rate biography. *Venustiano Carranza,* by Alfonso Taracena (Mexico: Editorial Jus, 1963), is the best one available. Two studies of ideology, nationalism, and Mexican perceptions of the United States are *La Ideología de la Revolución Mexicana, La Formación del Nuevo Régimen,* by Arnaldo Córdova (México, D.F.: Ediciones Era, 1973); and *The Dynamic of Mexican Nationalism,* by Frederick C. Turner (Chapel Hill: University of North Carolina

Press, 1968). A detailed account of Carranza's foreign policy is the two-volume work by Isidro Fabela, *Historia Diplomática de la Revolución Mexicana, 1912-1917* (Mexico: Fondo de Cultura Económica, 1959). Fabela served Carranza for a time as foreign minister and had access to official documents. He depicts Carranza in heroic terms. *Historia de las Relaciones entre México y los Estados Unidos de América, 1800-1958,* two volumes by Luis G. Zorrilla (Mexico: Editorial Porrua, 1966), is a solid work by a professional historian which contains a long section on diplomacy during the revolution. The Ph.D. dissertation by Floyd Ford Ewing, "Carranza's Foreign Relations: An Experiment in Nationalism" (University of Texas, 1952), though based on limited sources, ably shows the main thrust of Carranza's foreign policy.

Woodrow Wilson's crusade against Victoriano Huerta has attracted extensive attention. *An Affair of Honor; Woodrow Wilson and the Occupation of Veracruz,* by Robert E. Quirk (New York: McGraw Hill Book Co., 1964) is the standard account. Peter Calvert, in *The Mexican Revolution, 1910-1914, The Diplomacy of Anglo-American Conflict* (Cambridge: at the University Press, 1968), elucidates the development of British and American policy and shows that Wilson misunderstood British aims. *La Revolución Intervenida, Relaciones Diplomáticas entre México y Estados Unidas (1910-1914),* by Berta Ulloa (Mexico: Colegio de México, 1971), is a detailed, scholarly treatise, which avoids generalizations. Larry D. Hill's *Emissaries to a Revolution, Woodrow Wilson's Executive Agents in Mexico* (Baton Rouge: Louisiana State University Press, 1973) examines unconventional efforts to establish contact with Mexican leaders. In volume 2 of *William Jennings Bryan,* entitled *Progressive Politican and Moral Statesman, 1909-1915* (Lincoln: University of Nebraska Press, 1969), Paolo E. Coletta argues that Wilson's first secretary of state was less incompetent than critics have imagined. *Huerta, A Political Portrait,* by Michael C. Meyer (Lincoln: University of Nebraska Press, 1972), is the best work on the subject; it takes a revisionist stance and breaks with the traditional demonology of the revolution.

The collapse of the Constitutionalist coalition and the ensuing civil war are studied by Robert E. Quirk, in *The Mexican Revolution, 1914-1915; The Convention of Aguascalientes* (Bloomington: Indiana University Press, 1960). Louis Kahle's article, "Robert Lansing and the Recognition of Venustiano Carranza" [*Hispanic American Historical Review,* 38 (Aug. 1958, pp. 353-372], accurately follows the secretary of state's reasoning but attributes too much influence to Lansing over the president. Useful works on Carranza's rivals include *Francisco Villa y la Revolución,* by Federico Cervantes M. (México, D.F.: Ediciones Alonso, 1960), a partisan account by a one-time Villista; *Félix Díaz,* by Luis Liceága (Mexico: Editorial Jus,

1958), a partisan account by a one-time Felicista; "Counterrevolution in Mexico: Félix Díaz and the Struggle for National Supremacy 1910-1920," a Ph.D. dissertation by Peter Van Ness Henderson (University of Nebraska, 1973), a solid, well-researched account; *Doheny El Cruel, Valoración Histórica de la Lucha Sangrienta por el Petróleo Mexicano,* by Gabriel Antonio Menéndez (Mexico: Ediciones Bolsa Mexicano del Libro, 1958), a partisan account favorable to Manuel Peláez; and *Zapata and the Mexican Revolution,* by John Womack, Jr. (New York: Alfred A. Knopf, 1969), an outstanding study.

The Pershing punitive expedition into Mexico has inspired a great deal of writing, much of it superficial or polemical. Clarence C. Clendenen, in *Blood on the Border, The United States Army and the Mexican Irregulars* (n.p.: Macmillan Co., 1969), and Herbert Molloy Mason, Jr., in *The Great Pursuit* (New York: Random House, 1970), provide good introductions. Donald Smyth, in *Guerrilla Warrior, The Early Life of John J. Pershing* (New York: Charles Scribner's Sons, 1973), shows the role of the commanding general. "The Punitive Expedition: A Military, Diplomatic, and Political History of Pershing's Chase after Pancho Villa, 1916-1917," a Ph.D. dissertation by Robert Bruce Johnson (University of Southern California, 1964), contains much detail. Alberto Salinas Carranza, in *La Expedición Punitiva,* second edition (Mexico: Ediciones Botas, 1937), is sympathetic to Carranza. Among recent articles, Charles H. Harris, III, and Louis R. Sadler, in "Pancho Villa and the Columbus Raid" [*New Mexico Historical Review,* 50 (Oct. 1975), pp. 335-346], call for a new examination of Villa's aims in light of documents in the Records of the Adjutant General's Office. This study takes those documents into account. In "The Muddied Waters of Columbus, New Mexico" [*The Americas,* 32 (July 1975), pp. 72-91], E. Bruce White studies the historiographical controversies surrounding Villa's raid. "Pershing's Punitive Expedition: Pursuer of Bandits or Presidential Panacea?" an article in *The Americas* [32 (July 1975), pp. 46-72] by Michael L. Tate, shows that Wilson's goals shifted during the undertaking.

The question of Mexican relations with Germany is probed most fully by Friedrich Katz, in *Deutschland, Diaz und die mexikanische Revolution, Die deutsche Politik in Mexiko 1870-1920* (Berlin: VEB Deutscher Verlag der Wissenschaften, 1964). He employs a Marxian model of explanation and examines the inception of the Zimmermann note. Thomas Baecker, in *Die Deutsche Mexikopolitik 1913/1914* (Berlin: Colloquium Verlag, 1971), and in "Los Intereses Militares del Imperio Alemán en México: 1913-1914" [*Historia Mexicana,* 22 (enero-marzo 1973), pp. 347-362], shows that German policy toward Mexico proceeded opportunistically; he rejects the notion that the Zimmermann telegram had its origins during the Huerta presidency. My essay, "The United States and Carranza, 1917: The Question of *De Jure* Recognition" [*The Americas*, 29 (Oct. 1972), pp. 214-231], an early version of chapter 4, explores the Mexican response to the Zimmermann note in connection with the Constitution of 1917. Percy Alvin Martin's *Latin America and the War* (Baltimore, Md.: Johns Hopkins Press, 1925) is still the standard account.

For the Mexican Constitution of 1917, E. V. Niemeyer, Jr., in *Revolution at Querétaro, the Mexican Constitutional Convention of 1916-1917* (Austin: University of Texas Press, 1974), provides a useful study based on traditional methods. One should use it in conjunction with Peter H. Smith's "La Política Dentro de la Revolución: El Congreso Constituyente de 1916-1917" [*Historia Mexicana*, 22 (enero-marzo 1973), pp. 363-395], a statistical analysis of voting alignments. Robert E. Quirk's "Liberales y Radicales en la Revolución Mexicana" [*Historia Mexicana*, 2 (abril-junio 1953), pp. 513-528], presents an illuminating discussion of relationships between ideology and power. *México y Estados Unidos en el Conflicto Petrolero (1917-1942)*, by Lorenzo Meyer (Mexico: Colegio de México, 1968), and *The Mexican Mining Industry, 1890-1950: A Study of the Interaction of Politics, Economics and Technology,* by Marvin D. Bernstein (Albany: State University of New York, 1965) show the impact of the constitution on foreign interests. The article by María Eugenia López de Roux, "Relaciones Mexicano-Norteamericanas (1917-1918)" [*Historia Mexicana, 14* (enero-marzo 1965), pp. 445-468], surveys the war years. My essay, "Henry P. Fletcher in Mexico, 1917-1920: An Ambassador's Response to Revolution" [*The Rocky Mountain Social Science Journal,* 10 (Oct. 1973), pp. 61-70], looks at the view from the Embassy. Emily S. Rosenberg's article, "Economic Pressure in Anglo-American Diplomacy in Mexico, 1917-1918" [*Journal of Inter-American Studies and World Affairs,* 17 (May 1975), pp. 123-152], shows that economic pressure on Mexico became more intense during World War I.

Into the Twenties, The United States from Armistice to Normalcy, by Burl Noggle (Urbana: University of Illinois Press, 1974), studies the closing years of Wilson's administration. Gene Smith's *When the Cheering Stopped, The Last Years of Woodrow Wilson* (New York: William Morrow and Co., 1964) covers some of the same ground in a sentimental, sometimes maudlin, manner. Joseph S. Tulchin, in *The Aftermath of War, World War I and U.S. Policy toward Latin America* (New York: New York University Press, 1971), explains subtle shifts in the conduct of relationships. Daniel M. Smith, in *Aftermath of War: Bainbridge Colby and Wilsonian Diplomacy, 1920-1921* (Philadelphia, Pa.: American Philosophical Society, 1970), scrutinizes the work of Wilson's last secretary of state. *Politics is Adjourned, Woodrow Wilson and the War Congress, 1916-1918,* by Seward Livermore (Middletown, Conn.: Wesleyan University Press, 1966), sets the stage for the drama after the war and demonstrates that politics never was adjourned. An important contribution toward understanding Wilson's intransigeance is Edwin A. Weinstein's "Woodrow Wilson's Neurological Illness" [*Journal of American History*, 57 (Sept. 1970), pp. 324-351].

Historians have not devoted much attention to Carranza's last years. Most accounts conclude in 1917 with the promulgation of the constitution and the withdrawal of the punitive expedition. Two notable exceptions are *Mexican Revolution, The Constitutionalist Years*, by Cumberland, and volume 1, *Las Ideas — La Violencia*, of *La Revolución Social de México*, by González Ramírez. The overthrow of Carranza in 1920 merits much fuller study than it has received. Solid accounts are contained in *Yesterday in Mexico: A Chronicle of the Revolution, 1919-1936*, by John Watson Foster Dulles (Austin: University of Texas Press, 1961), and *Mexican Militarism, The Political Rise and Fall of the Revolutionary Army*, by Edwin Lieuwen (Albuquerque: University of New Mexico Press, 1968). Fabela, ed., in volume 19, *Testimonios sobre los Asesinatos de Don Venustiano y Jesús Carranza* (1971), of *Documentos Históricos de la Revolución Mexicana*, presents information on the Mexican president's death.

Chapter Notes

Abbreviations

AREM
: Archivo General de la Secretaría de Relaciones Exteriores de México, México, D. F., Mexico.

DHRM
: *Documentos Históricos de la Revolución Mexicana,* edited by Isidro Fabela and the Comisión de Investigaciones Históricas de la Revolución Mexicana, Mexico City.

FR, 1913-1921
: *Papers Relating to the Foreign Relations of the United States, 1913-1921,* Washington, D.C.

FRLP
: *Papers Relating to the Foreign Relations of the United States, The Lansing Papers, 1914-1920,* Washington, D.C.

IMA
: *Investigation of Mexican Affairs,* U.S. Congress, Senate, 66th Cong., 2d sess., Washington, D.C.

RAGODF
: Records of the Adjutant General's Office, Document Files — Mexican Border, R.G. 94, Department of War, National Archives, Washington, D.C.

RAGOPF
: Records of the Adjutant General's Office, Project Files 1917-1925, Mexican Border, R.G. 94, Department of War, National Archives, Washington, D.C.

RDS
: Records of the Department of State Relating to Political Relations between the United States and Mexico, 1910-1929, R.G. 59, Microfilm Publications, Microcopy 314, National Archives, Washington, D.C. A "711." decimal number refers to this collection.

RDS
: Records of the Department of State Relating to Internal Affairs of Mexico, 1910-1929, R.G. 59, Microfilm Publications, Microcopy 274, National Archives, Washington, D.C. An "812." decimal number refers to this collection.

RDWWCD
: Records of the Department of War, General Staff, War College Division, R.G. 165, National Archives, Washington, D.C.

Notes to Preface

1. Ray Stannard Baker, ed., *Woodrow Wilson: Life and Letters* (Garden City, N.Y.: Doubleday, Doran and Co., 1931), vol. 4, p. 55.
2. Arthur S. Link, *Wilson the Diplomatist, A Look at his Major Foreign Policies* (Chicago: Quadrangle Paperbacks, 1965), pp. 13, 15-16.
3. William Appleman Williams, *The Tragedy of American Diplomacy,* 2d ed. rev. (New York: Dell Publishing Co., Delta Books, 1972), chap. 2.
4. This study employs the terms "revolution" and "reform" in much the same sense as did the historical actors. Wilson and Carranza habitually spoke of reform as a goal of the revolution. "Revolution" refers to the great, violent struggle in Mexico between 1910 and 1920; "reform" to the sort of changes which Wilson and Carranza expected to issue from it.
5. The idealist model is employed by Clarence C. Clendenen, *The United States and Pancho Villa; A Study in Unconventional Diplomacy* (Ithaca, N.Y.: Cornell University Press, 1961); Howard F. Cline, *The United States and Mexico,* rev. ed. (New York: Atheneum, 1963); Kenneth J. Grieb, *The United States and Huerta* (Lincoln: University of Nebraska Press, 1969); P. Edward Haley, *Revolution and Intervention: The Diplomacy of Taft and Wilson with Mexico, 1910-1917* (Cambridge, Mass.: MIT Press, 1970); Arthur S. Link, *Wilson,* 5 vols. (Princeton, N.J.: Princeton University Press, 1947-1965); and Robert E. Quirk, *An Affair of Honor, Woodrow Wilson and the Occupation of Vera Cruz* (New York: McGraw-Hill Book Co., 1964). Examples of the materialist model are M. S. Alperovich and B. T. Rudenko, *La Revolución Mexicana de 1910-1917 y la Política de los Estados Unidos,* 3rd ed., trans. Makedonio Garza y Armén Ohanián *et al.* (México, D.F.: Fondo de Cultura Popular, 1969); Scott Nearing and Joseph Freeman, *Dollar Diplomacy: A Study in American Imperialism* (New York: Monthly Review Press, Modern Reader Paperbacks, 1969); and Robert Freeman Smith, *The United States and Revolutionary Nationalism in Mexico, 1916-1932* (Chicago: University of Chicago Press, 1972).
6. N. Gordon Levin, *Woodrow Wilson and World Politics, America's Response to War and Revolution* (New York: Oxford University Press, 1968).
7. Ibid., p. 3.
8. For a description of situational analysis, see Robert F. Berkhofer, Jr., *A Behavioral Approach to Historical Analysis* (New York: Free Press, 1969), pp. 32-49.

Notes to Chapter 1

❋ 1. David M. Pletcher, *Rails, Mines, and Progress: Seven American Promoters in Mexico, 1867-1922* (Ithaca, N.Y.: Cornell University Press, 1958), pp. 3, 313-314; Luis Nicolau D'Olwer, "Las Inversiones Extranjeras," *Historia Moderna de México, El Porfiriato, La Vida Económica,* ed. Daniel Cosío Villegas (Mexico: Editorial Hermes, 1965), vol. 7, tomo 2, chap. 10.
2. Charles C. Cumberland, *Mexican Revolution, Genesis under Madero* (Austin: University of Texas Press, 1952) and Stanley R. Ross, *Francisco I. Madero, Apostle of Mexican Democracy* (New York: Columbia University Press, 1955); Walter V. and Marie V. Scholes, *The Foreign Policies of the Taft Administration* (Columbia: University of Missouri Press, 1970), chap. 6; Berta Ulloa, *La Revolución Intervenida,*

Relaciones Diplomáticas entre México y Estados Unidos (1910-1914) (Mexico: Colegio de México, 1971), chaps. 2, 3.

3. ʹMichael C. Meyer, *Huerta, A Political Portrait* (Lincoln: University of Nebraska Press, 1972), chaps. 3, 4; Kenneth J. Grieb, *The United States and Huerta* (Lincoln: University of Nebraska Press, 1969), chap. 1.

4. The Chamizal controversy involved an ongoing dispute over a region of land near El Paso, Texas. Although the Treaty of Guadalupe Hidalgo in 1848 fixed the boundary between the United States and Mexico, the Rio Grande had an irritating habit of refusing to stay in its bed, thereby bringing the exact location of the border constantly into question. The two countries wrangled over the question for more than a century until 1963, when at last a Convention settled the problem. See Karl M. Schmitt, *Mexico and the United States, 1821-1973: Conflict and Coexistence* (New York: John Wiley & Sons, 1974), pp. 201-202.

5. *FR 1913*, pp. 728-729; Meyer, *Huerta*, pp. 71-82; Grieb, *U.S. and Huerta*, pp. 25-31.

6. *New York Times*, 12 Mar. 1913.

7. William Diamond, *The Economic Thought of Woodrow Wilson, The Johns Hopkins University Studies in Historical and Political Science*, vol. 61, no. 4 (Baltimore: Johns Hopkins University Press, 1943), pp. 132-137, 150.

8. *DHRM*, 1:3-6; entry for 19 Feb. 1913, Libro Actas del Congreso del Estado de Coahuila, Archivo de Venustiano Carranza, Centro de Estudios de Historia de México, Departamento Cultural de Condumex, S.A., México, D.F.

9. Alfonso Taracena, *Venustiano Carranza* (Mexico: Editorial Jus, S.A., 1963), chap. 1; Ildefonso Villarello Velez, *Historia de la Revolución Mexicana en Coahuila* (Mexico: Biblioteca del Instituto Nacional de Estudios Históricos de la Revolución Mexicana, 1970), chaps. 1-4, passim.

10. Taracena, *Carranza*, pp. 14-29; Villarello Velez, *Coahuila*, chap. 3.

11. Taracena, *Carranza*, pp. 30-84; Villarello Velez, *Coahuila*, chaps. 3, 4; Alfonso Junco, *Carranza y los Orígenes de su Rebelión* (Mexico: Ediciones Botas, 1935), pp. 17-43, charges Carranza with bad faith toward Madero; for an appraisal, see Mark T. Gilderhus, "Carranza and the Decision to Revolt, 1913: A Problem in Historical Interpretation," *The Americas*, 33 (Oct. 1976), pp. 298-310.

12. Quoted in Taracena, *Carranza*, pp. 75-76.

13. For elaboration, see Gilderhus, "Carranza and the Decision to Revolt." Kenneth J. Grieb, "The Causes of the Carranza Rebellion: A Reinterpretation," *The Americas*, 24 (July 1968), pp. 25-32, criticizes Carranza's conduct.

14. *DHRM*, 4:32-33, 14:94; 108-109; Alfredo Breceda, *México Revolucionario* (Madrid: Tipografía Artistica, 1920), vol. 1, pp. 169-175; Junco, *Orígenes*, pp. 99-101.

15. *DHRM*, 14:94-95; *FR 1913*, p. 767; Breceda, *México Revolucionario*, vol. 1, pp. 226-229; Charles C. Cumberland, *Mexican Revolution, The Constitutionalist Years* (Austin: University of Texas Press, 1972), pp. 23-57.

16. *DHRM*, 4:56-58; Taracena, *Carranza*, pp. 134-139.

17. E. David Cronon, ed., *The Cabinet Diaries of Josephus Daniels, 1913-1921* (Lincoln: University of Nebraska Press, 1963), pp. 6-7; Howard F. Cline, *The United States and Mexico*, rev. ed. (New York: Atheneum, 1963), pp. 142, 144.

18. Stuart A. MacCorkle, *American Policy of Recognition towards Mexico, The Johns Hopkins University Studies in Historical and Political Science*, vol. 51, no. 3 (Baltimore: Johns Hopkins University Press, 1933), pp. 22, 102; Arthur S. Link, *Wilson, The New Freedom* (Princeton, N.J.: Princeton University Press; 1956), vol. 2, pp. 105-107, 348-353; Grieb, *U.S. and Huerta*, pp. 71-73.

19. George J. Rausch, Jr., "Poison Pen Diplomacy: Mexico, 1913," *The Americas,* 24 (Jan. 1968), pp. 272-280; Larry D. Hill, *Emissaries to a Revolution, Woodrow Wilson's Executive Agents in Mexico* (Baton Rouge: Louisiana State University Press, 1973), chaps. 2, 3.

20. Oscar J. Braniff to Francisco L. de la Barra and Toribio Esquivel Obregón, 29 May 1913, Archivo de Francisco de la Barra, Centro de Estudios de Historia de México, Departamento Cultural de Condumex, S.A. México, D.F.

21. Hopkins to Carranza, 13 May 1913, Archivo de Carranza; *DHRM,* 1:31-33, 52, 76, 14:178-179, 208.

22. *DHRM,* 1:11-12, 26, 44, 79, 14:111-112, 20:22; decrees of 17 May and 7 June 1913, Carranza to Governor Oscar B. Colquitt of Texas, 17 May 1913, Carranza to Samuel Belden, 17 May 1913, Archivo de Carranza; see also Berta Ulloa Ortiz, "Carranza y el Armamento Norteamericano," *Historia Mexicana,* 17 (1967), pp. 253-261; I. Thord-Gray, *Gringo Rebel (Mexico, 1913-1914)* (Coral Gables, Fla.: University of Miami Press, 1960), pp. 53-61, 88-90.

23. *FR 1913,* pp. 820-822; George M. Stephenson, *John Lind of Minnesota* (Minneapolis: University of Minnesota Press, 1935), pp. 208-262; Hill, *Emissaries,* chap. 4.

24. *FR 1913,* pp. 820-827.

25. Meyer, *Huerta,* chap. 7, quote, p. 153.

26. Peter Calvert, *The Mexican Revolution, 1910-1914, The Diplomacy of Anglo-American Conflict* (Cambridge: At the University Press, 1968), pp. 23-26, chap. 7; Larry D. Hill, "The Progressive Politician as Diplomat: The Case of John Lind in Mexico," *The Americas,* 27 (Apr. 1971), pp. 362-373. Nevertheless, Mexican leaders such as Francisco de la Barra, the minister to France, regarded Carden as "our friend" who perhaps could neutralize "certain pretensions" of the American government; de la Barra to José I. Limantour, 23 Sept. 1913, Archivo de F. de la Barra.

27. Calvert, *The Mexican Revolution,* chaps. 7, 8.

28. Ray Stannard Baker and William E. Dodd, eds., *The Public Papers of Woodrow Wilson, The New Democracy* (New York: Harper and Brothers, 1926), vol. 1, pp. 64-69.

29. House Diary, 30 Oct. 1913, Edward M. House Papers, Yale University, New Haven, Conn.: Ray Stannard Baker, ed., *Woodrow Wilson, Life and Letters* (Garden City, N.Y.: Doubleday, Doran and Co., 1931), vol. 4, pp. 287-288.

30. *FR 1914,* pp. 443-444.

31. Calvert, *The Mexican Revolution,* quotes, pp. 255, 267. Calvert and other scholars recently have perceived little direct relationship between Mexico and the Panama tolls question; Walter V. and Marie V. Scholes, "Wilson, Grey, and Huerta," *Pacific Historical Review,* 37 (May 1968), pp. 151-158; William S. Coker, "Mediación Británica en el Conflicto Wilson-Huerta," *Historia Mexicana,* 18 (1968), pp. 244-257; William S. Coker, "The Panama Tolls Controversy: A Different Perspective," *Journal of American History,* 55 (Dec. 1968), pp. 555-564.

32. *DHRM,* 15:25; *FR 1914,* pp. 446-448.

33. Robert E. Quirk, *The Mexican Revolution, 1914-1915, The Convention of Aguascalientes* (New York: Citadel Press, 1963), pp. 18-24; Merrill Rippy, "The Mexican Oil Industry," *Essays in Mexican History,* ed. Thomas Cotner and Carlos E. Castañeda (Austin: University of Texas Press, 1958), pp. 248-267.

34. Robert E. Quirk, *An Affair of Honor, Woodrow Wilson and the Occupation of Vera Cruz* (New York: McGraw-Hill Book Co., 1964), p. 7; the following account, including quotations, is based on chaps. 1, 2, 3. Also see Ronald G. Woodbury, "Wilson y la Intervención de Veracruz, Análisis Historiográfica," *Historia Mexicana,* 17 (1967), pp. 263-290.

35. Meyer, *Huerta,* p. 196.
36. For details, see Michael C. Meyer, "The Arms of the *Ypiranga,"Hispanic American Historical Review,* 50 (Aug. 1970), pp. 543-556; Thomas Baecker, "The Arms of the *Ypiranga:* The German Side," *The Americas,* 30 (July 1973), pp. 1-17.
37. *FR 1914,* pp. 483-488; *DHRM,* 2:38-42, 79-80; Clarence C. Clendenen, *The United States and Pancho Villa, A Study in Unconventional Diplomacy* (Ithaca, N.Y.: Cornell University Press, 1961), chap. 7. Carranza would sanction no talk of cooperating with Huerta against the Americans; Carranza to Generals Alvaro Obregón, Pablo Gonzáles, Francisco Murguía, and Francisco Villa, 17 May 1914, Archivo de Carranza.
38. Isidro Fabela, *Historia Diplomática de la Revolución Mexicana, 1912-1917* (Mexico: Fondo de Cultura Económica, 1959), vol. 2, chap. 1.
39. Quirk, *Mexican Revolution,* chaps. 2, 3; Cumberland, *Mexican Revolution, Constitutionalist Years,* pp. 151-167.
40. John Womack, Jr., *Zapata and the Mexican Revolution* (New York: Alfred A. Knopf, 1969), chap. 7; see pp. 393-404 on the Plan of Ayala.
41. Womack, *Zapata,* p. 192; James D. Cockcroft, *Intellectual Precursors of the Mexican Revolution, 1910-1913* (Austin: University of Texas Press, 1968), p. 216; Robert E. Quirk, "Liberales y Radicales en la Revolución Mexicana," *Historia Mexicana,* 2 (abril-junio, 1953), pp. 502-528.
42. Quirk, *Mexican Revolution,* chap. 5; Cumberland, *Mexican Revolution, Constitutionalist Years,* pp. 170-181.

Notes to Chapter 2

1. Byran to George C. Carothers, 3 July 1914, 812.00/12425a, Bryan to Carranza and Villa, 23 July 1914, 812.00/14052, RDS.
2. Carranza's agents sought to mobilize support in the United States throughout 1914 and established an information bureau to disseminate propaganda through the newspapers; M. Aguirre Berlanga to Carranza, 3 Jan. 1914, J. Acevedo to Carranza, 4 Jan. 1914, R. Zubarán Capmany to Carranza, 24 Jan. 1914, *Mexican News Letter,* 19 Sept. 1914, Adolfo Carrillo to Carranza, 22 Sept. 1914, Archivo de Venustiano Carranza, Centro de Estudios de Historia de México, Departamento Cultural de Condumex, S.A., México, D.F. Late in July 1914 one agent, Rafael Zuburán Capmany, misled Carranza about American intentions by reporting that Secretary Bryan regarded him as "an absolute spirit of justice" who merited "strong and decided support"; *DHRM,* 1:317. Villa's agents, Felix Sommerfeld and Lázaro de la Garza, lobbied energetically in the summer of 1914 and complained that Carranza's men in Washington embarrassed them by interfering with the purchase of ammunition; see correspondence in wallets 1, 5, Archivo de Lázaro de la Garza Vidaurri, Latin American Collection, University of Texas, Austin.
3. De la Garza to Villa, 19 Sept. 1914, wallet 1, Archivo de L. de la Garza; Edward L. Doheny to Harold Walker, 1 Jan. 1915, Archivo de Carranza.
4. Larry D. Hill, *Emissaries to a Revolution, Woodrow Wilson's Executive Agents in Mexico* (Baton Rouge: Louisiana State University Press, 1973), pp. 229 ff.; Clarence C. Clendenen, *The United States and Pancho Villa, A Study in Unconventional Diplomacy* (Ithaca, N.Y.: Cornell University Press, 1961), chap. 8; Arthur S. Link, *Wilson, The Struggle for Neutrality, 1914-1915* (Princeton, N.J.: Princeton University Press, 1960), vol. 3, pp. 242-248.
5. Robert E. Quirk, *An Affair of Honor, Woodrow Wilson and the Occupation of Vera Cruz* (New York: McGraw-Hill Book Co., 1964), chap. 5; *FR 1914,* pp. 602-603.

6. Scott to Lindley M. Garrison, 17 Jan. 1915, box 17, Hugh L. Scott Papers, Library of Congress, Washington, D.C.

7. Juan Barragán Rodríguez, *Historia del Ejército y de la Revolución Constitucionalista* (Mexico: Talleres de la Editorial Stylo, 1946), vol. 2, pp. 201-202.

8. *DHRM,* 4:111.

9. Ray Stannard Baker and William E. Dodd, eds., *The Public Papers of Woodrow Wilson, The New Democracy* (New York: Harper and Brothers, 1926), vol. 1, pp. 111-122; *DHRM,* 4:122-124, 140; *FR 1915,* p. 872.

10. Robert E. Quirk, *The Mexican Revolution, 1914-1915, The Convention of Aguascalientes* (New York: Citadel Press, 1963), chaps. 7, 8; Charles C. Cumberland, *Mexican Revolution, The Constitutionalist Years* (Austin: University of Texas Press, 1972), pp. 184 ff.

11. Edgar Turlington, *Mexico and Her Foreign Creditors* (New York: Columbia University Press, 1930), p. 263; *FR 1915,* pp. 649-651, 654, 658; *DHRM,* 20:170-171.

12. *FR 1915,* p. 659; *FRLP,* 2:528-529.

13. Link, *Wilson,* vol. 3, p. 462; *FR 1915,* pp. 659-661, 667-668; Barragán Rodríguez, *Historia,* vol. 2, p. 234.

14. *FRLP,* 2:529-532; *FR 1915,* pp. 668-669.

15. Andrés G. García to Carranza, 5 Mar. 1915, Archivo de Carranza; Lind to Bryan, 23 July 1914, Lind to Douglas, 2 Apr. 1915, John Lind Papers, Minnesota State Historical Society, St. Paul, Minnesota; George M. Stephenson, *John Lind of Minnesota* (Minneapolis: University of Minnesota Press, 1935), pp. 289-303.

16. Adolfo Carrillo to Carranza, 22 Sept. 1914, Cole to Carranza, 11 Oct. 1914, Archivo de Carranza; *DHRM,* 20:168-169, 177-178, 242-250. The Constitutionalists compensated Cole with money for his aid; Cole to Lázaro de la Garza, 22 Dec. 1921, wallet 6, Archivo de L. de la Garza; Arredondo to Carranza, 1 June 1916, III 252/(72:73)/10, Expediente Personal de Carranza, L-E- 1443, tomo 3, leg. 1, AREM. Also see Jorge Vera-Estañol, *La Revolución Mexicana; Orígenes y Resultados* (Mexico: Editorial Jus, 1957), pp. 442-444; Federico Cervantes M., *Francisco Villa y la Revolución* (Mexico: Ediciones Alonso, 1960), pp. 512-521; Ignacio Muñoz. *Verdad y Mito de la Revolución Mexicana (Relatada por un Protagonista)* (Mexico: Ediciones Populares, 1960), vol. 2, pp. 30-39, which misleadingly interpret this episode to mean that Carranza prized American support more than Mexican interests.

17. *DHRM,* 20:180; Lind Memorandum, 16 Apr. 1915, Lind Papers; Ramón P. de Negri to Wilson, 10 Apr. 1915, ser. 4, file 471, Woodrow Wilson Papers, Library of Congress, Washington, D.C.

18. Lind memorandum, 16 Apr. 1915, Lind Papers.

19. Quirk, *Mexican Revolution,* pp. 220-226; Lind to Wilson, 19 Apr. 1915, Lind Papers.

20. Arredondo to Carranza, 22 Apr. 1915, Carranza to Arredondo, 23 Apr. 1915, H. 513″910-20/1, Revolución Mexicana durante los Años 1910-1920, Informaciones Diversas de la República y de las Oficinas de México en el Exterior, L-E- 861 R, leg. 2, AREM.

21. Arredondo to Carranza, 30 Apr., 1 May 1915, Ibid.

22. Carranza to Arredondo, 3 May 1915, Expediente Personal de Carranza, L-E- 1441, tomo 1, leg. 3, circular by Carranza, 3 May 1915, Revolución Mexicana, L-E- 861 R, leg. 2, AREM.

23. Carranza to Obregón, 5 May 1915, to Hill, 6 May 1915, to Manuel M. Diéguez, 6 May 1915, Revolución Mexicana, L-E- 861 R, leg. 2, AREM; Charles Douglas to Carranza, 19 May 1915, A. Bulnes Tavares to Carranza, 25 May 1915, Archivo de Carranza; Carranza to Arredondo, 20 May, 30 May 1915, to Douglas, 24 May 1915, Expediente Personal de Carranza, L-E- 1441, tomo 1, leg. 3, AREM.

This issue may have contributed to a cabinet crisis in June 1915; Barragán Rodríguez, *Historia*, vol. 2, pp. 367-369.

24. Quoted in Hill, *Emissaries*, pp. 310-311; see pp. 309 ff. for account; also Clendenen, *U.S. and Villa*, chap. 12.

25. West to Bryan, 5 Apr. 1915, 812.00/20721, RDS.

26. Quoted in Link, *Wilson*, 3:470.

27. Link, *Wilson*, vol. 3, pp. 471-478; Quirk, *Mexican Revolution*, pp. 255-256; Robert E. Quirk, "Cómo se Salvó Eduardo Iturbide," *Historia Mexicana*, 6 (julio-septiembre 1956), pp. 39-58.

28. Michael C. Meyer, *Mexican Rebel, Pascual Orozco and the Mexican Revolution, 1910-1915* (Lincoln: University of Nebraska Press, 1967), pp. 118-120.

29. Allen Gerlach, "Conditions Along the Border — 1915, The Plan of San Diego," *New Mexico Historical Review,* 43 (July 1968), pp. 195-208, quotes, pp. 198, 199; Charles C. Cumberland, "Border Raids in the Lower Rio Grande Valley — 1915," *Southwestern Historical Quarterly,* 57 (Jan. 1954), pp. 285-311; Walter Prescott Webb, *The Texas Rangers, A Century of Frontier Defense* (New York: Houghton-Mifflin Co., 1935), chap. 21.

30. George J. Rausch, Jr., "The Exile and Death of Victoriano Huerta," *Hispanic American Historical Review,* 42 (May 1962), pp. 133-151; Michael C. Meyer, "The Mexican-German Conspiracy of 1915," *The Americas,* 23 (July 1966), pp. 77-80; Michael C. Meyer, *Huerta, A Political Portrait* (Lincoln: University of Nebraska Press, 1972), chap. 11.

31. Bryan to Zachary Cobb, 26 Apr. 1915, 812.00/14928, RDS.

32. *FR 1915*, pp. 694-695.

33. *FRLP,* 2:534-535.

34. *FR 1915,* pp. 696-700, 711; Quirk, *Mexican Revolution,* pp. 256-260.

35. *FR 1915,* pp. 701-704.

36. Silliman to Bryan, 4 June 1915, 812.00/15133, RDS; *DHRM*, 3:191-194, 20:183-184; *FR 1915,* p. 698.

37. *DHRM*, 4:142-147.

38. Douglas to Lind, 7 June 1915, Lind to Samuel Untermeyer, 17 June 1915, Lind to Richard L. Metcalfe, 18 June 1915, Lind Papers; *DHRM*, 20:199. On the effort to win support in the United States during the summer and fall, see Francisco S. Elías to Carranza, 9 July 1915, Carranza to Henry Allen Tupper, 30 July 1915, Archivo de Carranza; Juan T. Burns to Ramón P. de Negri, 11 July 1915, Revolución Mexicana, L-E- 836 R, leg. 2, news releases and propaganda items, L-E- 811 R, leg. 1, AREM.

39. Lansing memorandum, 17 July 1915, 812.00/23137, Canova to Lansing, 812.00/23138, RDS.

40. Correspondence in "Mexican Situation" file, summer 1915, box 146, James R. Garfield Papers, Library of Congress, Washington, D.C.; Villa to Scott, 16 June 1915, Scott to Carlos Rusk, 19 May 1915, box 18, Scott Papers; Hugh Lenox Scott, *Some Memories of A Soldier* (New York: Century Co., 1928), pp. 504-506, 516.

41. Garfield to Lansing, 15 June, 3 July 1915, box 146, J. R. Garfield Papers.

42. Scott to McCoy, 3 July 1915, box 26, Frank Ross McCoy Papers, Library of Congress, Washington, D.C.; Franklin K. Lane memorandum, 1 July 1915, 812.00/23132, RDS.

43. Richard Challender, "William Jennings Bryan," *An Uncertain Tradition; American Secretaries of State in the Twentieth Century,* ed. Norman A. Graebner (New York: McGraw-Hill Book Co., 1961), p. 98.

44. James R. Garfield to Harry A. Garfield, 30 June 1915, box 36, Harry A. Garfield Papers, Library of Congress, Washington, D.C.; Daniel M. Smith, "Robert

Lansing," *Uncertain Tradition,* ed. Graebner, pp. 101-104; Louis Kahle, "Robert Lansing and the Recognition of Venustiano Carranza," *Hispanic American Historical Review,* 38 (Aug. 1958), pp. 353-372, exaggerates Lansing's influence over Wilson.

45. *FRLP,* 2:535-536; Lansing-Silliman, 18, 22 June 1915, 812.00/15261a, 15288, RDS; *DHRM,* 20:198.

46. *FRLP,* 2:538-539.

47. Ibid., 2:540-541.

48. House Diary, 24 July 1915, Edward M. House Papers, Yale University, New Haven, Conn.; *FRLP,* 2:536.

49. Lansing to Silliman, 22 July 1915, 812.00/15510, RDS.

50. Breckinridge-Funston, 24 July, 10 Aug. 1915, 812.00/15547, 15777, 15887, RDS.

51. Lansing to Silliman, enclosure, 28 Aug. 1915, 812.00/15956, Funston to War Dept., 30 Aug. 1915, 812.00/16002, RDS. William H. Hager, "The Plan of San Diego; Unrest on the Texas Border in 1915," *Arizona and the West,* 5 (winter 1963), pp. 326-336, argues unconvincingly that Carranza turned the violence off and on, seeking an advantage in his quest for recognition.

52. Oliveira to Lansing, 18 July, 3 Aug. 1915, 812.00/15473, 15629, American Society to Lansing, 29 July 1915, 812.00/15679, RDS.

53. Lansing Diary, 11 July 1915, Robert Lansing Papers, Library of Congress, Washington, D.C.

54. Lansing Diary, 10 Oct. 1915, Lansing Papers.

55. *FRLP,* 2:542-543. Lansing dealt with Ambassador Domicio da Gama of Brazil and Ministers Eduardo Súarez Múgica of Chile, Rómulo S. Naón of Argentina, Ignacio Calderón of Bolivia, Carlos María de la Peña of Uruguay, and Joaquín Méndez of Guatemala.

56. Cobb to Lansing, 26 July 1915, 812.00/15546, RDS; Carothers to Lansing, 5 Aug. 1915, box 19, Scott Papers.

57. *FRLP,* 2:545-548.

58. *FR 1915,* p. 736; *FRLP,* 2:547, 549.

59. Carranza to Obregón, 4 Aug. 1915, Archivo de Carranza; *DHRM,* 3:227-229, 20:209-210, 217; Carranza-Arredondo, 6, 8 Aug. 1915, Expediente Personal de Carranza, tomo 1, leg. 3, AREM; Douglas to Lind, 14 Aug. 1915, Lind to Lansing, to Wilson, 1, 2 Aug. 1915, Lind Papers.

60. *FR 1915,* pp. 738, 740; *DHRM,* 3:253-255.

61. *DHRM,* 20:221.

62. *FR 1915,* pp. 746-747.

63. Ibid., p. 837; *FRLP,* 2:550-552.

64. *FRLP,* 2:552-554; *DHRM,* 3:273, 20:233-236; *FR 1915,* pp. 755-761, 764-765; Douglas to Carranza, 21 Sept. 1915, Archivo de Carranza.

65. *FR 1915,* p. 766; Barragán Rodríquez, *Historia,* vol. 2, pp. 486-487.

66. Scott, *Some Memories,* p. 517; Scott to Carlos Rusk, 27 Sept. 1915, box 20, Scott Papers.

67. Lansing Diary, 10 Oct. 1915, Lansing Papers.

68. House Diary, 23 Sept. 1915, House Papers; Baker and Dodd, eds., *Public Papers, War and Peace,* vol. 3, pp. 408-409.

Notes to Chapter 3

1. *DHRM,* 3:298; Rafael Alducín, ed., *La Revolución Constitucionalista, Los Estados Unidos y el "A.B.C."* (Mexico: Talleres Linotipográficos de "Revista de Revistas," 1916), pp. 89-205.

2. *FR 1915,* pp. 772, 782. Carranza meanwhile considered the appointment of an ambassador to the United States; *DHRM,* 20:253; Carranza memorandum, 8 Dec. 1915, 1/131/258, Expediente Personal de Ing. Ignacio Bonillas, L-E- 1351, leg. 1, AREM. The Constitutionalist government also established an office of propaganda in New York, the Mexican Bureau of Information, to distribute press releases; Arredondo circular, 27 Dec. 1915, H. 513″910-20/1, Revolución Mexicana durante los Años 1910 a 1920, Informaciones Diversas de la República y de las Oficinas de México en el Exterior, L-E- 811 R, leg. 1, AREM.

3. House Diary, 14 Oct. 1915, Edward M. House Papers, Yale University, New Haven, Conn.; *New York Times,* 19 Oct., 17 Dec. 1915.

4. Clifford Wayne Trow, "Senator Albert B. Fall and Mexican Affairs: 1912-1921" (Ph.D. diss., University of Colorado, 1966), pp. 119, 121.

5. *New York Times,* 9, 10 Oct. 1915; Rhoades to Scott, 13 Oct. 1915, Scott to James R. Garfield, 14 Oct. 1915, box 20, Hugh L. Scott Papers, Library of Congress, Washington, D.C.; Hugh Lenox Scott, *Some Memories of A Soldier* (New York: Century Co., 1928), p. 517.

6. McAdoo to Wilson, 1 Oct. 1915, ser. 2, file 134, Woodrow Wilson Papers, Library of Congress, Washington, D.C.; *FR 1915,* pp. 769, 838.

7. *FR 1915,* pp. 775-779, 817-820; Clarence C. Clendenen, *The United States and Pancho Villa, A Study in Unconventional Diplomacy* (Ithaca, N.Y.: Cornell University Press, 1961), chap. 16.

8. *New York Times,* 1 Jan. 1916; *FR 1916,* pp. 463-464, 653, 656. Carranza ordered "energetic" pursuit; Carranza to Ramón P. de Negri, 13 Jan. 1916, Revolución Mexicana, L-E- 836 R, leg. 4, AREM.

9. Arthur S. Link, *Wilson, Confusions and Crises, 1915-1916* (Princeton, N.J.: Princeton University Press, 1964), vol. 4, pp. 202-204; Trow, "Fall," p. 124; *New York Times,* 13-16 Jan. 1916.

10. Fletcher to William Phillips, 24 Jan. 1916, oath of allegiance and office, 9 Mar. 1916, Henry P. Fletcher Papers, Library of Congress, Washington, D.C.; *New York Times,* 17 Jan. 1916; *FR 1916,* pp. 469-478.

11. *FR 1916,* pp. 478-480. Haldeen Braddy, *Pancho Villa at Columbus, The Raid of 1916 Restudied, Southwestern Studies,* vol. 3, no. 9 (El Paso: University of Texas, 1965); and Herbert Molloy Mason, Jr., *The Great Pursuit* (New York: Random House, 1970), chap. 1, provide accounts.

12. Villa to Zapata, 8 Jan. 1916, Box 8131, AG2384662, RAGODF.

13. The details of the Columbus raid and Villa's motives in undertaking it have provoked an esoteric controversy. Braddy, *Villa at Columbus,* holds that the guerrillas carried out the attack to obtain provisions, horses, and supplies. Another view, advanced by Alberto Calzadíaz Barrera, *Villa Contra Todo y . . . en pos de la Venganza sobre Columbus, N.M.* (Mexico: Libros de México, 1960), argues that Villa wanted revenge against Samuel and Louis Ravel. Isidro Fabela, *Historia Diplomática de la Revolución Mexicana, 1912-1917* (Mexico: Fondo de Cultural Económica, 1959), vol. 2, provides a more convincing variation on the revenge thesis. Larry Harris, *Pancho Villa and the Columbus Raid* (El Paso: McMath Co., 1949), also attributes the assault to Villa's desire for vengeance against the United States. Alberto Salinas Carranza, *La Expedición Punitiva,* 2d ed. (Mexico: Ediciones Botas, 1937), maintains that Villa wanted to embarrass Carranza by provoking a crisis with the United States. Friedrich Katz, "Alemania y Francisco Villa," *Historia Mexicana,* 12 (julio-septiembre 1962), pp. 88-102, and James A. Sandos, "German Involvement in Northern Mexico, 1915-1916: A New Look at the Columbus Raid," *Hispanic American Historical Review,* 50 (Feb. 1970), pp. 70-88, suggest that the

Columbus raid served German interests but refrain from asserting that official German policy inspired it. General Hugh Scott hesitated to belicve that Villa was responsible for the attack; Scott, *Some Memories,* pp. 517-518; Scott to F. A. Sommerfeld, 11 Mar. 1916, box 22, Scott Papers.

14. Cabrera to Carranza, 13 Mar. 1916, Revolución Mexicana, L-E- 729 R, leg. 8, AREM; *New York Times,* 12 Mar. 1916; Carnegie Endowment for International Peace, *Official German Documents Relating to the World War* (New York: Oxford University Press, 1923), vol. 2, p. 1292.

15. Desk diary, 9 Mar. 1916, Robert Lansing Papers, Library of Congress, Washington, D.C.; *FR 1916,* p. 481; Lansing memorandum, 9 Mar. 1916, 812.00/17510½, RDS; *Labor Internacional de la Revolución Constitucionalista de México (Libro Rojo)* (Mexico: n.p., 1960), pp. 126-127.

16. *FR 1916,* p. 482; Baker to Wilson, enclosures, 10 Mar. 1916, ser. 2, box 142, Wilson Papers; appeals from El Paso, Bisbee, Nogales, Tucson, box 8127, RAGODF.

17. Trow, "Fall," pp. 132 ff.; Robert Bruce Johnson, "The Punitive Expedition: A Military, Diplomatic and Political History of Pershing's Chase After Pancho Villa, 1916-1917" (Ph.D. diss., University of Southern California, 1964), pp. 94 ff.; U.S. Congress, Senate, *Congressional Record,* 64th Cong., 1st sess., 1916, 3883, pt. 4.

18. Johnson, "Punitive Expedition," pp. 90 ff.; Link, *Wilson,* vol. 4, pp. 206-208; *New York Times,* 11, 12 Mar. 1916.

19. *FR 1916,* pp. 483-484; Baker's statement, 10 Mar. 1916, ser. 2, box 142, Wilson Papers; War Dept. to Frederick Funston, 10 Mar. 1916, box 22, Scott Papers.

20. Desk diary, 10 Mar. 1916, Lansing Papers; quoted in Fabela, *Historia Diplomática,* vol. 2, pp. 195-196.

21. John W. Belt to Lansing, 10 Mar. 1916, 812.00/17413, RDS; *Labor Internacional,* pp. 127-128; J. Fred Rippy, "Some Precedents of the Pershing Expedition into Mexico," *Southwestern Historical Quarterly,* 24 (Apr. 1921), pp. 292-316.

22. Arredondo to Carranza, Carranza to Gutiérrez, 11 Mar. 1916, III 252/(72:73)/ 10, Expediente Personal de Carranza, L-E- 1443, tomo 3, leg. 1, AREM; quoted in Fabela, *Historia Diplomática,* vol. 2, p. 195.

23. *FR 1916,* pp. 486-487.

24. Desk diary, 12 Mar. 1916, Lansing Papers; Lane to Wilson, 13 Mar. 1916, ser. 2, box 143, Wilson Papers; *FR 1916,* pp. 487-489.

25. *FR 1916,* p. 488; Scott to Baker, 13 Mar. 1916, box 22, Scott Papers; Luis Cabrera to Carranza, 13 Mar. 1916, Revolución Mexicana, L-E- 729 R, leg. 8, AREM.

26. Link, *Wilson,* vol. 4, pp. 211-215; Tumulty to Wilson, 15 Mar. 1916, ser. 2, box 143, Wilson Papers; House Diary, 15, 17 Mar., House Papers.

27. *FR 1916,* pp. 490, 491; Arredondo to Carranza, 15 Mar. 1916, Expediente Personal de Carranza, L-E- 1443, tomo 3, leg. 1, AREM; *Labor Internacional,* p. 136; *DHRM,* 12:82.

28. McCain to Funston, 15 Mar. 1916, ser. 2, box 143, Wilson Papers; *FR 1916,* pp. 491-492.

29. Johnson, "Punitive Expedition," pp. 192-194, 204; Baker to Wilson, enclosures, 16 Mar. 1916, ser. 2, box 143, Wilson Papers; Scott to J. W. Prude, 17 Mar. 1916, box 22, Scott Papers.

30. *Labor Internacional,* pp. 136-143; Polk Memorandum, 18 Mar. 1916, Frank Lyon Polk Papers, Yale University, New Haven, Conn.; *FR 1916,* pp. 495-496; *FRLP,* 2:555-556.

31. *FR 1916,* pp. 499-502, 507-508; Polk Memorandum, 21 Mar. 1916, Polk Papers; *DHRM,* 20:299-301; Arredondo to Carranza, 5 Apr. 1916, Expediente Personal de Carranza, L-E- 1443, tomo 3, leg. 1, AREM.

32. *New York Times,* 17 Mar. 1916.
33. New York *Tribune,* 3 Apr. 1916, clipping in William Frank Buckley Papers, Latin American Collection, University of Texas, Austin, Texas.
34. House Diary, 29 Mar. 1916, House Papers; *FR 1916,* p. 505.
35. Desk diary, 4, 5, 8, 10, 11 Apr. 1916, Lansing Papers; House Diary, 6, 11 Apr. 1916, House Papers; *New York Times,* 7 Apr. 1916.
36. Scott to Funston, 17 Mar. 1916, box 80, John J. Pershing Papers, Library of Congress, Washington, D.C.; *DHRM*, 12:124; Colonel Frank Tompkins, *Chasing Villa: The Story Behind the Story of Pershing's Expedition into Mexico* (Harrisburg, Pa.: Military Service Publishing Co., 1934), pp. 118-157.
37. *FR 1916,* pp. 513-514; *DHRM*, 12:253-254.
38. Funston to McCain, enclosures, 17 Apr., 30 Apr. 1916, Box 8128, AG2379210, RAGODF.
39. Lansing to Special Agent James Linn Rodgers, 22 Apr. 1916, 812.00/17966a, RDS; Scott to Baker, 22 Apr. 1916, Scott-Bliss, 27 Apr. 1916, box 22, Scott Papers.
40. *FR 1916,* pp. 530-532; Carranza to Obregón, 30 Apr. 1916, Expediente Personal de Carranza, L-E- 1443, tomo 3, leg. 2, AREM.
41. Scott and Funston to Baker, 30 Apr., 1 May 1916, 812.00/18020, 18039, McCain to Scott, 30 Apr. 1916, 812.00/18030, RDS; *DHRM*, 12:281-284.
42. *FR 1916,* pp. 535, 536; Funston to Baker, McCain to Scott, 1 May 1916, box 1, Newton D. Baker Papers, Library of Congress, Washington, D.C.; Funston to Pershing, box 8128, AG2379210, RAGODF.
43. Obregón-Carranza, 1, 2 May 1916, Expediente Personal de Carranza, L-E- 1443, tomo 3, leg. 2, AREM; Fabela, *Historia Diplomática,* vol. 2, pp. 217-219.
44. Scott and Funston to Baker, 3 May 1916, 812.00/18097, RDS.
45. Lansing to Wilson, 4 May 1916, ser. 2, box 144, Wilson Papers; Baker to Scott, 4 May 1916, box 8131, AG2394312, RAGODF; Carranza to Obregón, 6 May 1916, Expediente Personal de Carranza, L-E- 1443, tomo 3, leg. 2, AREM.
46. Clarence C. Clendenen, *Blood on the Border, The United States Army and the Mexican Irregulars* (n.p.: Macmillan Co., 1969), pp. 279-281; *DHRM,* 12:309, 312.
47. *FR 1916,* p. 689; Funston to Pershing, Bliss to McCain, Baker to governors of Texas, Arizona, New Mexico, 9 May 1916, AG2379210, AG2394312, AG2396936, RAGODF.
48. *Labor Internacional,* p. 191; Polk memorandum, 10 May 1916, Polk Papers; Carranza to Fernando Peraldí, 11 May 1916, Carranza to Plutarco Elías Calles, 15 May 1916, Expediente Personal de Carranza, L-E- 1443, tomo 3, leg. 2, AREM; Scott to Baker, 12 May 1916, box 8131, AG2394312, RAGODF.
49. Arredondo to Carranza, 19 May 1916, Expediente Personal de Carranza, L-E- 1443, tomo 3, leg. 1, AREM; *Labor Internacional,* pp. 196-210.
50. Quoted in Link, *Wilson,* vol. 4, p. 298.
51. Desk diary, 7 June 1916, Lansing Papers; Arredondo to Carranza, 7 June 1916, Expediente Personal de Carranza, L-E- 1443, tomo 3, leg. 1, AREM; Pershing-Roosevelt, 24 May, 6 June 1916, box 177, Pershing Papers.
52. *FR 1916,* pp. 568-569, 573-575; Major Alonso Gray report, 15 June 1916, box 8135, AG2413024, Pershing to Funston, box 8128, AG2379210, RAGODF; Scott to War College, 16 June 1916, Scott Papers.
53. Carranza to Treviño, 13 June 1916, Expediente Personal de Carranza, L-E- 1443, tomo 3, leg. 2, AREM; *DHRM,* 12:369-371; Funston to McCain, 18 June 1916, box 8128, AG2379210, Special Agent Barnes to Bruce Bielaski, 19 June 1916, box 8129, AG2381442, RAGODF; Funston to McCain, 18 June 1916, 5761-1130, RDWWCD.

54. *FR 1916,* pp. 578-580.

55. Desk diary, 17, 18 June 1916, Lansing Papers; *FRLP,* 2:557-558; Link, *Wilson,* vol. 4, p. 301; Johnson, "Punitive Expedition," p. 682.

56. Arredondo to Carranza, 18 June 1916, Expediente Personal de Carranza, L-E- 1443, tomo 3, leg. 1, AREM; *Labor Internacional,* p. 213.

57. Lansing to Arredondo, 20 June 1916, 812.00/18450, RDS.

58. Scott to H. J. Slocum, 20 June 1916, box 23, Scott Papers; *FRLP,* 2:558-560.

59. Clendenen, *Blood on the Border,* pp. 303-310.

60. *Congressional Record,* 64th Cong., 1st sess., 1916, 9983, pt. 10; Funston to McCain, 22 June 1916, Baker to Funston, 22, 25 June 1916, box 8136, AG2417328, AG2416998, AG2418482, RAGODF.

61. Ray Stannard Baker, *Woodrow Wilson, Life and Letters* (Garden City, N.Y.: Doubleday, Doran and Co., 1937), vol. 6, p. 76.

62. *Labor Internacional,* pp. 230-231; Arredondo-Carranza, 21, 24 June 1916, Expediente Personal de Carranza, L-E- 1443, tomo 3, leg. 1, AREM; Arredondo to Lansing, 24 June 1916, 812.00/18574, RDS.

63. *FR 1916,* p. 595; Fabela, *Historia Diplomática,* vol. 2, p. 289.

64. Canova to Lansing, 22 June 1916, box 4, Fletcher Papers; Tumulty to Lansing, 24 June 1916, vol. 19, desk diary, 23-25 June 1916, Lansing Papers; Joseph P. Tumulty, *Woodrow Wilson as I Know Him* (Garden City, N.Y.: Doubleday, Page and Co., 1921), p. 158.

65. Draft, file 2, box 100, Wilson Papers.

66. Carranza to Emiliano Nafarrete, Arredondo to Carranza, 28 June 1916, Expediente Personal de Carranza, L-E- 1443, tomo 3, leg. 1, 2, AREM; Desk diary, 30 June 1916, Lansing Papers.

67. Quoted in John A. Garraty, *Henry Cabot Lodge, A Biography* (New York: Alfred A. Knopf, 1953), p. 329.

68. Trow, "Fall," pp. 122, 152-154, 172; Kirk H. Porter and Donald Bruce Johnson, eds., *National Party Platforms,* 3d ed. (Urbana: University of Illinois Press, 1966), p. 204; Roosevelt to McCoy, 9 July 1916, box 14, Frank Ross McCoy Papers, Library of Congress, Washington, D.C.

69. Porter and Johnson, eds., *National Party Platforms,* p. 197.

70. Ray Stannard Baker and William E. Dodd, eds., *The Public Papers of Woodrow Wilson, The New Democracy* (New York: Harper & Row, 1926), vol. 2, p. 218; Arredondo to Carranza, 30 June 1916, Expediente Personal de Carranza, L-E- 1443, tomo 3, leg. 1, AREM.

71. Arredondo to Carranza, 30 June 1916, Expediente Personal de Carranza, L-E- 1443, tomo 3, leg. 1, AREM; *FRLP,* 2:560-562; Arredondo to Lansing, 4 July 1916, 812.00/19066, RDS.

72. Memoranda, 10, 12, 14, 18, 19, 27, 28 July 1916, Polk Papers; Polk to Arredondo, 28 July 1916, 812.00/19039, RDS.

73. Memoranda, 18, 19, 28 July 1916, Polk Papers; *FR 1916,* pp. 601-604; *Labor Internacional,* pp. 265-266.

74. Polk to Lansing, 3 Aug. 1916, vol. 20, Lansing Papers; Memoranda, 6, 8, 9 Aug. 1916, Polk Papers.

75. *FR 1917,* pp. 916-917; *FRLP,* 2:563-564; Alberto J. Pani, *Mi Contribución al Nuevo Régimen* (México, D.F.: Editorial Cultura, 1936), pp. 230-231.

76. *FR 1916,* p. 608; Funston to McCain, 17 Aug. 1916, Baker to Bliss, box 1, Baker Papers; Pershing to Scott, 23 Sept. 1916, box 25, Scott Papers; *Labor Internacional.* pp. 272-274.

77. *FR 1916,* pp. 610-614; *FR 1917,* p. 918; Pershing to Funston, 2 Nov. 1916, box 8138; AG2490520, RAGODF; Desk diary, 26 Oct. 1916, Lansing Papers; Aguilar to Cabrera, 5 Oct. 1916, Revolución Mexicana, L-E- 859 R, leg. 1, AREM; *Labor Internacional,* pp. 281-282; *DHRM,* 13:284.
78. Pani, *Mi Contribución,* p. 236; *Labor Internacional,* p. 294; Baker and Dodd, eds., *Public Papers, The New Democracy,* vol. 2, pp. 342-343; Baker to Bliss, 15 Oct. 1916, box 1, Baker Papers.
79. *FR 1917,* pp. 918-927.
80. Pani, *Mi Contribución,* pp. 236, 241-242; Polk-Frederick Watriss, 27 Nov. 26 Dec. 1916, 2, 4 Jan. 1917, Polk Papers; *FR 1917,* pp. 928-933.
81. Baker to Wilson, 23 Dec. 1916, box 1, Baker Papers; Fletcher to House, 31 Dec. 1916, House Papers.
82. *FR 1917,* pp. 935-938.
83. Tompkins, *Chasing Villa,* p. 184; Scott, *Some Memories,* p. 521; Pershing to Leonard Wood, 10 Sept. 1916, box 215, Pershing Papers. Clarence C. Clendenen, "The Punitive Expedition of 1916: A Re-evaluation," *Arizona and the West,* 3 (winter 1961), pp. 311-320, develops a similar point.

Notes to Chapter 4

1. Baker to Lansing, 8 Feb. 1917, box 8139, AG2532462, RAGODF; Wilson to Carranza, 2 Feb. 1917, box 4, Henry P. Fletcher Papers, Library of Congress, Washington, D.C.
2. Charles C. Cumberland, *Mexican Revolution, The Constitutionalist Years* (Austin: University of Texas Press, 1972), pp. 326 ff.; E. V. Niemyer, Jr., *Revolution at Querétaro, The Mexican Constitutional Convention of 1916-1917* (Austin: University of Texas Press, 1974), pp. 39-42.
3. Cumberland, *Mexican Revolution, Constitutionalist Years,* chap. 9; Niemeyer, *Revolution at Querétaro,* pp. 221-222.
4. Niemeyer, *Revolution at Querétaro,* p. 222; México, Cámara de Diputados, *Diario de los Debates del Congreso Constituyente* (México, D.F.: Imprenta de Cámara de Diputados, 1922), tomo 1, pp. 260 ff.
5. For the Spanish text, Felipe Tena Ramírez, ed., *Leyes Fundamentales de México, 1808-1957* (Mexico: Editorial Porrua, 1957), pp. 817-881; for an English translation, H. N. Branch, tr., *The Mexican Constitution of 1917 as Compared with the Constitution of 1857, Annals of the American Academy of Political and Social Science,* vol. 71, supp. (Philadelphia, Pa., 1917).
6. Robert E. Quirk, *The Mexican Revolution and the Catholic Church, 1910-1929* (Bloomington: University of Indiana Press, 1973), chap. 4.
7. Branch, *Mexican Constitution,* pp. 15-25.
8. Luis Nicolau D'Olwer, "Las Inversiones Extranjeras," *Historia Moderna de México, El Porfiriato, La Vida Económica,* ed. Daniel Cosío Villegas (Mexico: Editorial Hermes, 1965), vol. 7, tomo 2, chap. 10; David M. Pletcher, *Rails, Mines, and Progress: Seven American Promoters in Mexico, 1867-1911* (Ithaca, N.Y.: Cornell University Press, 1958), p. 313; Merrill Rippy, "The Mexican Oil Industry," *Essays in Mexican History,* ed. Thomas E. Cotner and Carlos E. Casteñada (Austin: University of Texas Press, 1958), p. 253; Lorenzo Meyer, *México y Estados Unidos en el Conflicto Petroleo (1917-1942)* (México, D.F.: Colegio de México, 1968), pp. 25, 82;

Merrill Rippy, *Oil and the Mexican Revolution* (Leiden, Netherlands: E. J. Brill, 1972), chaps. 1, 2.

9. Meyer, *Conflicto Petroleo,* pp. 28-34, 87-88; Cumberland, *Mexican Revolution, Constitutionalist Years,* pp. 350 ff.; Niemeyer, *Revolution at Querétaro,* chap. 5; *Diario de los Debates,* tomo 2, pp. 781-813; J. Scott Keltie, ed., *The Statesman's Year-Book, 1917* (London: Macmillan and Co., 1917), pp. 1049-1050.

10. *Diario de los Debates,* tomo 1, p. 264; Frank Tannenbaum, *Mexico: The Struggle for Peace and Bread* (New York: Alfred A. Knopf, 1950), pp. 104-105.

11. Pastor Rouaix, *Génesis de los Artículos 27 y 123 de la Constitución Política de 1917* (Mexico: Biblioteca del Instituto Nacional de Estudios Históricos de la Revolución, 1959), p. 161; Meyer, *Conflicto Petroleo,* chap. 4.

12. Memorandum for Polk, 27 Mar. 1917, Frank Lyon Polk Papers, Yale University, New Haven, Conn.

13. Anderson Diary, 15 Nov., 29 Dec. 1916, Chandler P. Anderson Papers, Library of Congress, Washington, D.C.; for examples, Frederick Watriss to Polk, 21 Nov. 1916, Harold Walker to Polk, 11 Feb. 1917, Polk Papers; L. C. Neale to Polk, 3 Feb. 1917, 812.011/27, L. C. Neale to Lansing, 14 April 1917, 812.63/452, William Loeb memorandum, 24 Feb. 1917, 812.011/33, Mine and Smelter Operators Assoc. to Lansing, 23, 25 Apr. 1917, 812.63/456, 459, Harold Walker memorandum, 18 Apr. 1917, 812.6363/296, RDS.

14. Lansing to Special Agent Charles B. Parker, 22, 25 Jan. 1917, 812.011/11a, 812.512/1540, RDS.

15. *FR 1917,* p. 1044; William Loeb memorandum, 24 Feb. 1917, 812.011/33, Fletcher to Lansing, 26 Feb. 1917, 812.63/380, RDS.

16. Anderson Diary, 8, 10 Mar. 1917, Anderson Papers; Anderson-Polk, 19-21 Mar. 1917, Polk Papers; Anderson to Polk, 8 Mar. 1917, 812.011/57, memorandum for Polk, 19 Mar. 1917, 812.011/57, RDS.

17. Anderson Diary, 3 Jan. 1917, Anderson Papers; *War Memoirs of Robert Lansing, Secretary of State* (New York: Bobbs-Merrill Co., 1935), p. 308; E. David Cronon, ed., *The Cabinet Diaries of Josephus Daniels, 1913-1921* (Lincoln: University of Nebraska Press, 1963), p. 107.

18. Keltie, ed., *Statesman's Year-Book, 1917,* p. 1089; Warren Schiff, "The Germans in Mexican Trade and Industry during the Díaz Period," *The Americas,* 23 (Jan. 1967), pp. 279-296; Warren Schiff, "German Military Penetration into Mexico during the Late Díaz Period," *Hispanic American Historical Review,* 39 (Nov. 1959), pp. 568-579, quote, p. 578.

19. Friedrich Katz, *Deutschland, Diaz und die mexikanische Revolution, Die deutsche Politik in Mexiko 1870-1920* (Berlin: VEB Deutscher Verlag der Wissenschaften, 1964), pp. 338-339, 348-350; James A. Sandos, "The Plan of San Diego, War and Revolution on the Texas Border, 1915-1916," *Arizona and the West,* 14 (spring 1972), pp. 5-24.

20. *Labor Internacional de la Revolución Constitucionalista de México (Libro Rojo)* (México: n.p., 1960), p. 333; FRLP, 1:86-87, 90-91; DHRM, 20:255.

21. Friedrich Katz, "Alemania y Francisco Villa," *Historia Mexicana,* 12 (julio-septiembre 1962), pp. 88-102; Parker to Lansing, 1 May 1916, ser. 2, box 144, Woodrow Wilson Papers, Library of Congress, Washington, D.C.; Enrique A. González-Aguilar, 26 May, 2 June 1916, H. 513″910-20/1, Revolución Mexicana durante los Años 1910 a 1920, Informaciones Diversas de la República y de las Oficinas de México en el Exterior, L-E- 800 R, leg. 9, AREM.

22. Katz, *Deutschland,* pp. 353-355; *Lansing War Memoirs,* p. 311; Alfonso Taracena, *La Verdadera Revolución Mexicana (1916 a 1918)* (Mexico: Editorial Jus, S.A., 1960), pp. 10-11; Fletcher to Lansing, 14 May 1918, 712.62/4, box 6708, State

Decimal File 1910-1929, R.G. 59, Records of the Department of State, U.S. National Archives, Washington, D.C., recounts rumors of Carranza's overture to Germany; a classified document of 8 December 1916 in RDWWCD alleges that Carranza refused to provide a base.

23. Parker to Polk, 1, 3 Nov. 1916, 712.94/7, 8, box 6708, State Decimal File, RDS.

24. Katz, *Deutschland,* pp. 356-382.

25. Carnegie Endowment for International Peace, *Official German Documents Relating to the World War* (New York: Oxford University Press, 1923), vol. 2, pp. 1337-1338; Burton J. Hendrick, *The Life and Letters of Walter Hines Page* (New York: Doubleday, Page and Co., 1925), vol. 3, p. 349.

26. Barbara W. Tuchman, *The Zimmermann Telegram* (New York: Dell Publishing Co., 1965), chaps. 9-12; Arthur S. Link, *Wilson, Campaigns for Progressivism and Peace* (Princeton, N.J.: Princeton University Press, 1965), vol. 5, pp. 342 ff., 433-436.

27. Link *Wilson,* vol. 5, p. 346; House to Wilson, 27 Feb. 1917, ser. 2, box 158, Wilson Papers; Desk diary, 27, 28 Feb. 1917, Lansing Diary, 4 Mar. 1917, Robert Lansing Papers, Library of Congress, Washington, D.C.

28. Charles B. Burdick, "A House on Navidad Street. The Celebrated Zimmermann Note on the Texas Border?," *Arizona and the West,* 8 (spring 1966), pp. 19-34.

29. *New York Times,* 1-3 March 1917; *FR 1917,* supp. 1, pp. 160-161.

30. *FR 1917,* supp. 1, pp. 234-235, 238-239; Fletcher to Lansing, 13 Mar. 1917, box 4, Fletcher Papers.

31. *FR 1917,* pp. 911-912; *FR 1917,* supp. 1, pp. 238-239; Fletcher to Lansing, 13 Mar. 1917, box 4, Fletcher Papers. In *DHRM,* 3:284-285, Isidro Fabela charged that Fletcher was instructed to present an ultimatum at Guadalajara — either Mexico should break relations with Germany or the United States would declare war on Mexico. The evidence fails to substantiate the allegation.

32. *Labor Internacional,* pp. 372-375; Fletcher to Lansing, 13 Mar. 1917, box 4, Fletcher Papers.

33. *FR 1917,* supp. 1, pp. 238-239.

34. This writer searched the Archivo de la Secretaría de Relaciones Exteriores in Mexico City with the hope of finding evidence upon which to base an appraisal of Mexico's response to the Zimmermann telegram. In the archival index, he found reference to a file entitled "Documentos sobre Relaciones entre México y Alemania durante los Años 1915-1920, Especialmente sobre el Telegrama Zimmermann de 1917." He received permission from the appropriate authorities to examine the file, but when the archival staff looked for it, the documents could not be found. Regrettably they appeared to be lost, misplaced, or perhaps destroyed. It was possible to use a file relating generally to Mexican-German relations from 1880 to 1920, but it revealed nothing about the Zimmermann note.

35. Burdick, "House on Navidad Street," p. 28, note 23; *DHRM,* 3:284; José López Portillo y Weber, "Cómo Perdío Carranza el Apoyo de Estados Unidos y Cómo se Relacionó esto con la Proposición que a México Presentó Alemania en 1917," *Memoria de la Academia Mexicana de la Historia,* 19 (enero-marzo 1960), pp. 31-33.

36. Hendrick, *Life and Letters,* vol. 3, pp. 351-360; Katz, *Deutschland,* pp. 381-382.

37. Fletcher to Lansing, 30 Mar. 1917, 711.12/36, RDS; *Labor Internacional,* pp. 370-371; *FR 1917,* supp. 1, pp. 67-68, 242, 262.

38. Fletcher to Lansing, 30 Mar. 1917, 711.12/36, Wilson to Lansing, 19 Apr. 1917, 711.12/36½, RDS; *FR 1917,* supp. 1, p. 262.

39. *Labor Internacional,* p. 407; *FR 1917,* supp. 1, pp. 265-266; Fletcher's statement, 24 Apr. 1917, 711.12/44, RDS.

40. Frank R. McCoy report, 4 Apr. 1917, 9700-91, RDWWCD; Pershing to Adjutant General, 5 Apr. 1917, ser. 2, box 159, Wilson Papers; Pershing to Scott, 7 Apr. 1917, box 181, John J. Pershing Papers, Library of Congress, Washington, D.C.; Scott to McCoy, 30 Apr. 1917, box 14, Frank Ross McCoy Papers, Library of Congress, Washington, D.C.; Lansing to Wilson, 18 Apr. 1917, 711.12/43a, RDS.

41. *IMA,* 1:1229; *New York Times,* 28 Sept. 1917.

42. Percy Alvin Martin, *Latin America and the War* (Baltimore: Johns Hopkins Press, 1925), pp. 522-527; *IMA,* 2:3025-3026; for example, Lansing to Wilson, 18 Apr. 1917, 711.12/43a, Zachary Cobb to Polk, 21 Apr. 1917, 711.12/40, John R. Silliman to Lansing, 26 June 1917, 711.12/52, Walter Hines Page to Lansing, 11 Nov. 1917, 812.6363/317, Weekly Report #247, 8 Dec. 1917, 812.00/21592, Matthew Hanna to Lansing, 30 May 1917, 712.62/1, box 6708, State Decimal File, RDS; Auchincloss Diary, 4 Sept. 1917, Gordon Auchincloss Papers, Yale University, New Haven, Conn.; L. Witzke statement, n.d., wallet 154, William Frank Buckley Papers, Latin American Collection, University of Texas, Austin; Wilson to Creel, 31 July 1918, vol. 2, George Creel Papers, Library of Congress, Washington, D.C.

43. O. W. Fowler to chief of naval operations, 10 Nov. 1917, box 658, Roger Welles to chief of naval operations, 31 May 1918, box 652, Naval Records Collection of the Office of Naval Records Library, Subject File 1911-1927, R.G. 45, Records of the Department of the Navy, U.S. National Archives, Washington, D.C.; this file, boxes 650-660, contains a number of such reports.

44. Capt. Hunt to Capt. Keppel, 13 June 1918, 11012-6, RDWWCD; Campbell report, 30 Jan. 1919, box 6, Fletcher Papers.

45. Lansing-Silliman, 1, 3 Sept. 1917, 711.12/54, 55, Boaz Long memorandum, 10 Aug, 1918, 711.12/130, RDS; *FR 1917,* supp. 1, pp. 349, 392.

46. Ramón P. de Negri to Aguilar, 23 Mar. 1918, Juan B. Vegas to Mexican consuls, 25 Apr. 1918, Revolución Mexicana, L-E- 837 R, leg. 6, AREM.

47. Auchincloss Diary, 8 Feb. 1918, Auchincloss Papers; Creel to Wilson, 23 July 1918, vol. 2, Creel Papers; George Creel, *How We Advertised America* (New York: Harper and Brothers, 1920), pt. 2, chap. 7, quotes, pp. 303-304; James R. Mock and Cedric Larson, "Activities of the Mexico Section of the Creel Committee, 1917-1918," *Journalism Quarterly,* 16 (June 1939), pp. 136-150, quote, p. 144; James R. Mock, "The Creel Committee in Latin America," *Hispanic American Historical Review,* 22 (May 1942), pp. 262-279.

48. Fletcher to Henry Cabot Lodge, 10 Aug. 1917, box 4, to William Phillips, 13 Nov. 1917, to Frank Polk, 13 Nov. 1917, to Lansing, 13 Mar. 1918, box 5, Fletcher Papers.

49. Cumberland, *Mexican Revolution, Constitutionalist Years,* pp. 361 ff.; Carranza to Aguilar, 13 Feb. 1917, Lansing to de Negri, 10 March 1917, Bonillas to E. Garza Pérez, 17 Apr. 1917, 1/131/258, Ing. Ignacio Bonillas; Su Expediente Personal, L-E- 1351, leg. 1, AREM.

50. *FR 1917,* pp. 1060-1061, 1065-1067. On Mexico's financial and economic condition, see Edwin Walter Kemmerer, *Inflation and Revolution, Mexico's Experience of 1912-1917* (Princeton, N.J.: Princeton University Press, 1940); Edgar Turlington, *Mexico and Her Foreign Creditors* (New York: Columbia Press, 1930).

51. Fletcher to Lansing, 23 Apr. 1917, 712.4/1, box 6708, State Decimal File, 26 Apr. 1917, 812.63/460, RDS.

52. Lansing to Wilson, 25 Apr. 1917, 812.01/a, RDS; *FRLP,* 2:567.

53. Anderson Diary, 29 Mar., 6, 16 Apr., 7, 16 May, 4 June 1917, Anderson Papers; Anderson to Polk, 9, 13 Apr. 1917, 812.011/55, Anderson memorandum, 711.12/47½, RDS.
54. Lansing to Fletcher, 6 June 1917, 812.011/48a, RDS.
55. *FR 1917,* pp. 1068-1069; Fletcher to Lansing, 5 June 1917, 711.12/50, RDS.
56. Anderson Diary, 13 June, 11 July 1917, Anderson Papers.
57. *FR 1917,* p. 939; Desk diary, 12 June 1917, Lansing Papers; Lansing to Fletcher, 13 June 1917, 812.00/21039a, RDS.
58. Fletcher married Beatrice Bend at Westbury, Long Island, on 25 July 1917, box 4, Fletcher Papers; Anderson Diary, 7, 12, 16, 17, 23 July 1917, Anderson Papers.
59. *FR 1917,* p. 1083; Wilson to Polk, 9 July 1917, ser. 4, file 471, Wilson Papers; Carl W. Ackerman, *Mexico's Dilemma* (New York: George H. Doran Co., 1918), pp. 28-29.
60. Polk to Summerlin, 19 July 1917, 812.113/8386, Fletcher to Lansing, 2 Aug. 1917, 812.113/8767, 812.51/312, 812.63/481, 5 Sept. 1917, 812.6363/301, RDS; Fletcher to Lansing, 8 Aug. 1917, box 8, Fletcher Papers.
61. Wilson to Carranza, 31 Aug. 1917, 812.001C23/1, Fletcher to Lansing, 26 Sept. 1917, 812.001C23/6, RDS.
62. Anderson Diary, 8, 11, 20 Sept. 1917, Anderson Papers.

Notes to Chapter 5

1. Carothers to Lansing, 25 Mar. 1917, 812.00/20732, RDS.
2. Luis Licéaga, *Felix Díaz* (Mexico: Editorial Jus, 1958), pp. 349-375, 396-404, 421-426, 489-505; Peter Van Ness Henderson, "Counterrevolution in Mexico: Félix Díaz and the Struggle for National Supremacy 1910-1920" (Ph.D. diss., University of Nebraska, 1973), pp. 265-266; Alberto Salinas Carranza, *La Expedición Punitiva,* 2d ed. (Mexico: Ediciones Botas, 1937), p. 210; Federico Cervantes M., *Francisco Villa y la Revolución* (México, D.F.: Ediciones Alonso, 1960), p. 585; Manuel González Ramírez, *La Revolución Social de México, Las Ideas — La Violencia* (Mexico: Fondo de Cultura Económica, 1960), vol. 1, pp. 666-667; Charles E. Jones report, 13 July 1918, H. 513″910-20/1, Revolución Mexicana durante los Años 1910 a 1920, Informaciones Diversas de la República y de las Oficinas de México en el Exterior, L-E- 837 R, leg. 12, AREM.
3. Group H, Chas. F. Hunt correspondence, Senate Office File, reel 31, Albert B. Fall Papers, microfilm copy, University of Nebraska, Lincoln; Eduardo Soriano Bravo to Cándido Aguilar, 10 Mar. 1917, I. Bonillas to E. Garza Pérez, 9 Apr. 1917, Revolución Mexicana, L-E- 799 R, leg. 6, L-E- 838 R, leg. 2, AREM.
4. List of secret service agents, 22 May 1918, E. Garza Pérez memoranda, 7 Sept. 1917, 17 Sept. 1918, Charles E. Jones reports, June-Sept. 1918, Revolución Mexicana, L-E- 837 R, leg. 3, 11, 12, AREM; *IMA,* 2:2897. Intelligence reports are scattered throughout the file Revolución Mexicana in the AREM, the Archivo de Venustiano Carranza, Centro Estudios de Historia de México, Departamento Cultural de Condumex, S.A., Mexico City, and *DHRM.*
5. Clarence C. Clendenen, *Blood on the Border, The United States Army and the Mexican Irregulars* (n.p.: Macmillan Co., 1969), pp. 343-350; Walter Prescott Webb, *The Texas Rangers, A Century of Frontier Defense* (New York: Houghton Mifflin Co., 1935), pp. 504-513; Baker to Wilson, 16 Feb. 1917, enclosures, box 4, Newton D. Baker Papers, Library of Congress, Washington, D.C.; Cobb to Lansing, 19 Apr. 1917, 812.00/20801, Carothers to Lansing, 27 Apr. 1917, 812.00/20848,

RDS; Fall to Hugh Scott, to Baker, 6 Feb., 5 Apr. 1917, Papers on Mexican Affairs, reel 40, Fall Papers; Juan Gualberto Amaya, *Venustiano Carranza, Caudillo Constitucionalista; Segunda Etapa, Febrero de 1913 a Mayo de 1920* (México, D.F.: n.p., 1947), pp. 365-391; *FR 1917,* pp. 1074-1077; Thomas Edwards to Lansing, 15 Apr., 23, 26 May, 14 June, 14 July 1917, 812.00/20795, 20933, 20960, 21017, 21113, RDS.

6. Matthew Hanna to Lansing, 7 Nov. 1917, 812.00/21444, Edwards to Fletcher, 11 Dec. 1917, 812.00/21556, RDS.

7. *FR 1917,* pp. 940-946; *FR 1918,* pp. 548-576.

8. Bonillas-Lansing, 11, 26 Feb. 1918, 812.0144/53, RDS.

9. Alfonso Fabila, *Las Tribus Yaquis de Sonora, Su Cultura y Anhelada Autodeterminación* (Mexico: Departamento de Asuntos Indígenas, 1940), pp. 70-110; Jack D. Forbes, "Historical Survey of the Indians of Sonora, 1821-1910," *Ethnohistory,* 4 (fall 1957), pp. 335-368; *FR 1917,* pp. 1025-1027; Weekly Reports 230, 233, 239, 241, 242, 243, 244, 23 Aug.-10 Nov. 1917, 812.00/21221, 21279, 21336, 21421, 21485, RDS.

10. *FR 1917,* pp. 1031-1036.

11. *FR 1917,* pp. 667-669; American authorities arranged for Americans in Sonora to obtain weapons and ammunition to defend themselves; Watriss-Polk, 22 Dec. 1917, 11 Jan., 7 Feb., 5, 7 June 1918, Frank Lyon Polk Papers, Yale University, New Haven, Conn.

12. Polk to Fletcher, 9 Mar. 1918, 711.12/68a, Fletcher to Lansing, 10 Apr. 1918, 711.12/75, RDS.

13. Ruckman to McCain, 11 Apr. 1917, 812.00/21886, Bonillas to Lansing, 11 Apr. 1917, 812.0144/53, RDS; *FR 1918,* pp. 557-558.

14. Canova memoranda, 13, 17 Apr. 1918, 812.00/21907, 22032, Lansing to Baker, 17 Apr. 1918, 812.00/21884, Wilson to Lansing, 25 Apr. 1918, Lansing to Fletcher, 27 Apr. 1918, 812.00/21933, RDS; Baker to Wilson, 24 Apr. 1918, box 8, Baker Papers.

15. Pablo L. Martínez, *A History of Lower California,* trans. Ethel Duffy Turner (México, D.F.: Editorial Baja California, 1960), pp. 504-514; Eugene Keith Chamberlain, "Mexican Colonization versus American Interests in Lower California," *Pacific Historical Review,* 20 (Feb. 1951), pp. 46-47; Carothers to Lansing, 25 Mar. 1917, 812.00/22171, Woodrome to Fullam, 2 Aug. 1917, 812.00/22171, report from Intelligence Officer Fred Chamberlain, 16 Aug. 1917, 812.00 Cantú, Daniels to Lansing, enclosures, 20 Aug. 1917, 812.00/21206, RDS.

16. Gibbon to Franklin K. Lane, 24 Oct. 1916, Papers on Mexican Affairs, reel 39, Fall Papers; Gibbon to Polk, 23 July 1917, 812.00/21138, RDS. Gibbon wrote *Mexico under Carranza: A Lawyer's Indictment of the Crowning Infamy of Four Hundred Years of Misrule* (Garden City, N.Y.: Doubleday, Page and Co., 1919).

17. Lowell L. Blaisdell, *The Desert Revolution; Baja California, 1911* (Madison: University of Wisconsin Press, 1962), pp. 27-35; Canova to Auchincloss, 12 Sept. 1917, 812.00/21260, RDS.

18. *IMA,* 1:318-321, 2:2994-3050; Dave Gershon report, 9 May 1918, Leland Harrison to Auchincloss, 14 May 1918, Roger Welles to Harrison, 3 June 1918, C. Shelden to Harrison, 30 Aug. 1918, 812.00 Cantú, RDS.

19. *FR 1918,* p. 571; Records of the Investigation of the Nogales Incident, 27-30 Aug. 1918, 812.00/22299, RDS; Francisco R. Almada, "El Conflicto Internacional de Nogales," *Boletín de la Sociedad Chihuahuense de Estudios Históricos,* 9 (Sept. 1953), pp. 826-827; Holbrook to Adjutant General, 13 June 1918, 319.1, box 274, RAGOPF. Also see Lawton to Lansing, 18 July, 9 Aug. 1918, 812.00/22116, 22160,

Burlingham to Lansing, 19 July 1918, 812.00/22119, Stewart to Lansing, 31 Aug. 1918, 711.12/137, RDS; *FR 1918,* p. 573.

20. Harold F. Williamson, Ralph L. Andreano, Arnold R. Daun, and Gilbert C. Klose, *The American Petroleum Industry, The Age of Energy, 1899-1959* (Evanston, Ill.: Northwestern University Press, 1963), vol. 2, pp. 28-29, 261-270; Gerald D. Nash, *United States Oil Policy 1890-1964, Business and Government in Twentieth Century America* (Pittsburgh, Pa.: University of Pittsburgh Press, 1968), pp. 29-30; *War Memoirs of Robert Lansing, Secretary of State* (New York: Bobbs-Merrill Co., 1935), pp. 314-316.

21. Canova to Lansing, 14 Apr. 1917, 812.6363/308, Lansing-Wilson, 18, 19 Apr. 1917, 711.12/43a, 43½, RDS.

22. *Lansing War Memoirs,* p. 316.

23. Gabriel Antonio Menéndez, *Doheny el Cruel, Valoración Histórica de la Lucha Sangrienta por el Petróleo Méxicano* (Mexico: Ediciones Bolsa Mexicana de Libro, S.C., 1958), p. 75 ff., depicts Peláez as a responsible landowner who reacted against the excesses of the revolution and used the oilmen to obtain financial support; Robert Blanco Moheno, *Crónica de la Revolución Mexicana* (Mexico: Libro Mex Editores, 1959), vol. 2, chap. 16, portrays Peláez as a reactionary and counter-revolutionary who served as an agent of American imperialism. *IMA,* 1:277-283, 296-297, 533, 839; Charles W. Hamilton, *Early Day Oil Tales of Mexico* (Houston: Gulf Publishing Co., 1966), p. 170; *The Autobiography of John Hays Hammond* (New York: Farrar and Rinehart, 1935), vol. 2, pp. 748-749; L. J. De Bekker, *The Plot against Mexico* (New York: Alfred A. Knopf, 1919), p. 28.

24. Fletcher to Lansing, 10 Apr. 1918, 711.12/75, RDS; Report from the Mexican Consulate, New York, 7 May 1918, Archivo de Carranza; *IMA,* 1:282, 533; Hamilton, *Oil Tales,* p. 169.

25. *IMA,* 1:280-283, 297; Claude I. Dawson to Lansing, 11 Aug. 1916, 812.6363/245, RDS; Anderson Diary, 10 Mar., 13 Apr. 1917, Chandler P. Anderson Papers, Library of Congress, Washington, D.C.

26. Summary of Bandit Outrages and Holdups in 1918, wallet 152, William Frank Buckley Papers, Latin American Collection, University of Texas, Austin; *FR 1918,* p. 670; Boaz Long memorandum, 10 Aug. 1918, 711.12/130, Dawson to Lansing, 17 Aug., 6 Sept. 1917, 812.00/21230, 21272, Walker to Auchincloss, 9 Sept. 1917, 812.6363/312, RDS.

27. Fletcher to Lansing, 9, 18 Oct. 1917, 812.00/21335, 21378, RDS; Alfonso Taracena, *La Verdadera Revolución Mexicana, Quinta Etapa (1916 a 1918)* (Mexico: Editorial Jus, S.A., 1960), p. 153.

28. Richardson to Navy Dept., 26 Sept. 1917, 812.00/21362, Dawson to Lansing, 13 Oct. 1917, 812.00/21381, William Canada to Lansing, 17 Nov. 1917, 812.00/21499, RDS; Richardson to Navy Dept., 26 Sept., 24 Nov. 1917, WE-5, box 651, R.G. 45, Naval Records Collection of the Office of Naval Records and Library, Subject File 1911-1927, U.S. National Archives, Washington, D.C.; Fletcher to Polk, 13 Nov. 1917, box 5, Henry P. Fletcher Papers, Library of Congress, Washington, D.C.; E. David Cronon, ed., *The Cabinet Diaries of Josephus Daniels, 1913-1921* (Lincoln: University of Nebraska Press, 1963), p. 233.

29. Dawson to Lansing, 7 Dec. 1917, 3, 10, 24 Jan. 1918, 812.00/21557, 21627, 21649, 21675, RDS; Richardson to Navy Dept., 18 Dec. 1917, 15 Jan. 1918, WE-5, box 651, R.G. 45, Naval Records Collection, Subject File; Taracena, *Verdadera Revolución (1916 a 1918),* p. 212; *El Demócrata,* 12 Dec. 1917, 25 Jan. 1918, Hemeroteca Nacional, Mexico City.

30. Auchincloss Diary, 1, 17 Feb. 1918, Gordon Auchincloss Papers, Yale University, New Haven, Conn.; Lansing to Fletcher, 17 Feb. 1918, 812.6363/341, RDS.
31. *FR 1918*, pp. 687-688.
32. México, Secretaría de Industria, Comercio y Trabajo, *Documentos Relacionados con la Legislación Petrolera Mexicana* (Mexico: Poder Ejecutivo Federal, 1919), pp. 399-402; *FR 1918*, pp. 700-704; Merrill Rippy, *Oil and the Mexican Revolution* (Leiden, Netherlands: E. J. Brill, 1972), pp. 43-48.
33. Taracena, *Verdadera Revolución (1916 a 1918)*, pp. 221, 229; Daniels to Lansing, enclosures, 2 Mar. 1918, 812.00/21774, RDS; *IMA*, 1:251, 267-268; Protest of the Chamber of Commerce and Landowners of Tampico, June 1918, box 174, James R. Garfield Papers, Library of Congress, Washington, D.C.
34. Walker to Doheny, 8 Mar. 1918, 812.6363/372, RDS; Auchincloss regarded Canova as an "incompetent;" Polk and Lansing had "absolutely no confidence" in him and suspected that Canova on occasion sought bribes from Chandler Anderson and his clients, an allegation which Anderson denied; Auchincloss Diary, 13 Aug. 1917, Auchincloss Papers; Anderson Diary, 3 Oct. 1917, Anderson Papers.
35. *FR 1918*, pp. 698, 700, 705-707.
36. Fletcher to Aguilar, 2 Apr. 1918, 711.12/104, RDS.
37. Fletcher to Lansing, 3 Apr. 1918, 711.12/77½, RDS; *FR 1918*, pp. 720-722.
38. *IMA*, 1:290-291; List of clients, A. W. Ivins to Rhoades, enclosure, 10 Jan. 1918, box 174, J. R. Garfield Papers.
39. Garfield memorandum of conference with Carranza on 20 May 1918, box 127, Harry A. Garfield Papers, Library of Congress, Washington, D.C.; *FR 1918*, pp. 724-732; *Legislación Petrolera Mexicana*, pp. 427-434.
40. Auchincloss Diary, 3, 4 June 1918, Auchincloss Papers; Lansing-Wilson, 4, 6 June 1918, Daniels-Wilson, 10 June 1918, box 14, Josephus Daniels Papers, Library of Congress, Washington, D.C.
41. *FR 1918*, pp. 577-579; James R. Mock and Cedric Larson, "Activities of the Mexico Section of the Creel Committee, 1917-1918," *Journalism Quarterly*, 16 (June 1939), pp. 136-150.
42. *FR 1918*, pp. 580, 584-586; *El Demócrata*, 13, 14 June 1918, *El Pueblo*, 13-17, 29, 30 June 1918, Hemeroteca Nacional; Antonio Manero, *México y la Solidaridad Americana, La Doctrina Carranza* (Madrid: Editorial-América, n.d.) and Hermila Galindo, *La Doctrina Carranza y el Acercamiento Indo-Latino* (Mexico: n.p., 1919); *Labor Internacional de la Revolución Constitucionalista de México (Libro Rojo)* (Mexico: n.p., 1960), p. 421.
43. Murray to Creel, 14 June 1918, 711.12/95, Fletcher to Lansing, 3, 13 July 1918, 711.12/116, 119, RDS; Fletcher to House, 19 June 1918, Edward M. House Papers, Yale University, New Haven, Conn.
44. Auchincloss Diary, 23, 26 June 1918, Auchincloss Papers; Lansing-Fletcher, 24, 27, 28 June, 1, 3, July 1918, 711.12/102, 104, 108, 112, 115, RDS.
45. Lansing to Fletcher, 26 June 1918, 711.12/103, Lansing to Wilbur J. Carr, 22 July 1918, 711.12/132a, RDS; Polk to Wilson, 31 July, ser. 2, box 180, Woodrow Wilson Papers, Library of Congress, Washington, D.C. Also see María Eugenia López de Roux, "Relaciones Mexicana-Norteamericanas (1917-1918)," *Historia Mexicana*, 14 (enero-marzo 1965), pp. 445-466.
46. *FR 1918*, pp. 736-743; Fletcher to House, 17 July 1918, House Papers.
47. *FR 1918*, p. 743; Mark L. Requa memorandum, 19 July 1918, H. A. Garfield Papers.
48. *FR 1918*, pp. 743-745; Joseph Wheless, *Compendium of the Laws of Mexico* (St. Louis: F. H. Thomas Law Book Co., 1910), p. 516.

49. Auchincloss Diary, 20, 24, 25, 30 July 1918, Auchincloss Papers.
50. Fletcher to Lansing, enclosures, 21 July 1918, box 127, H. A. Garfield Papers; J. R. Garfield to Fletcher, 27 July 1918, Fletcher Papers; *Legislación Petrolera Mexicana,* pp. 435-444; *FR 1918,* pp. 746-754; *IMA,* 1:837.
51. *FR 1918,* pp. 749-750; Requa to Bernard Baruch, 7 Aug. 1918, box 127, H. A. Garfield Papers.
52. *FR 1918,* pp. 750-751; Auchincloss Diary, 1, 6, 8 Aug. 1918, Auchincloss Papers.
53. Watriss to Polk, 9 Aug. 1918, Polk Papers; Auchincloss Diary, 9 Aug. 1918, Auchincloss Papers; Josephus Daniels, *The Wilson Era, Years of War and After, 1917-1923* (Chapel Hill: University of North Carolina Press, 1946), vol. 2, p. 248; Cronon, ed., *Cabinet Diaries,* p. 328.
54. Long memorandum, 10 Aug. 1918, 711.12/130, RDS.
55. *FR 1918,* pp. 754-755, 757-770; *Legislación Petrolera Mexicana,* p. 766.
56. Fletcher to Polk, 3 Dec. 1918, Polk Papers.

Notes to Chapter 6

1. Auchincloss Diary, 4 Sept. 1918, Gordon Auchincloss Papers, Yale University, New Haven, Conn.; Fletcher to Polk, 30 Oct. 1918, 711.12/150, RDS.
2. Memorandum, 12 Nov. 1918, 812.6363/415, RDS; *FR 1918,* pp. 772-783; Memorandum of a conference on 12 Nov. 1918, Watriss to Polk, 31 Dec. 1918, Frank Lyon Polk Papers, Yale University, New Haven, Conn.
3. *FR 1918,* pp. 784-789.
4. Harold F. Williamson, Ralph L. Andreano, Arnold R. Daum, and Gilbert C. Klose, *The American Petroleum Industry, The Age of Energy, 1899-1959* (Evanston, Ill.: Northwestern University Press, 1963), vol. 2, pp. 294-295; Gerald D. Nash, *United States Oil Policy 1890-1964, Business and Government in Twentieth Century America* (Pittsburgh, Pa.: University of Pittsburgh Press, 1968), pp. 43-49.
5. *FR 1919 Paris Peace Conference,* 1:315; Percy Alvin Martin, *Latin America and the War* (Baltimore: Md.: Johns Hopkins University Press, 1925), pp. 539-541; Warren H. Kelcher, *Latin American Relations with the League of Nations, World Peace Foundation Pamphlets,* vol. 12, no. 6 (Boston, Mass., 1929), p. 1062; Floyd F. Ewing, "Carranza's Foreign Relations: An Experiment in Nationalism" (Ph.D. diss., University of Texas, 1952), pp. 344-356.
6. Alberto J. Pani, *Mi Contribución al Nuevo Régimen* (México, D.F.: Editorial Cultura, 1936), pp. 250-254; Pani to Carranza, 11, 13 Feb., 25 May 1919, III/510 (72:73) (04)/1, Venustiano Carranza: Su Expediente Personal, L-E- 1445, AREM; this file containing Pani's reports was published in Alberto J. Pani, *Cuestiones Diversas* (Mexico: Imprenta Nacional, S.A., 1922).
7. Edgar Turlington, *Mexico and Her Foreign Creditors* (New York: Columbia University Press, 1930), pp. 276-278; Robert Freeman Smith, *The United States and Revolutionary Nationalism in Mexico, 1916-1932* (Chicago: University of Chicago Press, 1972), pp. 128-132.
8. Thomas W. Lamont-Fletcher, 24 Oct., enclosures, 4, 18 Dec. 1918, box 5, 6, Henry P. Fletcher Papers, Library of Congress, Washington, D.C.
9. Polk to Fletcher, 10 Jan. 1919, departmental order, 20 Feb. 1919, box 6, Fletcher Papers; Fletcher memorandum, 1 Mar. 1919, 711.12/187, RDS.

10. Group N, National Association, Senate Office File, reel 32, Albert B. Fall Papers, microfilm copy, University of Nebraska, Lincoln; *IMA*, 1:290-291, 403-423; Watriss-Polk, 18 Dec. 1918-15 Jan. 1919, Polk Papers.

11. Clifford W. Trow, "Senator Albert B. Fall and Mexican Affairs: 1912-1921" (Ph.D. diss., University of Colorado, 1966), *passim*, pp. 225 ff.; David H. Stratton, "New Mexico Machiavellian? The Story of Albert B. Fall," *Montana, The Magazine of Western History*, 7 (autumn 1957), pp. 2-14; David H. Stratton, ed., *The Memoirs of Albert B. Fall, Southwestern Studies*, vol. 4, no. 3, monograph 15 (El Paso: Texas Western Press, 1966); *IMA*. 1:1130-1134.

12. Seward Livermore, *Politics Is Adjourned, Woodrow Wilson and the War Congress* (Middletown, Conn.: Wesleyan University Press, 1966), pp. 203-205; Walker to Fall, 14 Feb. 1919, Senate Office File, reel 36, Fall Papers.

13. Lansing Diary, 27 May 1919, Robert Lansing Papers, Library of Congress, Washington, D.C.

14. *IMA*, 1:80, 189-191; Samuel Guy Inman, *Intervention in Mexico* (New York: George H. Doran Co., 1919); John Kenneth Turner, *Hands off Mexico* (New York: Rand School of Social Science, 1920); Leander J. De Bekker, *The Plot against Mexico* (New York: Alfred A. Knopf, 1919); Arthur Thomson, *The Conspiracy against Mexico* (California: International press, n.d.).

15. Federico Cervantes M., *Francisco Villa y la Revolución* (México, D.F.: Ediciones Alonso, 1960), pp. 586-592; government authorities later captured Angeles and executed him on 26 Nov. 1919, pp. 606-607; *FR 1919*, 2:565-569.

16. John Womack, Jr., *Zapata and the Mexican Revolution* (New York: Alfred A. Knopf, 1969), pp. 316-317; Luis Licéaga, *Félix Díaz* (Mexico: Editorial Jus, 1958), pp.529 ff.; Pedro del Villar manifesto, 5 Feb. 1919, 812.00/22520, Weekly reports 305, 306, 8, 15 Feb. 1919, 812.00/22522, 22535, Gayón to Woodrow Wilson, 4 Mar. 1919, 812.00/22599, RDS.

17. Womack, *Zapata*, pp. 322-329; *DHRM*, 18:217-219, 231-232; 237-240; Ramón Sánchez Ainslie to E. Garza Pérez, 10 Feb. 1919, H. 513″910-20/1, Revolución Mexicana durante los Años 1910 a 1920, Informaciones Diversas de la República y de las Oficinas de México en el Exterior, L-E- 837 R, leg. 8, AREM; Bonillas to Carranza, 24 Feb. 1919, Luis Déol to U.S. Commissioner Hitchcock, 15 May 1919, Archivo de Venustiano Carranza, Centro de Estudios de Historia de México, Departamento Cultural de Condumex, S.A., Mexico City; *FR 1919*, 2:548-549.

18. *FR 1919*, 2:593-597; Fletcher memorandum, Polk to Summerlin, 11 Apr. 1919, 812.6363/444, Summerlin to Lansing, 16 Apr. 1919, 812.6363/455, RDS.

19. Pani to Carranza, 6 May 1919, Venustiano Carranza: Su Expediente Personal, L-E- 1445, AREM; *FR 1919*, 2:545-548.

20. *FR 1919*, 2:597-603; Fletcher to Polk, 21 May 1919, box 6, Fletcher Papers.

21. Weekly reports, 317, 321, 325, 10 May, 7, 21 June 1919, 812.00/22703, 22803, 22864, RDS; E. David Cronon, ed., *The Cabinet Diaries of Josephus Daniels, 1913-1921* (Lincoln: University of Nebraska Press, 1963), p. 419; Peyton C. March to De R. C. Cabell, 11 June 1919, 319.2, box 272, RAGOPF; *FR 1919*, 2:550.

22. Clarence C. Clendenen, *Blood on the Border, The United States Army and the Mexican Irregulars* (n.p.: Macmillan Co., 1969), pp. 351-356; Crossing of Border by U.S. Troops at El Paso, Texas, 15-16 June 1919, 319.1, box 272, RAGOPF; Baker to Wilson, 18 June 1919, 812.00/22831, Juan B. Rojo to Polk, 17, 18 June 1919, 812.00/22830, 22855, RDS.

23. *DHRM*, 20:2:250-254, 357-372; Jara to Carranza, 3 June 1919, Aguilar to Carranza, 2 June 1919, Archivo de Carranza; Aguilar to Eliseo Arredondo, 6 June 1919, Mexican Affairs, reel 37, Fall Papers; Aguilar to Carranza, 2 July 1919, III/

628 (010)/1, 1914-1928 — Reglamentación de la Ley del Petróleo Mexicano, Controversia entre México y los Estados Unidos de A. con motivo de la Reglamentación de la Fracción I del Artículo 27 Constitucional, AREM.

24. *New York Times,* 22 June 1919; U.S. Congress, House, Committee on Rules, *Hearings on H.R. Res. 124, Appointment of a Committee for Investigation of Mexican Situation,* 66th Cong., 1st sess., 1919, pp. 4-14.

25. William Gates to Root, 3 June 1919, box 137, Elihu Root Papers, Library of Congress, Washington, D.C.; Womack, *Zapata,* pp. 298 ff.; Watriss to Polk, 27 June 1919, Polk Papers; *Bulletin* of the National Association, 1 July 1919, Group N, Senate Office File, reel 32, Fall Papers.

26. *New York Times,* 10 July 1919; List of persons present at an interview, 9 July 1919, box 7, Fletcher Papers; Conference with Mexican Oil Men, 9 July 1919, Polk Papers; *FR 1919,* 2:551-553; Baker-Wilson, 15, 18 July 1919, box 11, Newton D. Baker Papers, Library of Congress, Washington, D.C.; Polk to Fletcher, 17 July 1919, 711.12/181, RDS.

27. *FR 1919,* 2:572, 606-607; William Phillips-Fletcher, 22 July 1919, 711.12/179, RDS.

28. Summerlin to Lansing, enclosures, 28, 29 July, 2, 20, 24, 25 Aug. 1919, 711.12/176, 177, 180, 189, 198, 200, RDS; *FR 1919* 2:573-574; Aguilar to Carranza, 15 Aug. 1919, Reglamentación de la Ley del Petróleo Mexicano, L-E- 533, tomo 1, leg. 1, AREM; González to Carranza, 18 Aug. 1919, Archivo de Carranza.

29. Roosevelt to Lansing, 19 Aug. 1919, 711.12/195½, Foster to Lansing, 30 Aug. 1919, 812.23/64, RDS.

30. Fletcher to Lansing, 30 July 1919, 711.12/216, Wilson to Lansing, 4 Aug. 1919, Fletcher to Wilson, 18 Aug. 1919, 711.12/187, RDS.

31. Fletcher to Wilson, 20 Aug. 1919, 711.12/192½, Lansing to Wilson, 21 Aug. 1919, 812.00/23111C, RDS; the latter contains copies of Hermila Galindo, *La Doctrina Carranza y El Acercamiento Indo-Latino* (Mexico: n.p., 1919) and the "Bluebook," Secretaría de Relaciones Exteriores, *Labor Internacional de la Revolución Constitucionalista de México* (México, D.F.: Imprenta de la Secretaría de Gobernación, n.d. [1919]).

32. Fletcher to Wilson, 20 Aug. 1919, vol. 45, Lansing Papers; Wilson to Lansing, 22 Aug. 1919, 711.12/193½, RDS.

33. *IMA,* 1:3-4, 1131-1133; Trow, "Fall," pp. 270 ff.; Dennis W. Lou, "Fall Committee: An Investigation of Mexican Affairs" (Ph.D. diss., University of Indiana, 1963).

34. *IMA,* testimony of McDonald, Inman, Winton, Lind, De Bekker, Thomson; Lou, "Fall Investigation," pp. 53-64, 91-97; McDonald to Alvey Adee, 18 Aug. 1919, 812.6363/522, RDS. Inman was a personal friend of Carranza; Inman to Lansing, 29 June 1916, Inman memorandum, 20 Sept. 1919, box 13, Samuel Guy Inman Papers, Library of Congress, Washington, D.C. Carrancista authorities appreciated and encouraged the efforts of their apologists in the United States; Emeterio de la Garza to Carranza, 18 May 1919, De Bekker to Carranza, 21 April 1919, Archivo de Carranza.

35. *IMA,* 1:64-67, 116, 333-334, 2:2093-2110.

36. *IMA,* testimony of Doheny, Boynton, Kellogg, Beaty, Buckley, Wilson, O'Shaugnessy; Lou, "Fall Investigation," pp. 49-51; spokesmen for large oil companies in the Oil Producers Association and those for the independents in the so-called Murray Hill group headed by William F. Buckley often disagreed on questions of goals and tactics, with the latter group pushing for the toughest line; Trow, "Fall," pp. 398-401.

37. *IMA,* 2:2863-2873; George Agnew Chamberlain, *Is Mexico Worth Saving?* (Indianapolis, Ind.: Bobbs-Merrill Co., 1920), pp. 221-222.

38. Mark T. Gilderhus, "Senator Albert B. Fall and 'The Plot against Mexico,'" *New Mexico Historical Review,* 48 (Oct. 1973), pp. 299-311. In contrast, Clifford W. Trow, "Woodrow Wilson and the Mexican Interventionist Movement of 1919," *Journal of American History,* 58 (June 1971), pp. 46-72, depicts Fall, Doheny, and their allies as unswerving proponents of military intervention.

39. W. H. Field to Fall, 28 July 1919, 8 Sept. 1919, Senate Office File, reel 31, Fall Papers; Licéaga, *Félix Díaz,* pp. 579-585; Interview with Pedro del Villar, 4 Nov. 1919, wallet 113, statements by del Villar and A. Mariscal, 28 Nov. 1919, wallet 123, statement by T. Esquivel Obregón, 12 Dec. 1919, wallet 253, William Frank Buckley Papers, Latin American Collection, University of Texas, Austin; Manifesto, 3 Sept. 1919, 812.00/23060, RDS.

40. Fall to Lansing, 13 Nov. 1919, 711.12/227, RDS; Arthur Thomson to Gus Klumpner, 15 Nov. 1919, memorandum, 31 Dec. 1919, Senate Office File, reel 35, Fall Papers; W. M. Hansen to F. J. Kearful, 21 Dec. 1919, folio 177, Buckley Papers; Fall Committee to Fletcher, 4 Dec. 1919, box 6, Fletcher Papers; *New York Times,* 4 Dec. 1919; *El Universal,* 5 Dec. 1919, Hemeroteca Nacional, Mexico City.

41. Fletcher to Lansing, enclosures, Dec. 1919, 812.202/4, RDS; Lansing Diary, 26 July, 1 Sept. 1919, Lansing Papers.

42. Ramón P. de Negri to Salvador Diego Fernández, 23 Aug. 1919, Reglamentación de la Ley del Petróleo Mexicano, L-E- 533, tomo 1, leg. 1, AREM; *El Universal, El Demócrata,* Aug. 1919, Hemeroteca Nacional; *IMA,* 2:2954, 2970.

43. Edwin A. Weinstein, "Woodrow Wilson's Neurological Illness," *Journal of American History,* 57 (Sept. 1970), pp. 324-351; Daniel M. Smith, "Robert Lansing and the Wilson Interregnum, 1919-1920," *The Historian,* 21 (Nov. 1959), pp. 135-142.

44. Charles C. Cumberland, "The Jenkins Case and Mexican-American Relations," *Hispanic American Historical Review,* 31 (Nov. 1951), pp. 586-607; Manuel A. Machado, Jr., and James T. Judge, "Tempest in a Teapot? The Mexican-United States Intervention Crisis of 1919," *Southwestern Historical Quarterly,* 74 (July 1970), pp. 1-23; David Glaser, "1919: William Jenkins, Robert Lansing, and the Mexican Interlude," *Southwestern Historical Quarterly,* 74 (Jan. 1971), pp. 337-356. Critics held that Jenkins brought his misfortune on himself by speculating in depreciated Mexican currency and acquiring a fortune in real estate; Isaac Joslin Cox to Fall, 8 Dec. 1919, Mexican Affairs, reel 40, Fall Papers. Some Mexicans believed that the kidnapping was part of a large conspiracy by "the interests" and anti-Carranza rebels to bring about United States intervention; Manuel González Ramírez, *La Revolución Social de México, Las Ideas — La Violencia* (Mexico: Fondo de Cultura Económica, 1960), vol. 1, pp. 664-666; *El Universal Gráfica,* 12-24 Mar. 1924, Hemeroteca Nacional.

45. Texas Co. to Lansing, 16 Nov. 1919, Union Oil Co. to Lansing, 17 Nov. 1919, vol. 49, Lansing Papers; Harold Walker to Joseph Tumulty, 22 Nov. 1919, file 471, Woodrow Wilson Papers, Library of Congress, Washington, D.C.

46. Desk diary, 12-17 Nov. 1919, Lansing Diary, 17 Nov. 1919, Lansing Papers.

47. Desk diary, 18, 22, 24 Nov. 1919, Lansing Papers; Cronon, ed., *Cabinet Diaries,* p. 461; *FR 1919,* 2:612-613; Fletcher to Lansing, 21 Nov. 1919, box 7, Fletcher Papers; Charles V. Safford to Fall, enclosures, 24 Nov. 1919, Senate Office File, reel 31, Fall Papers.

48. *FR 1919,* 2:583-586; Womack, *Zapata,* p. 347; the death of Señora Carranza on 9 Nov. may have also contributed to his rigidity; Summerlin to Lansing, 9 Nov. 1919, 812.001C23/23, RDS.

49. Lansing memorandum, 28 Nov. 1919, 711.12/229 3/4, RDS; Lansing Diary, 28 Nov. 1919, Lansing Papers; *FR 1919,* 2:586-589.

50. Lansing Diary, 28 Nov. 1919, Lansing Papers.

51. Desk diary, 28 Nov. 1919, Lansing Papers: Cronon, ed., *Cabinet Diaries,* p. 365; Josephus Daniels, *The Wilson Era, Years of War and After, 1917-1923* (Chapel Hill: University of North Carolina Press, 1946), vol. 2, pp. 519-521, 529-530.

52. Memorandum, 29 Nov. 1919, vol. 49, Lansing Papers; Fletcher to Lansing, 2 Dec. 1919, box 7, Fletcher Papers; Fletcher-Lansing, 3 Dec. 1919, 812.6363/547, RDS.

53. Desk diary, 1, 2 Dec. 1919, Lansing Papers; Lane to Lansing, early Dec. 1919, 711.12/224½, RDS; *IMA,* 1:843a-843b; F. J. Kearful to W. F. Buckley, 5 Dec. 1922, wallet 220, Buckley Papers.

54. Concurrent Resolution, 3 Dec. 1919, W. E. D. Stokes to Fall, 28 Nov. 1919, Senate Office File, reel 31, 34, Fall Papers; Desk diary, 3 Dec. 1919, Lansing Papers.

55. Desk diary, 4 Dec. 1919, Lansing Diary, 4, 5 Dec. 1919, Lansing Papers; Fletcher memorandum, 9 Dec. 1919, box 7, Fletcher Papers; *IMA,* 1:843b-843d.

56. Desk diary, Lansing Diary, 4 Dec. 1919, Lansing Papers; Lansing to Wilson, 5 Dec. 1919, 711.12/225½, RDS.

57. David H. Stratton, "President Wilson's Smelling Committee," *The Colorado Quarterly,* 5 (autumn, 1956), pp. 164-184; Edith Bolling Wilson, *My Memoir* (New York: Bobbs-Merrill Co., 1938), pp. 298-299; Daniels, *Wilson Era,* vol. 2, 511-517.

58. *IMA,* 1:843d-843j; Wilson to Fall, 8 Dec. 1919, Mexican Affairs, reel 40, Fall Papers; *New York Times,* 5, 7, 9 Dec. 1919.

59. Lodge to James H. Wilson, 22 Dec. 1919, Henry Cabot Lodge Papers, Mass. State Historical Society, Boston; Cronon, ed., *Cabinet Diaries,* p. 471; Fletcher to Lansing, 11 Dec. 1919, box 7, Fletcher Papers; Long to Lansing, enclosures, 7 Dec. 1919, 711.12/228½, Long-Fletcher memorandum, 12 Dec. 1919, 711.12/299½, RDS.

60. Desk diary, 12 Dec. 1919, Lansing Papers; Memorandum, 20 Dec. 1919, box 7, Fletcher Papers; Lansing to Wilson, enclosures, 19 Dec. 1919, 812.6363/620, 3 Jan. 1919, 711.12/263a, RDS.

61. Lansing Diary, 7 Jan. 1920, Lansing to Wilson, 21 Jan. 1920, vol. 20, Lansing Papers; Fletcher to Lansing, 20 Jan. 1920, box 8, Fletcher Papers. Wilson accepted the resignation but later expressed his regret that Fletcher had turned out to be "a quitter." Wilson to Colby, 13 Apr. 1920, box 2, Bainbridge Colby Papers, Library of Congress, Washington, D.C.

62. Oil Producers Assoc.-Carranza, 13, 17 Jan. 1920, 812.6363/624, 628a, RDS; Fletcher to Polk, 22 Jan. 1920, box 8, Fletcher Papers; *FR 1920,* 3:203-205.

63. Anne Wintermute Lane and Louise Herrick Wall, eds., *The Letters of Franklin K. Lane, Personal and Political* (New York: Houghton-Mifflin Co., 1922), p. 337; Lane then took a position with Edward L. Doheny; Smith, "Lansing and the Wilson Interregnum," pp. 158-161.

Notes to Chapter 7

1. Daniel M. Smith, *Aftermath of War, Bainbridge Colby and Wilsonian Diplomacy, 1920-1921* (Philadelphia, Pa.: American Philosophical Society, 1970), pp. 10-31. Joseph S. Tulchin, *The Aftermath of War, World War I and U.S. Policy toward Latin America* (New York: New York University Press, 1971), pp. 56-57, disputes

Smith's claim that Colby played an active and independent role in forming policy but agrees that Wilson and Colby got on well together.

2. Clifford Wayne Trow, "Senator Albert B. Fall and Mexican Affairs" (Ph.D. diss., University of Colorado, 1966), pp. 395-398; Baker to Lansing, enclosure, 27 Feb. 1920, 812.6363/648, RDS.

3. Mexican courts failed to exonerate Jenkins until December 1920; Charles C. Cumberland, "The Jenkins Case and Mexican-American Relations," *Hispanic American Historical Review,* 31 (Nov. 1951), pp. 604-607. Senator Fall and his aides retained connections with anti-Carranza leaders; Gus T. Jones to Dan M. Jackson, 28 Dec. 1919, Senate Office File, reel 35, F. J. Kearful to Fall, 11 Feb. 1920, Papers on Mexican Affairs, reel 40, Albert B. Fall Papers, microfilm copy, University of Nebraska, Lincoln. Fall's aides hoped to bring Henry Fletcher before the committee for testimony, perhaps to compensate for the reluctance of other possible witnesses who feared reprisals in Mexico; Wallace Thompson to Kearful, Fall to Kearful, 25 Feb. 1920, Senate Office File, reel 35, Kearful to Fall, 3 Mar. 1920, Papers on Mexican Affairs, reel 40, Fall Papers; *El Universal,* 17 Jan. 1920, Hemeroteca Nacional, Mexico City.

4. Noticias and propaganda, Mar.-May 1920, H. 513″910-20/1, Revolución Mexicana durante los Años 1910 a 1920, Informaciones Diversas de la República y de las Oficinas de México en el Exterior, L-E- 849 R, leg. 1, AREM; Mexican releases gave special prominence to statements by Joseph Guffey and other oilmen in the so-called AGWI group who chose to submit to Carranza's decrees; Summerlin to Colby, 6 Feb., 20 Mar. 1920, 711.12/317, 812.6363/653, RDS; *FR 1920,* 3:205-217.

5. Lodge-Fall, 2, 11, 17 Apr. 1920, Senate Office File, reel 30, Fall Papers; Emeterio de la Garza to Carranza, 14 Apr. 1920, Archivo de Venustiano Carranza, Centro de Estudios de Historia de México, Departamento Cultural de Condumex, S.A., Mexico City.

6. Manuel González Ramírez, *La Revolución Social de México, Las Ideas — La Violencia* (Mexico: Fondo de Cultura Económica, 1960), vol. 1; John W. F. Dulles, *Yesterday in Mexico, A Chronicle of the Revolution, 1919-1936* (Austin: University of Texas Press, 1961); Charles C. Cumberland, *Mexican Revolution, The Constitutionalist Years* (Austin: University of Texas Press, 1972) provide accounts.

7. Alvaro Obregón, *Ocho Mil Kilómetros en Campaña, Fuentes para la Historia de la Revolución Mexicana,* ed. Manuel González Ramírez, (Mexico: Fondo de Cultura Económica, 1959), vol. 5, pp. 550-564; Dulles, *Yesterday,* p. 19.

8. Cumberland, *Mexican Revolution, Constitutionalist Years,* pp. 402-405.

9. Alfonso Taracena, *Venustiano Carranza* (Mexico: Editorial Jus, 1963), p. 294; Jesús Romero Flores, *Anales Históricos de la Revolución Mexicana* (Mexico: Edicones Encaudernables, 1939), vol. 2, pp. 285-286; Summerlin to Fletcher, 16 Dec. 1919, box 7, Henry P. Fletcher Papers, Library of Congress, Washington, D.C.

10. Dulles, *Yesterday,* p. 22.

11. Cumberland, *Mexican Revolution, Constitutionalist Years,* p. 406; *El Universal,* 26 Nov. 1919, Hemeroteca Nacional; Dulles, *Yesterday,* p. 22.

12. Romero Flores, *Anales Históricos,* vol. 2, pp. 281-288; Amado Chaverri Matamoros and Clodoveo Valenzuela, eds., *Sonora y Carranza* (México, D.F.: Casa Editorial "Renacimiento" de G. Sisniega y Hno., 1921); and José Vasconcelos, ed., *La Caída de Carranza, de la Dictadura a la Libertad* (Mexico: n.p., 1920), provide documentation.

13. *DHRM,* 18:435-439; Manuel González Ramírez, ed., *Planes Políticas y Otros Documentos, Fuentes para la Historia de la Revolución Mexicana* (México, D.F.: Fondo de Cultura Económica, 1954), vol. 1, pp. 251-255.

14. Romero Flores, *Anales Históricos,* vol. 2, pp. 290-301; Dulles, *Yesterday,* chaps. 3, 4; *DHRM,* 4:152.

15. W. E. Chapman to Lansing, 10 Nov. 1919, 812.00/23209, Summerlin to Lansing, 20 Jan. 1920, 812.00/23359, Summerlin to Colby, 17 Mar. 1920, 812.00/23532, Matthew E. Hanna to Colby, 14 Apr. 1920, 812.00/23687, RDS; Memorandum, Mexico, Estimate of Military Situation, Office of Naval Intelligence, 5 Mar. 1920, R.G. 45, Naval Records Collection of the Office of Naval Records and Library, Subject File 1911-1927, WE-5, box 658, U.S. National Archives, Washington, D.C.; Colby-Wilson, 17, 19, 20 Apr. 1920, box 2, Bainbridge Colby Papers, Library of Congress, Washington, D.C.

16. *FR 1920,* 3:133-147; Josephus Daniels to Colby, 23 Apr. 1920, 812.00/23706, 23707, Colby to Hanna, 14 Apr. 1920, 812.00/23578, Carr to Francis J. Dyer, 29 Apr. 1920, 812.00/23726, RDS; Daniels to Wilson, enclosure, 3 May 1920, box 14, Josephus Daniels Papers, Library of Congress, Washington, D.C.

17. Carr to Yost, 27 Apr. 1920, 812.00/23682, RDS; J. M. Arredondo to Hilario Medina, 30 Mar. 3, 15 Apr. 1920, Revolución Mexicana, L-E- 866 R, leg. 1, AREM.

18. Luis N. Ruvulcaba, ed., *Campaña Política de C. Alvaro Obregón, Candidato a la Presidencia de la República, 1920-1924* (Mexico: n.p., 1923), vol. 3, pp. 367-368; Chaverri Matamoros and Valenzuela, *Sonora y Carranza,* pp. 221, 230; Hanna to Colby, 13 Apr. 1920, 812.00/23580, Myron T. Parker to Colby, 17 Apr. 1920, 812. 2311/384, Adolfo de la Huerta to Wilson, 17 Apr. 1920, 812.2311/392, Salvador Alvarado to Colby, 21 Apr. 1920, 812.00/23665, memorandum, 17 Apr. 1920, 812.2311/ 402, RDS.

19. Mexican Embassy to State Dept., 19 Apr. 1920, 812.2311/387, RDS; J. M. Arredondo to Gustavo G. Hernández, 30 Apr. 1920, Revolución Mexicana, L-E- 866 R, leg. 3, AREM. Studies such as Adolfo Manero Suárez and José Paniagua Arredondo, *Los Tratados de Bucareli, Traición y Sangre Sobre México* (Mexico: n.p., 1958), vol. 1, pp. 137-138, and Luis Zorrilla, *Historia de las Relaciones entre México y los Estados Unidos de América, 1800-1958* (Mexico: Editorial Porrua, 1966), vol. 2, p. 349, perpetuate such misimpressions.

20. Colby to Wilson, 23 Apr., 7 May 1920, boxes 2, 3a, Colby Papers; *FR 1920,* 3:241-242; S. Diego Fernández to J. M. Arredondo, 27, 29 Apr. 1920, Arredondo to C. Nicefaro Zambrano, 28 Apr. 1920, Revolución Mexicana, L-E- 866 R, legs. 2, 3, AREM.

21. Taracena, *Carranza,* pp. 302-318; *DHRM,* vol. 19.

22. Dulles, *Yesterday,* chaps. 5, 6; Summerlin to Colby, 25 May 1920, 812.00/ 24177, RDS.

23. Dulles, *Yesterday,* chaps. 7, 8; John Womack, Jr., *Zapata and the Mexican Revolution* (New York: Alfred A. Knopf, 1969), pp. 361 ff.; Federico Cervantes M., *Francisco Villa y la Revolución* (México, D.F.: Ediciones Alonso, 1960), pp. 616-630; Luis Licéaga, *Félix Díaz* (Mexico: Editorial Jus, 1958), pp. 625-650.

24. Salvador Alvarado to Colby, 21 Apr. 1920, 812.00/23665, Dyer to Colby, 13, 15, 18 May 1920, 812.00/23969, 23995, 24013, Zachary Cobb to Colby, 17 May 1920, 812.00/24158, memoranda, 4, 12, 24 May 1920, 812.00/23837, 23980, 24169, RDS; Parker to Fall, 29 Dec. 1919, Senate Office File, reel 32, Fall Papers. In contrast, William F. Buckley, a spokesman for independent oil producers, advised against recognition, warning that radicalism permeated the new regime: Buckley to Colby, 22 May 1920, wallet 443, William Frank Buckley Papers, Latin American Collection, University of Texas, Austin.

25. Colby to Wilson, 20 May 1920, box 3a, Colby Papers; notation by Johnston, 22 May 1920, 812.00/24158, Dyer-Colby, 20, 21, 22 May 1920, 812.00/24013, 24032, Colby to Summerlin, 812.00/24071, RDS.

26. *IMA,* 2:3369-3373.

27. Alvaro Torre Díaz to Colby, 20 May 1920, 812.00/24044, RDS; *FR 1920,* 3:171.

28. Johnston to Colby, 16 June 1920, 812.00/24912, RDS.

29. Colby to Wilson, enclosure, 23 June 1920, 812.00/24227, RDS; *FR 1920,* 3:174; Memoranda, 30 June, 9 July 1920, box 9, Norman H. Davis Papers, Library of Congress, Washington, D.C.

30. *FR 1920,* 3:219-220; Summerlin-Colby, 6 July, 7 Sept. 1920, 812.6363/696, 724, Oil Producers Assoc. to Colby, 3 Aug. 1920, Alvey Adee to Summerlin, 18 Aug. 1920, 812.6363/707, Summerlin to Cutberto Hidalgo, 16, 31 Aug. 1920, 812. 6363/724, Summerlin memorandum, 14 Sept. 1920, 812.6363/722½, RDS.

31. Dulles, *Yesterday,* chap. 8; Pablo L. Martínez, *A History of Lower California,* trans. Ethel Duffey Turner (México, D.F.: Editorial Baja California, 1960), pp. 517-520; Summerlin Colby, 14, 28, 30 July 1920, 812.00/24393, 24400, RDS.

32. Trow, "Fall," pp. 439 ff.; Fall to Frank Brandegee, 9 June 1920, Senate Office File, reel 30, Fall Papers; Kirk H. Porter and Donald Bruce Johnson, *National Party Platforms, 1840-1964,* 3d ed. (Urbana: University of Illinois Press, 1966), pp. 221-222, 230; *New York Times,* 10, 15, Oct. 1920.

33. Davis to Wilson, 21 July 1920, ser. 4, file 471, Woodrow Wilson Papers, Library of Congress, Washington, D.C.; Memoranda, 24, 30 Aug. 1920, box 9, Davis Papers.

34. Memorandum, 28 Sept. 1920, box 9, Davis Papers.

35. Dulles, *Yesterday,* chap. 9; *FR 1920,* 3:182-183; see Aug.-Nov. 1920, 812.00/ 24426-24800, RDS.

36. *FR 1920,* 3:182; Memorandum, 23 Sept. 1920, box 9, Davis Papers; Wilson to Colby, 27 Sept. 1920, box 3b, Colby Papers.

37. Scrapbook, 9 Oct.-15 Dec. 1920, vol. 12, George Creel Papers, Library of Congress, Washington, D.C.; Creel to Colby, 23 Oct. 1920, 812.00/24746½, Pesqueira to Colby, 26 Oct. 1920, 812.00/24701½, RDS.

38. Johnston to Davis, 26 Oct. 1920, 812.6363/734½, Colby-Wilson, enclosure, 28 Oct. 1920, Colby to Pesqueira, 28 Oct. 1920, Colby's statement, 29 Oct. 1920, 812.00/24757a, RDS.

39. De la Huerta circular telegram, 5 Nov. 1920, 812.00/24764, Creel to Colby, 17, 20 Nov. 1920, 812.00/24764, 24774½, RDS.

40. Johnston to Colby, 9 Nov. 1920, 812.00/24765, Summerlin-Colby, 18, 20 Nov. 1920, 812.00/24775, 24776, RDS; *El Excélsior,* 4, 13 Nov. 1920, Hemeroteca Nacional; *FR 1920,* 3:197.

41. Patrick Gardiner, ed., *Theories of History* (New York: Free Press, 1959), p. 281.

Index